Conservation at the Crossroads

Conservation at the Crossroads

Science, Society, and the Future of India's Wildlife

GHAZALA SHAHABUDDIN

permanent black

in association with

THE NEW INDIA FOUNDATION

Published by
PERMANENT BLACK
'Himalayana', Mall Road, Ranikhet Cantt,
Ranikhet 263645
Email: perblack@gmail.com

In association with
THE NEW INDIA FOUNDATION

Distributed by
ORIENT BLACKSWAN PRIVATE LIMITED
Bangalore Bhopal Bhubaneshwar Chandigarh Chennai
Ernakulam Guwahati Hyderabad Jaipur Kolkata
Lucknow Mumbai New Delhi Patna
www.orientblackswan.com

First published 2010
First paperback printing 2018

ISBN 978-81-7824-534-8

Typeset in Agaramond
by Guru Typograph Technology, Dwarka, New Delhi 110075
Printed and bound by Sapra Brothers, New Delhi 110092

Contents

ILLUSTRATIONS

Preface

Forests of the Living Dead

A crisp December morning. I was in Sitamata, one of India's little-known wildlife sanctuaries. Situated in the state of Rajasthan, Sitamata was established in 1979, and, at more than 422 sq. km, is much larger than the average Indian Protected Area (PA). It encompasses undulating country with permanent springs, cliffs, and thick riverine forest stretches. Dry tropical forests flourish here, protected from the extreme weather of the Thar desert by the ancient range of the Aravalli mountains. Sitamata is extremely interesting biologically: several peninsular animal and plant species—including the Indian giant flying squirrel, the grey junglefowl, and natural teak—reach their north-western distributional limits here.

My trip here had been arranged by Dr Justus Joshua of the Foundation for Ecological Security, who was making an inventory of the sanctuary's flora and fauna. Mapping biodiversity patterns and understanding their relationship with human use is the first step towards developing a scientific management plan, a task he was carrying out together with the Rajasthan Forest Department.

Exploring a new area is always interesting and full of surprises. Travelling with the research team, I was intrigued by the vegetation, which was dominated by very short-statured teak trees. Whereas this tree normally reaches 10 to 15 metres in this part of the country, hardly any reached even 4 metres here. In fact, there were very few large trees, and even the ones that seemed to exist occurred only in patches. The understorey, which under normal circumstances should have comprised native saplings and shrubs of varying height, was dominated by *Lantana camara*, an exotic invasive species from South America which snuffs out other plants. The monotony of the teak stands, coupled with the visibly low regeneration of the already sparse native trees, told me the whole story: there had been diverse forest here in the past, but it was gone now and the future held declining biological diversity.

Ecologists are often derided for speculating on possible causes. But that is what I will do in the absence of a detailed history of this region. Discussions with forest personnel revealed that there had been a phase of commercial clear-felling of teak trees in the 1960s, much before the sanctuary was established. This period of clear-felling is likely to have been followed by a phase of chronic disturbance caused by fire, lopping, and grazing by local villagers. It is possible that such repeated disturbances prevented tree saplings and re-sprouting trees in the logged areas to grow to their natural height. Adverse changes in soil and micro-climate,[1] which are inevitable after logging, may have further constrained the establishment of new saplings. With repeated exposure to cattle-grazing and extremes of temperature, forest soil tends to get compacted, hard, and dry, and is therefore far less conducive to seed germination and plant growth. A senior forest officer told us that there had been teak-planting in the past to enrich the forest stands for this commercially valuable species. This is likely to have led to a further decline in other tree species in parts of the sanctuary.

I also found it interesting that ungulates such as nilgai, sambar, and chital, common in peninsular India's forests, were missing here despite the larger-than-average size of the sanctuary. The only wild ungulate that occurs here, the four-horned antelope, exists, according to Joshua, at extremely low densities. This is only to be expected, given the insufficient forage in the forest: herbivores need tree saplings, edible shrubs, and grasses. It was not surprising to find that predators such as tigers and wild dogs disappeared long ago from Sitamata, and even leopard signs are now uncommon. A once-common omnivore of the area, the

[1] 'Micro-climate' refers to a set of climatic conditions, measured at a very local level, which directly affects the growth and reproduction of animals and plants.

sloth bear, has become extinct as well—as it has from much of the Aravallis. A recent history reveals that Sitamata had a low herbivore density even as far back as 1994, when it was studied as a possible second home for the Asiatic lion—it was rejected on that account (Divyabhanusinh 2005). Joshua had, however, found evidence of rare small cats, such as the rusty spotted cat, and other endemic species such as the Indian star tortoise and the Aravalli spurfowl in the better-protected parts of the sanctuary. On a walk along a patch of thick riverine forest, hiding away in less accessible valleys, we were rewarded by the rare sight of the grey-headed canary flycatcher, the stork-billed kingfisher, and the crested serpent eagle. These bird species are known to live only in forests along perennial streams in the Aravallis.

The forest here had obviously suffered from intense commercial use in the past. Today, it bears the additional brunt of the numerous villages and towns located around it whose people extract whatever they need from it. Over a walk of 2 km I saw numerous tree stumps, some cut very recently. Tendu trees,[2] whose leaves are collected for the manufacture of country cigarettes (*bidis*) all over India, presented a particularly pathetic sight. They had been reduced to stumps because of repeated lopping and firing practices that encourage new leaf growth. I could see livestock grazing on the fringes of the sanctuary as well as around the small hamlets located inside its boundaries. The forest around each of the villages was degraded too, with only stunted teak saplings, harvested trees, and *Lantana* bushes. Along the highways I could see evidence of log extraction, obviously illegal, which the local forest functionaries seemed powerless to stop.

The sanctuary appeared to be run abysmally. Forest protection levels seemed very low. During the three days I spent inside the sanctuary I saw only a few guards at the entry gates, never patrolling inside. There were no facilities for tourists despite the considerable revenue-earning potential of the sanctuary. The local villagers seemed poor, underemployed, and lacking any facilities for education or health-care. There had been no initiative by the sanctuary managers to employ local people in forest protection duties or other remunerative activities. Many of the villagers here are descendants of those who moved to the

[2] *Diospyros melanoxylon*, commercially one of India's most important trees.

sanctuary after being displaced from the submergence zone of a dam in nearby Gujarat. Although they now live close to the state highway that connects them to nearby towns, they lack the skills for any substantial form of employment. Only daily wage labour supplements their income from subsistence agriculture in their rain-fed fields.

Disappearing Biodiversity

Wildlife sanctuaries were established in India with the aim of protecting all types of living organisms as well as the ecological and evolutionary processes that guarantee their long-term survival. However, it is obvious that Sitamata has become just a 'paper park' with high potential but limited actual value for biodiversity conservation. Its forests have failed to protect the range of flora and fauna that they originally harboured. Its trees have to do without fruit-eaters, such as the sloth bear and cheetal, which are responsible for seed dispersal and germination. Big cats cannot survive here as their prey-base does not come anywhere near the densities required. Even the rather more generalist herbivores, such as sambar, cannot find the plant diversity that they need. The serene-looking green canopy hides a dysfunctional forest ecosystem that can no longer shelter the diversity of tropical life that it is meant to.

It is apparent that the Indian government does not have this vulnerable patch of forest on its priority list. It is not a tiger reserve, nor is it visited by high-profile tourists—as are tiger reserves such as Corbett in Uttarakhand and Periyar in Kerala, for instance. Less than a hundred kilometres from Sitamata is the historic city of Udaipur, which has just woken up to shopping malls, world-class highways, and heritage tourism. But Sitamata, a treasure chest of biological values, lies forgotten and degraded, virtually wiped out from bureaucratic memory.

As an ecologist I have worked in numerous Indian wild places that are managed for conservation, both by the government as well as local communities. My experience tells me that Sitamata is not unique. Indian forests, whether inside PAs or outside, no longer support the range of biodiversity, wildlife habitat, and ecological functions that they were created and mandated to protect. The condition of the Sitamata Wildlife Sanctuary is more or less the same as that of countless stretches of 'forest land' all over the country. Forests of varying canopy-cover show up in the satellite imagery produced by remote-sensing agencies, and estimates of forest area in the country are now more accurate. However, no one really knows how much of this forest is still ecologically functional and how much of it has joined the ranks of 'the living dead',[3] as Sitamata apparently has.

Recent scientific studies point to widespread habitat degradation inside areas set aside for biodiversity conservation in India. For instance, intensive surveys of carnivorous mammals and prey species in the Namdapha Tiger Reserve in Arunachal Pradesh show that their densities have greatly reduced in recent times. The tiger has disappeared from the lowland rainforest areas of the reserve, where it was once reported (Datta *et al.* 2008). At the Bhadra Tiger Reserve in Karnataka between 8 and 10 per cent of reserve area was found degraded by biomass extraction activities (K. Karanth *et al.* 2005). Studies in the Pin Valley National Park in the Indian Himalaya indicate that there may be competition for pastures between domestic goats/sheep and the wild ibex (Bagchi *et al.* 2004). Vegetation and threat studies in the Biligirirangan Hills Temple Sanctuary in Karnataka show that roads, plantations, grazing, wood collection, and other human activities have affected the sanctuary. If the diversity of native tree species is considered an indicator, a considerable portion of the sanctuary is degraded (Barve *et al.* 2005). Long-term studies in the same sanctuary report the reduced regeneration of some extracted non-timber forest products (NTFP) species and changes in tree composition because of long-term use (Murali *et al.* 1996, Ganeshaiah *et al.* 1998, Shankar *et al.* 1998a). One can go for miles in vast areas of reserved forests in any state of the country without finding healthy tree regeneration or a diverse understorey.

The Monster of 'Development'

These biological changes in natural ecosystems may actually be reversible. A far more pernicious threat hangs over the fate of our forests:

[3] A phrase originally coined by John Terborgh, the pioneering rainforest biologist, in his book *Requiem for Nature* (Terborgh 1999).

Illustr. 1: Due to increasing degradation and fragmentation, Indian forests are losing many seed dispersers that are important to tree regeneration, such as the Great Hornbill. (*Photo: Jawed Ashraf*)

the voracious demands of development, the highways and dams to be built; agriculture, plantations, mining, and urbanization.[4] Few developing nations, least of all India, appear able to withstand the onslaught of rapidly expanding urbanization and industrial growth that can irreversibly destroy natural ecosystems. Developmental threats to natural ecosystems in India are mounting by the day. It would be instructive to take a look at a recent issue of the popular newsletter *Protected Areas Update.*[5] A single issue of this in 2007 documents at least four cases of developmental threats to PAs: a proposed wind energy project in the Kudremukh National Park, a narrow-gauge railway line in the Senchal Wildlife Sanctuary, height increase of the Mullaperiyar Dam (which will affect rainforests inside the Periyar Tiger Reserve), and a hydro-electric project within the Askot Wildlife Sanctuary. Another issue of the newsletter documents a legal dispute over

[4] See the journal *PAs Update*, which documents innumerable such cases each month: http://www.kalpavriksh.org/f1/f1.2/pa_update/index_html

[5] Published in India by the Kalpavriksh Environmental Action Group.

the diversion of forest land in the Mahatma Gandhi National Park, located in the Andaman Islands, for the laying of a water pipeline. Recent pollution threats have also been documented: such as the death of 111 gharials in the National Chambal River Sanctuary from industrial pollution; and a proposed thermal power plant which is likely to affect the Bandipur–Nagarhole forests—these form part of the largest contiguous tiger habitat in the country.[6] A large port at Dhamra in Orissa, being built jointly by major Indian corporate groups, threatens to destroy the last remaining nesting habitat of the Olive Ridley sea turtle in India. The list is endless.

The tragedy is that the developmental juggernaut is not going to spare even some of the biologically richest and most remote areas known to mankind. The north-eastern mountain state of Arunachal Pradesh lies in one of the designated twenty-five biodiversity hotspots of the world. The endangered tropical rainforest ecosystem reaches its northernmost Indian limit here. A mind-boggling 50 per cent of Indian flowering plants, 50 per cent of India's birds, and as much as 25 per cent of India's mammal species have been recorded in Arunachal Pradesh (Datta 2007). Several mammal species have been discovered here even as recently as in the past five years by scientists from the Nature Conservation Foundation and the Wildlife Conservation Society. Yet the escalating demand for electricity in the Indian plains has encouraged plans for thirteen massive hydro-electric projects in the state. These are together expected to generate more than 40,000 megawatts of electricity but will wipe out large swathes of globally important forests, fragmenting them into unviable habitats with impoverished fauna. The state administration has brushed aside objections by experts on the unfeasibility of the project, including seismic threats to the new structures, the immeasurable ecological impact, and large-scale dispossession of tribal lands and livelihoods in the region.

The development of road infrastructure, construction, mining, industries, and commercial plantations immediately outside PAs lead to undesirable changes within them as well. Buffer zones shrink, water is polluted, forests are degraded, invasive species creep in and spread,

[6] *PAs Update*, vol. XIV, no. 2.

and road-kills of animals increase. Hydrological changes and habitat fragmentation can represent a direct impact on PAs. In India, the Wildlife Protection Act includes a clause for declaring land within a 10-km radius of a PA as an ecologically sensitive zone where damaging developmental activities can be prohibited. Yet very few PA managers have actually used this provision to stop mining or urbanization in their backyards (Menon and Kohli 2003). On the, contrary, the years 2000–8 have seen an unprecedented use of power by the state machinery to protect promoters of such projects from objections by ecologists and local communities (ibid.).

What went Wrong?

India has a separate government department controlling as much as 23 per cent of the country's land area; its primary mandate is to maintain biodiversity, protect ecological functions, and incorporate vital environmental concerns into the development process. Despite India's high population density and low per capita income, PAs comprise 5.2 per cent of the country. In addition, huge forest areas are today under the joint management of local villages and the government, whereby protection and forest benefits are shared by the two parties. India, unlike most other developing countries in Asia, has a reasonably active judiciary and democratic governance that, however sporadic, allows a voice to marginalized people, and a media quick to expose environmental degradation. Above all, the Indian people have a richly recorded culture of wildlife protection and observation dating back to ancient times. Because of this, a substantial degree of tolerance exists among the common people towards the animals and plants that share their space—certainly much more so than in many developed countries. In comparison with many countries in South America, Africa, and Asia, India has far more stringent wildlife protection standards and a complex set of forest laws. Nor does the country lack biological expertise: there is a vast scientific establishment researching ecological issues. So where exactly has Indian conservation gone wrong?

This book is an attempt to try and understand the shortcomings of the varied strategies that have been adopted for biodiversity conservation by India since Independence, both in terms of policy as well

Illustr. 2: Due to their structural complexity, the native sal forests in and around the Corbett Tiger Reserve support a large diversity of woodpeckers. Over the past century such old-growth forests have shrunk considerably because of timber-working and conversion to teak plantations. (*Photo: Raman Kumar*)

as implementation.[7] What have our policies been? How are these policies formulated and translated from the drawing board to the field? Who, really, are the players, visible and invisible, in contemporary Indian conservation?

In the first chapter I look at the case of the Sariska Tiger Reserve to understand the socio-economic and political processes that led to it becoming an 'exclusive' preserve in the early twentieth century and, more lately, its decline as a premium tiger habitat. I hope that by applying a lens to the micro-level processes involved in PA management, people–forest relations, and the resultant ecological impact, one can

[7] I deliberately use the term 'biodiversity' rather than the more popularly used 'wildlife'. Most people take wildlife to denote principally large mammals, such as tigers, bears, and elephants in thick remote forests. Instead, I use the term biodiversity to include all manner of living creatures, including insects, amphibians, and microscopic plants which all exist in functional relationships with each other.

begin to understand where the failures lie. In most of India's PAs, issues pertinent to people's displacement have been central to management. The question of governmental control over biological research is also relevant to the way scientific knowledge is manufactured and then utilized for wilderness management. I attempt to convey the complexities and inadequacies of Indian policies relating to the displacement of people in the second chapter; in the third I look at biological research.

The earlier part of the book is really a critique of the principally exclusionary paradigm that has been adopted by the Indian government, particularly since the advent of Project Tiger in 1972. Influenced by the West, the Indian conservation establishment has traditionally been led by a belief that the creation of people-free wildernesses, such as national parks, is the best way to protect nature (Guha 2000). In this perspective, while the weaknesses of state governance institutions are recognized, the policing of ecosystems and their protection from local use gets the most importance and attention. Efforts to develop channels of economic benefit for local communities are thought of as misguided and impractical, particularly given India's high population density (for instance, see Thapar 2005, and K.U. Karanth 2006). This approach to conservation finds resonance in the writings of an influential set of international wildlife biologists and institutions that have considerable reach in the developing world (see, for instance, Terborgh 1999, Kramer *et al.* 1997, K.U. Karanth 2006, and Terborgh and van Schaik 2002). However, it is also easy to swing to the other extreme position which claims to represent the people living in and depending on forests, wetlands, and coastal areas for their day-to-day sustenance (see Kothari 2000, Kothari *et al.* 2000). Sustainable extraction as a means of incorporating local interests in forests is often overrated by these scholars, who can tend to gloss over the difficult biological issues that are involved. This view is based on an almost complete negation of the positive role of science to solve conservation problems. Yet another constituency—that of the political ecologist and environmental historian—emphasizes the political exclusion of people from natural resources and the colonial subversion of the 'conservation agenda'; this tends to overlook the more local causes of ecological degradation (see Chhatre and Saberwal 2006, Gadgil and Guha 1992). It can be argued that 'Biologists and social scientists often examine different parts of a large complex picture and also have different ways of asserting an argument. Biologists mostly focus on the impact of differing kinds of human use of the ecosystem, with species and ecosystems at the epicentre. Social scientists have largely examined process and pattern of conservation-induced displacement of communities and the resultant impoverishment of cultures and livelihoods. Their study revolves around people as actors, with nature as a mere backdrop' (Rangarajan and Shahabuddin 2006: 360). The chasm between biologists and social scientists seems insurmountable.

As a biologist who has engaged, though only superficially, with the politics of conservation and its socio-economic context, I have found that there are no easy answers either to the question of the causes of ecosystem erosion or of the best ways ahead. But through my book I attempt to pick out some of the common chords within the numerous disparate voices speaking for Indian conservation. I hope to carve out a middle ground that encompasses equally the views of the social scientist and the biologist.

Emerging Voices

While the principal mode of conservation adopted in India has been exclusionary in its orientation, it would not be accurate to say that alternative paradigms have not been experimented with at all. Pioneering participatory work in forest conservation has been undertaken in Independent India. In 1990 an innovative forest officer in West Bengal sowed the seeds of a revolutionary Joint Forest Management (JFM) Programme which worked towards re-greening the degraded landscape on which millions of people depended for their livelihoods and energy sources. Around the same time, community-initiated conservation movements were rapidly spreading in the Indian countryside, often as a reaction against industrial interests—with their aggressive demand for valuable resources such as bamboo and timber—that threatened to undermine local livelihoods. Such movements frequently had their historical roots in subaltern movements in the late nineteenth and early twentieth century. They were, in fact, often closely connected with popular demands for greater empowerment and decentralized governance. In the later part of the book I focus on participatory conservation strategies that have been adopted by the Indian government as well as those initiated locally. My aim is to evaluate both their larger role in and their limitations for biological conservation, and to distil from this some lessons for the future.

During recent times, India has become home to a diversity of state-sponsored programmes and grassroots movements. Many recent conservation initiatives are piecemeal in their approach to biodiversity, while others are more holistic. Some are ambitious in their scale while others are limited to a single district, PA, or even village. All of these efforts, if they are given an honest chance, promise to alter the narrow ways in which Indians tend to think about conservation and biodiversity. Together they form a jigsaw puzzle, however fragmented and unstable, that will form the vital framework for more viable and effective conservation in the future. In the last chapter of the book I try to piece together ingredients for a more effective strategy for nature protection in India, based on past experience and emerging efforts. I hope my proposed conservation paradigm will address many of the important

Illustr. 3: A villager being fined for an offence in the Palamau Tiger Reserve, Jharkhand. Millions of people in India continue to be dependent on forest resources due to lack of alternatives, and continually come into conflict with forest department staff. (*Photo: Jagdish Krishnaswamy*)

concerns—of equity, ecology, and participation—that have dogged conservation for decades.

These concerns have to be addressed, and soon. India is one of only seventeen 'megadiversity' countries of the world (Mittermeier *et al.* 1997). It has an astonishing array of habitats and species, many of which are yet to be documented, let alone studied. The country's ecological heterogeneity makes it possible to travel from deserts to mangroves, and from temperate meadows to swamps, within a few hours. India also possesses many species that are not found anywhere else, such as the charismatic Nilgiri tahr and the elusive Malabar trogon of the Western Ghats. Human interaction with different ecologies has spawned an equally rich array of cultures in India. To allow such tremendous diversity of wildlife and peoples to disappear would be a monumental tragedy, one that would leave Indians much the poorer not only materially, but also in spirit.

Acknowledgements

I would like to thank the New India Foundation for their generous support of this book through their fellowship which I availed of during 2007 and 2008. I am grateful to Ramachandra Guha and Mahesh Rangarajan for taking time to send me their extremely useful and detailed comments on the first draft of this book. A special thanks to Ravi Kumar and Manish Shrivastava for their generosity in allowing me to use the results of our joint research (at the Council for Social Development) for the first chapter of this book.

I also thank the Center for Wildlife Studies, Ministry of Environment and Forests, Wildlife Conservation Society's India Programme, National Foundation for India, Wildlife Protection Society of India, Oriental Bird Club, Ford Foundation, International Union for Forestry Research Organizations, and Winrock-International India for their financial support of the research projects on which this book is based. The Council for Social Development provided a valuable base for my research activities over 2002–7 and for that I am extremely grateful. I would also like to acknowledge Dr Ullas Karanth of the Wildife Conservation Society, Dr Mahesh Rangarajan, and Professor Muchkund Dubey of the Council for Social Development for their unstinting support to all my academic ventures during the last several years. A special thanks to Rukun Advani and Anuradha Roy for their help with publication and to Raman Kumar for assisting me with references and many other tasks.

My journey into the world of wildlife conservation started long ago, when I was still at school. In 1985, I participated in what must have been one of the most engaging debates I have ever been part of—a meeting of members of the Kalpavriksh Environmental Action Group in Delhi. By asking some of the most difficult environmental questions of the time, Kalpavriksh opened my eyes to the complexity of the task of protecting India's biodiversity. I walked into hazardous terrain but the journey has been well worth it. I would like to specially thank Ajay Mahajan, Anchal Khemka, Ashish Kothari, Chiranjeev Bedi, Farhad Vania, Jagdish Krishnaswamy, Kanchi Kohli, Krishnendu Bose, Pankaj Sekhsaria, Prabhakar Rao, Pradeep Malhotra, Pratibha Pande, Seema Bhatt, Shekhar Singh, and Sunita Rao for frequent and stimulating discussions. I would like to specially thank Ranjit Lal for continually showing me humour not only in the environmental movement but also in the birds of field and forest!

Back in the early 1990s my friends and colleagues in Kodaikanal's exciting Sustainable Development Programme helped me gain real-life exposure to how conservation projects can or cannot work—in an environment that could not have been more dramatically different from the Delhi-based environmental movement. Rauf Ali, particularly, introduced me to my first real-life problem in conservation by hiring me in my first job ever, a valuable vantage point from where I gained many insights. His unorthodox approach to conservation has won him many admirers and I am certainly in that league. Neelu Sharma, Farshid Ahrestani, Jayshree Ratnam, Sonali Saha, Jagdish Krishnaswamy, Gyanendra Singh, Pratim Roy, Amartya Saha, and Matthew John were part of the team I worked with and provided stimulating company. As professors in Pondicherry University, Devi Prasad, N. Parthasarathy, and Priya Davidar opened many doors to learning and I am grateful to them.

Duke University's Nicholas School of the Environment was where I learnt the tools of the trade and worked with inspiring professors—John Terborgh, Dean Urban, Steve Nijhout, Martha Groom, and Laura Snook—each of whom wonderful supervisors. They were the reason I left Duke with a tremendous sense of empowerment for taking on tricky research questions in the chaotic environmental landscape of India.

I also thank numerous other friends and colleagues for their support and encouragement through the years and for openly sharing their ideas and thoughts, all of which contributed to the germination and culmination of this book: Ajay Mehta, Amit Nair, Amita Baviskar, Amita Shah, Ankila Hiremath, Arpan Sharma, Asad Rahmani, Asmita Kabra, Belinda Wright, Bharati Chaturvedi, C.R. Babu, D.V. Girish, Deepshikha Mehra, Dunu Roy, Farida Tampal, G. Areendran, Gopi Sundar, Gunnel Cederlöf, Harini Nagendra, Hilaluddin, Jagdeesh Rao, Joanna van Gruisen, John Seidensticker, K. Sivaramakrishnan, K.C. Malhotra, Kamal Bawa, Kartik Shankar, Kartik Vasudevan, Kim Beazley, Kinsuk Mitra, Krithi Karanth, M.D. Madhusudan, Madhu Rao, Mahesh Rangarajan, Mohan Hirabai Hiralal, Nitin Sethi, Pia Sethi, Raghubir Chundawat, Raman Kumar, Raman Sukumar, Ravi Chellam, Rohan D'Souza, Rucha Ghate, Samba Kumar, Savyasaachi, Sharad Lele, Soumya Prasad, Tapan Mishra, Vasant Saberwal, Vidya Athreya, and Vikram Dayal.

At the Indian Forest Service I would like to thank P.K. Sen, A.S. Negi, Promode Kant, H. Somashekhara, Rajiv Bhartari, Rajiv Shrivastava, Gopal V. Reddy, and Sanjeeva Pandey, who continue their battle for nature on various fronts. Their work truly inspires and gives me hope that we can still make it with all our wildlife into the next century. They generously shared their insights and information with me for the purposes of this book.

For this book, my travels into Sitamata Wildlife Sanctuary were anchored by Jagdeesh Rao, Sanjeev Joshi, and Justus Joshua; in West Bengal by Tapan Mishra; and in Mendha (Lekha) and Tadoba-Andhari Tiger Reserve by Mohan Hiralal, Kim Beazley, Rucha Ghate, and Deepshikha Mehra. Without the local support of all these friends, much of the information herein could not have been collected.

Our competent field assistants in Sariska—Mangu Singh, Om Prakash Gujjar, and Khagesh Kumar—not only enriched the quality of our research but considerably and unfailingly livened our field experience. I am grateful to them for their efficient help and generosity at all times.

Last, but not least, I would like to thank my husband Jawed Ashraf for his unstinting support through every journey, both academic and personal.

1

The Anatomy of a Failing Paradigm

Crisis and Response

The extinction of the Bengal tiger from Rajasthan's Sariska Tiger Reserve in February 2005 made prominent newspaper headlines.[1] Biologists, wildlife-lovers, social activists, and the public were shocked. The tiger, along with the rhinoceros, the lion, and the elephant, is one of the few animal species for which most Indians feel considerable pride. It has been the prime flagship species for conservation in India since the 1970s when Project Tiger, one of the largest conservation projects in the world at the time, was initiated.

Most commentators attributed the tiger's local extinction in Sariska to large-scale poaching (Wright 2005). However, biologists familiar with Sariska maintained that the tiger was bound to disappear sooner or later, given the visible degradation of forests in the reserve and the fact that the tiger population had reached an all-time low (Johnsingh *et al.* 1997).[2] Thus for many conservationists this news was no more than a dramatic manifestation of the general failure of India's PA network in protecting biodiversity.

[1] *Indian Express*, 15 February 2005, p. 1: 'No Evidence of Tigers in Sariska-WWF-India'; *Times of India*, 30 January 2005, 'Big Cat Vanishes from Sariska; Will Ranthambhore be Next?'

[2] However, the official figure, based on the officially conducted annual tiger census, had fluctuated between 16 and 25 animals from 1991 to 2004. In 2004, the last season when tigers were spotted in Sariska, the official figure was 16–18.

Sariska had always been a high-profile tiger habitat. Being one of the tiger reserves established during the early years of Project Tiger, it was frequented by ministers and bureaucrats, partly because of its proximity to both Delhi and Jaipur. The tourists came in droves—Sariska being only a slight detour on the popular tourist circuit from Delhi to Jaipur—in the hope of spotting one of the big cats. The reserve got considerable attention from biologists as well: many a doctoral thesis was based there and it was a field training site for forest officers. Because of its prominence, it had comparatively better infrastructure and management resources than many other tiger reserves; for example, it had one of the highest guard-to-forest area ratios in the country (Ministry of Environment & Forests 2005).

The 'tiger crisis' was puzzling for another reason. Sariska had been the site of a village-based initiative in forest and water conservation since the late 1980s spearheaded by the Tarun Bharat Sangh, an influential voluntary organization working in Rajasthan.[3] Many conservationists had argued that a certain level of coexistence had been established between local communities and wildlife over the years through the efforts of the Tarun Bharat Sangh, which was working among the village people on projects relating to water and forest conservation. If there ever was a place where wildlife had a fighting chance, it was here in Sariska. So, clearly, something had gone terribly wrong in the Reserve.

The immediate response of the state forest department of Rajasthan was to take steps to increase armed protection of the reserve, using paramilitary and police forces.[4] Since commercial poaching, aided and abetted by the local villagers, was thought to be the primary cause behind the disappearance of the tiger, villagers suspected to be part of the tiger-poaching ring were arrested. Some observers felt that the arrests had been made without significant corroborative evidence (Gupta 2005). For the first time in its history the reserve

[3] 'A Role for Villagers in Managing Sariska', *The Hindu*, New Delhi, 12 September 2000, p. 5.

[4] 'Roar Like a Tiger, Mr. Prime Minister', *Indian Express* (online edition), New Delhi, 18 May 2005.

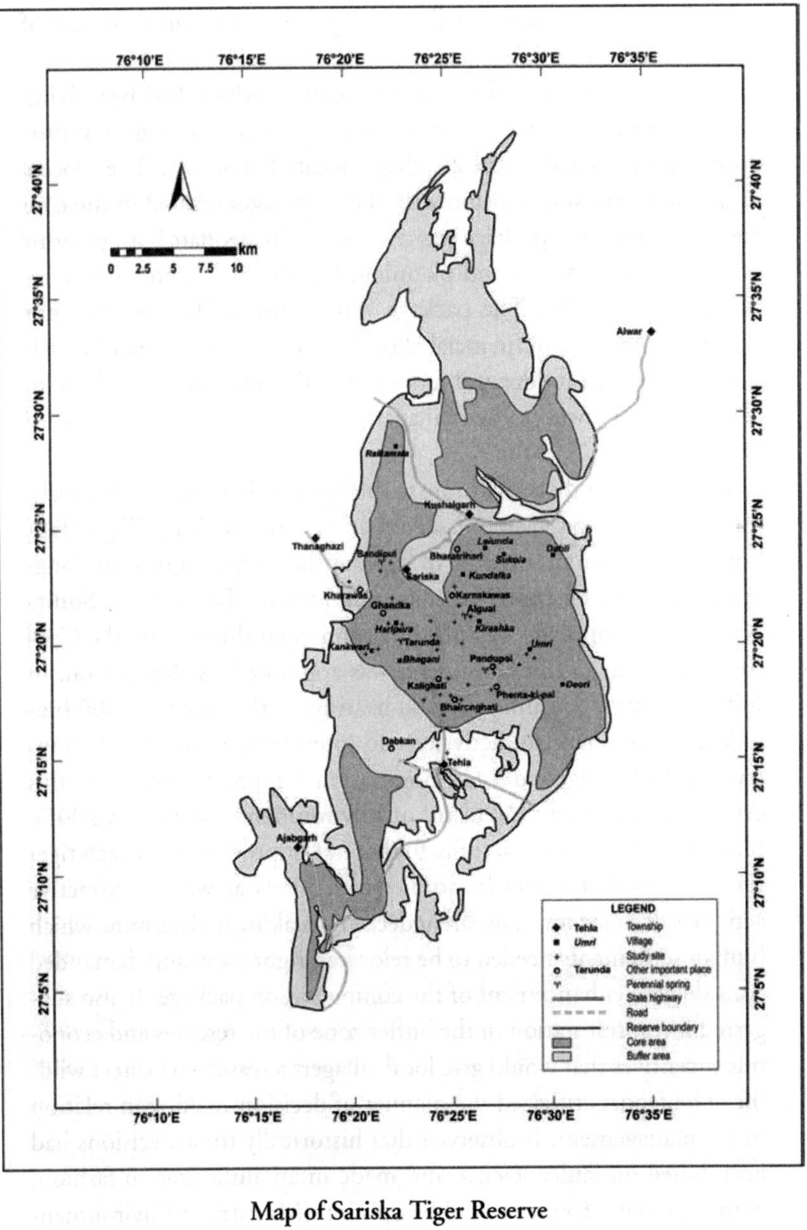

Map of Sariska Tiger Reserve

was closed to the public for a period of four months. Investigations aided by India's premier intelligence agency, the Central Bureau of Investigation, began.

In July 2005 a plan for village relocation, which had been lying dormant for three years, was revived by the reserve's managers. It proposed moving out all of the 27 villages located in Sariska. The process of displacement was to begin with the 11 villages located in the core area. The relocation package was criticized as inadequate both in terms of financial allocations and planning, but this was ignored (Shahabuddin *et al.* 2005). The package was riddled with problems, not least being the lack of financial allocation for irrigation and of provision for livestock fodder and fuelwood in the new site (Shahabuddin *et al.* 2007). However, the managers were eager to push ahead with this plan.

Realizing that there was more to the 'tiger crisis' than merely poaching, the Indian government set up an expert panel, the Tiger Task Force (TTF), in an attempt to explore the deeper and more long-term causes of declining tiger populations in the country. Sunita Narain, director of the reputed environmental think-tank, the Centre for Science and Environment, was appointed its chairperson. In July 2005, after consultations and hearings with more than 300 biologists, social scientists, activists, and forest officers across the country, the TTF suggested a far more rational approach to resolve this crisis of conservation (Ministry of Environment and Forests 2005). It advocated planning carefully for habitat improvement in each tiger reserve, based on scientific studies of habitats as well as extractive activities. It called for transparent decision-making to determine which human settlements needed to be relocated right away and demanded considerable enhancement of the compensation package. It also suggested forest restoration in the buffer zone of the reserves and economic incentives that would give local villagers a reason to protect wildlife. The report criticized the manner of decision-making in relation to PA management. It observed that historically these decisions had been based on faulty science and made in an authoritarian fashion, with minimal reference to public opinion (Ministry of Environment and Forests 2005). The TTF also suggested that biologists, including the growing number of independent scientists in India, be involved in designing the future management of tiger reserves.

The report was published in July 2005 and the response to it underlined the extreme divisions among the country's conservationists. Valmik Thapar, an influential wildlifer who has written extensively on tigers, was scathing about the report, saying it did not give enough importance to tiger conservation needs. He saw its recommendations as 'the final nail in the coffin' for the tiger.[5] He saw little possibility for coexistence between people and tigers and supported comprehensive village displacement from reserves (Thapar 2005). K. Ullas Karanth, a renowned tiger biologist, while appreciating the data-based and transparent approach of the TTF, opposed its suggestion of enhancing coexistence between villagers and wildlife by allowing multiple use in some of the tiger habitats (K.U. Karanth 2005). On the other hand, some conservationists hailed the TTF report as representing a significant step forward in India's conservation history given its transparent mode of functioning, high degree of public participation, and emphasis on scientific rigour (Shahabuddin 2005).

Poaching, seen as the primary cause for tiger extermination in Sariska and other tiger reserves, became a target for longer-term action as well. As suggested by the TTF, the Tiger and Other Endangered Species Crime Control Bureau was established. This would have special powers to investigate wildlife crime. The National Tiger Conservation Authority was set up in New Delhi; it delegated considerable power to the union ministry of environment and forests to make decisions on management issues relating to tiger reserves.[6] In November 2006 legal amendments to the Wildlife Protection Act of 1972 were passed in parliament, giving more powers to local authorities to apprehend illegal poaching and forest use and considerably enhancing the punishment for wildlife-related crime. And in July 2007 fresh financial

[5] Interviewed in *Frontline* magazine, 9 September 2005.

[6] 'Tiger Protection: Centre Threatens to Block State Funds', *Times of India* (online edition), 22 March 2008.

provisions were made to establish an elite Tiger Protection Force comprising ex-servicemen and people living around tiger reserves.[7]

In November 2005 another important recommendation of the TTF was taken up for action: a mammoth proposal to conduct a fresh countrywide census with the aim of establishing more accurate tiger numbers. One of the failings in reserve management was thought to be the technique of counting individual tigers using primarily their pugmarks. This technique had long been criticized as leading to the over-reporting of tiger numbers in Sariska and other tiger reserves in the country, and was therefore seen as partly responsible for obscuring the crisis. The pugmark method was finally to be phased out during the new census. This time, the census was to assume the form of a multi-stage, scientifically rigorous process that would take field researchers from the Wildlife Institute of India to every tiger reserve in the country. Tigers would be counted using statistically definitive methods based on intensive camera-trapping, backed up by remote sensing as well as field studies of vegetation to assess the available habitat.

Earlier in 2005 a bold government decision had been made: to reintroduce tigers in Sariska as soon as possible.[8] A feasibility study was therefore carried out in 2007 by the Wildlife Institute. It recommended shifting three adult tigers from the Ranthambhore Tiger Reserve, located approximately 200 km away in a similar ecosystem. However, most conservationists felt that the reintroduction of tigers without the necessary improvements in management infrastructure, forest restoration, development of local partnerships, and strengthened buffer zone management would be doomed. The viable habitat for tigers in 2007 was 70–80 sq. km at most, because one had to discount the forest area degraded by forest overexploitation or occupied by villages. Such a small area was unlikely to maintain a significant tiger population for too long.

[7] 'Exclusive Space for Tigers Soon', *Times of India*, New Delhi, 23 July 2007, p. 9.

[8] 'Rajasthan Panel Wants Tigers Relocated', *Indian Express* (online edition), 8 September 2005.

In the meantime the reserve managers pressed ahead with the relocation plan for the eleven villages located inside the core area, a plan that was expected to pave the way for tiger reintroductions. In September 2007 this phase of relocation began with the small village of Bhagani, comprising twenty households: they were moved out from Sariska to a denotified forest site 70 km away. When I visited the resettlement site just a few weeks after the relocation had begun, only seven houses had been completely constructed. Not surprisingly, the financial allotment of Rs 84,000 for house construction in the relocation site turned out to be too low for the kind of housing expected by the villagers. As the cost of construction of each house had risen to Rs 1.1 lakh, the forest department reported that the initial financial allocation for land-tilling and transportation of the villagers' belongings had now been diverted to house construction. A failed winter crop (the result of sowing too late in the monsoon) was already visible in the villagers' fields. While road connections, agricultural land development, and electricity connections were satisfactory in the resettlement site, budget constraints restricted water supply to only a single deep borewell. This catered to drinking water demands but left no provision for irrigation; irrigation was necessary if the villagers were to plant more than a single crop each year. Livestock fodder was another major limiting factor as there were no forests near the resettlement site where livestock could be grazed. A certain degree of optimism was, all the same, evident among the displaced villagers. They had been desperate to move out of Sariska because of their wretched condition inside the reserve; several families also possessed some agricultural land in other villages outside the reserve which was tiding them over the first year after relocation. But it would take a long time before they could reach a degree of livelihood security in the resettlement site.

In February 2008 the final report on the national tiger population, which confirmed dwindling tiger numbers in the country, was published by the Wildlife Institute of India.[9] The estimate of the number of tigers in the country had gone down to 1411 from the

[9] National Tiger Conservation Authority and Wildlife Institute of India 2008.

nearly 3600 counted in 2003, a period of just five years.[10] Yet there were doubts about the accuracy of the new census, given that several tiger reserves and known habitats outside PAs could not be surveyed for logistical reasons. While the census was peer-reviewed, the reviewing did not coincide with the design of the census and suffered from several shortcomings which considerably reduced its credibility.[11] For instance, field methodology was not consistent across the numerous tiger reserves with respect to assessing forest quality and herbivore abundance. The extrapolation of tiger density figures calculated for unrepresentative sampling areas to entire tiger reserves could have been another critical source of error in tiger population estimation.

In July 2008 Bhagani continued to face problems of irrigation and insecurity of livelihood, though the villagers appeared more confident about making a transition to modern living. The financial allocation for village relocation had officially been enhanced to Rs 10 lakhs in 2008,[12] but the beneficiary families had not yet gained. The reserve managers felt that the villagers, egged on by local politicians, were increasing their demands. Further, they felt that the final rehabilitation would be particularly difficult because, as one of the senior forest personnel said, 'They are not people who are willing to work hard and make their land productive.' According to a newspaper report there was opposition to the new villagers at Badhod Rund, the village where the resettlement site was located. The original residents of the area formed a committee to protest against the move to resettle villagers in the area.[13] There were also indications of resistance to displacement in other villages of Sariska if appropriate adjustments were not made in the compensation package and better implementation not ensured.

Meanwhile, at the insistence of the Rajasthan state forest department, a pair of tigers was reintroduced into Sariska in June 2008.[14] The

[10] 'Just 1411 Tigers in India', *Times of India* (online edition), 13 February 2008.

[11] Maraj and Seidensticker 2006.

[12] Press Release of the Ministry of Environment and Forests, 23 March 2008.

[13] 'Behror Doesn't Want People to Shift from Sariska', *Times of India*, New Delhi, 29 November 2006, p. 5.

[14] 'After 4 Years, Sariska Gets a Tiger', *Times of India* (online edition), New Delhi, 29 June 2008.

reintroduction took place under heavy secrecy, with only a few favoured conservationists and media persons allowed inside the reserve during that period. It was reported that airlifting the animals from Ranthambhore and fitting them with state-of-the-art satellite radio-collars had cost at least Rs 15 crore. The two reintroduced tigers continue to be guarded heavily by forest personnel, their every move reported each day by the reserve managers.

Apart from the enforced reappearance of the tiger, or rather a pair of them, not much has changed in Sariska Tiger Reserve in terms of governance or forest condition even three years after the crisis of 2005. Forest habitat continues to degrade, particularly in the buffer zone. Buffer zone management is still restricted to policing. There have been no efforts to design ways for local villages to share in the revenues earned by the reserve, or to develop tourism infrastructure from which they can gain. Still less has been done to regulate the ever-increasing numbers of pilgrims and tourists who pass through the reserve,[15] or manage the state highway which causes numerous road-kills each year.[16] The pollution of ecologically important permanent springs continues. The threat of poaching remains, given the hostility towards the forest department among most people living in and around the reserve. Nine of the ten core villages inside the reserve are years away from being relocated, given the difficulties in successful resettlement of the first village. The habitat is far from restored or secured, yet the reserve managers saw it fit to bring back tigers at enormous cost.

Why did the situation in Sariska reach such a gridlock? I try here to explore the historical and social causes of the conservation crisis in Sariska, a tiger reserve that has much in common with other Indian PAs. It seems important to understand the crisis by studying the history of rights and management, the relationship between biodiversity patterns and people's livelihoods, as well as state responses to human–wildlife conflict in colonial India. Much of the information in this chapter was collected during a series of research projects in the Sariska

[15] 'Sariska to Ban Private Vehicles', *Times of India* (online edition), 13 February 2008.

[16] 'Highway Traffic Threatens Animals in Sariska', *Times of India* (online edition), 5 May 2008.

Tiger Reserve. I have worked there since 2003 with my colleagues Raman Kumar, Ravi Kumar, and Manish Shrivastava, whose assistance, ideas, and analysis have been indispensable. Initially our research was focused on patterns in the distribution and occurrence of forest bird species across the mosaic of used and intact tiger habitat, and the threat to them from grazing and biomass extraction. Later we began studying the socio-economics, politics, and history of this intriguing tiger reserve. Perhaps this detailed micro-analysis of the relationships between people, animals, and the state can help illuminate exactly where Indian conservation is going wrong.

Diversity at the Edge of the Desert

The Sariska Tiger Reserve was one of the most important conservation areas in Rajasthan, representing the westernmost limit of the tiger in India in the semi-arid north-west (Divyabhanusinh 1987). It still has the potential for sustaining a high density of tigers, being similar in habitat to the better-known Ranthambhore Tiger Reserve (Sankhala 1964, 1969). At first glance the dry forests of Sariska appear to be an unlikely sanctuary for wildlife. The monotonous dhok stands (leafless for a large part of the year) and thorny scrub forest seem to be rather inhospitable. A walk through the forest, however, reveals a diversity of plants and animals, all uniquely adapted to the extremes of temperature experienced in this part of Rajasthan.[17] Sariska is hot and dry in the summer, with temperatures sometimes reaching 45°C. Nor does the monsoon in July substantially alleviate the heat: the annual rainfall is less than 650 mm per year, restricted to a few weeks each year. The winter makes up, with its sunny and pleasant days and close-to-freezing temperatures at night.

The most widespread forest type in Sariska is dry deciduous,[18] dominated by trees of dhok (*Anogeissus pendula*), salar (*Boswellia serrata*),

[17] See for instance studies and notes by Reddy 1994, Sankar and Johnsingh 2002, Sankar 1994, Sankar *et al.* 1993, Sharma 1981, Sharma 1986, and Sharma 2001.

[18] A type of forest located in a region where there is less than 2000 mm of rainfall annually. Most trees shed their leaves synchronously, so the forest appears leafless at a particular time of the year.

and jhingan (*Lannea coromandelica*). These cover the hill slopes right up to the steep ridges. In the drier and flatter terrain thorny scrub forest occurs, with small trees of palash (*Butea monosperma*), ber (*Ziziphus mauritiana*), raunj (*Acacia leucophloea*), and khair (*Acacia catechu*), interspersed with a variety of grasses. The scrubby plains are where the nilgai graze contentedly even in the midday heat while chital gather at waterholes and small reservoirs, many of which are man-made.

But it is the cool confines of the tall riverside forest, now restricted to fragments scattered throughout the reserve, with its lush trees of gular (*Ficus infectoria*), baans (*Dendrocalamus strictus*), kadamb (*Mitragyna parvifolia*), and khajur (*Phoenix sylvestris*), that holds many a surprise for the visitor. These narrow and sometimes deep valleys have streams running through them, many of which are perennial and harbour very diverse forest in comparison to the scrub or dhok stands. One can often startle a sambar stag (*Cervus duvauceli*), a crested serpent eagle (*Spilornis cheela*), or a brown fish owl (*Ketupa zeylonensis*), here, early on a summer morning, or run into families of painted spurfowl and peafowl scratching up leaf litter. I have observed usually elusive insect-eating birds such as the red-throated flycatcher (*Ficedula parva*), Tickell's blue flycatcher (*Cyornis tickelliae*), and the grey-headed canary flycatcher (*Culicicapa ceylonensis*) by the streamside.

Scientists (mostly from the Wildlife Institute of India) have carried out a number of studies on flora and fauna in the reserve since the 1990s.[19] Carnivores such as the leopard (*Panthera pardus*) and the jungle cat (*Felis chaus*) are commonly seen in Sariska (Mukherjee 2000). There also exist a number of intriguing small mammals, including the ruddy mongoose (*Herpestes smithii*), the common palm civet (*Paradoxurus hermaphroditus*), the rarely seen caracal (*Caracal caracal*), and the ratel (*Mellivora capensis*); not much is known as yet about the ecology of these animal species. The four-horned antelope, which lives singly or in pairs (*Tetracerus quadricornis*), was always rare in Sariska but may have become extinct during the last few years (A.J.T. Johnsingh, pers. comm.). The chinkara (*Gazella bennetti*) is reported to have been commonly observed in the 1960s but had obviously disappeared by

[19] See Mukherjee 2000, Sharma 2001, Sankar 1994, Sankar *et al.* 1993, Rodgers 1990, Sankar and Johnsingh 2002.

the 1990s, as can be inferred from the lack of references to it in accounts by naturalists after that period (Sankhala 1964). Wolves (*Canis lupus*) and Indian wild dogs (*Cuon alpinus*), which have been spotted occasionally in the past, are likely to be occasional visitors. The rich mammalian diversity in the reserve, despite the low rainfall and extreme temperatures, can be attributed at least partly to the presence of several permanent springs (Rodgers 1990).

Sariska is astonishingly rich in bird species, too, rivalling many of the other tiger reserves in India: 236 species have been recorded so far. It has been identified as one of the Important Bird Areas in the state of Rajasthan by Birdlife International (Shahabuddin *et al.* 2006; Bombay Natural History Society 2001).[20] Much of the avifauna is typical of the tropical dry forests of peninsular India, such as the painted spurfowl (*Galloperdix lunulata*), the yellow-eyed babbler (*Chrysomma sinense*), the grey francolin (*Francolinus pondicerianus*), and the black-shouldered kite (*Elanus caeruleus*) (Bombay Natural History Society 2001). With its rugged and open landscape and tall cliffs, Sariska is particularly rich in raptors. The list of raptors includes the crested serpent-eagle and the brown fish owl that stick to the forested stream tracts. It is still common to see flocks of vultures circling over carnivore kills and livestock carcasses in the forest, a sight that is becoming rare in other parts of northern India. While the long-billed vulture (*Gyps indicus*) is most commonly seen, the white-backed vulture (*Gyps bengalensis*) and the red-headed vulture (*Sarcogyps calvus*), which are listed as critically endangered, can also be occasionally spotted. During autumn and spring the scrub forests in Sariska come alive with the calls of passage migrants such as the common rosefinch (*Carpodacus erythrinus*) and the rosy starling (*Sturnus roseus*), which migrate in large flocks. The diversity of habitats—riverain forest, hill slopes, evergreen scrub forest, waterbodies, the degraded parts around villages—is collectively responsible for the rich birdlife, which is augmented by large numbers of seasonal migrants. The riverain forest is

[20] Important Bird Areas (IBA) is a scientific category based on richness of species and endemism (distribution only in a delimited area), indicating importance as a conservation site for birds.

in particular crucial for birdlife, providing a largely evergreen habitat and rich diversity of trees that provide for roosting cover, fruit, and insects throughout the year (Rodgers 1990).

From Hunter's Paradise to Tiger Reserve

What has become the Sariska Tiger Reserve was originally a hunting reserve for Maharaja Jaisingh of Alwar. Photographs of tiger-hunts from the early twentieth century show carcasses of gigantic tigers shot by the maharaja and his British guests—with the assistance of over a hundred game-beaters. The glamorous shooting accounts conceal a brutal history. Records from the nineteenth century onward show how cattle-camps of nomadic graziers were shifted out of the forest and portions closed for grazing and wood-cutting. During the same period the state allowed parts of Sariska's central valley to be opened up for the commercial sale of forest produce such as wood. By all accounts the forests of Sariska contributed considerably to the state treasury. Records indicate that several of the villages that exist today inside the reserve were established under the *lamberdaari* system to enhance revenue collection from forest products such as timber, charcoal, and fodder grasses (Johari 2007).[21] During this period people also received grazing passes for a fee based on the number of cattle they owned. The fee differed for cows, buffaloes, and goats. The minimum amount reported was 50 paise per buffalo per year during the rule of the maharaja of Alwar. By the time the maharaja's repressive regime was brought to an end in 1933 and the British took over the forests of Sariska, timber and bamboo had become important sources of income for the government (Johari 2007). The forest department formulated a regime for the collection of forest produce which continued up to Independence. In the post-Independence period, however, there was extensive working of the forests for charcoal and timber extraction. While some villages and cattle-camps were moved out after 1947, others were allowed to remain.

[21] Lamberdaari was a system of tax collection wherein one person (the *lamberdaar*) was assigned the task of revenue collection from a revenue unit comprising one or more villages.

Sariska was brought under the purview of the Rajasthan Wild Animals and Birds Protection Act of 1951 after a notification by the state government in 1955. After recommendations from eminent naturalists such as Dharmakumarsinhji (1952), Sariska was declared a Wildlife Sanctuary with an area of 492 sq. km on 18 September 1958 with an amended notification under the Rajasthan Wild Animals and Birds Protection Act. It is important to note that the area had not been legally declared a Reserved Forest under the Rajasthan Forest Act.[22] Because game reserves under the erstwhile Alwar princely state did not have any legal status in Independent India, the question of a wildlife sanctuary did not legally arise. There had been no settlement of rights, which is obligatory for the formal establishment of reserved forests or wildlife sanctuaries. So the villages and cattle-camps remained where they were even after the sanctuary notification.[23]

In the 1960s measures were taken to shift some of the habitations within the Sariska sanctuary. Cattle-camps, referred to as *guadas* by the forest department, were relocated over 1966–7 from Kalighati and Slopka—today part of the core area—to some of the existing villages outside the sanctuary. Later, in 1976–7, two villages, Karnakawas and Kiraska, were relocated in a more organized fashion. This was the first attempt to relocate full-fledged villages (rather than just cattle-camps) in the post-Independence period. Several of those moved out returned to live close to the present-day reserve, due to inadequate resettlement.

In 1979 Sariska was officially declared a Project Tiger Reserve with a total area of 866 sq. km. The years 1980–2 were the beginning of an era of rapidly tightening controls on forest use by local people. Commercial felling of dhok was stopped by the forest department. Restrictions on grazing and agriculture by the local villages were now more strictly enforced. A formal 'Intention' to notify a part of the Core Zone of Sariska Tiger Reserve as National Park was issued in 1982. Following this, in 1987, the forest department issued a statement to the effect

[22] Only declared Reserved Forests, where rights have been settled, can be upgraded to the status of a Wildlife Sanctuary or National Park, according to the WLPA 1972.

[23] For further detail on this aspect of the matter, see the Project Tiger Website: http://projecttiger.nic.in/sariska.htm

that all villages inside the reserve were 'illegal'. All activities relating to forest use by locals were banned and people were left with mainly informal rights of forest use.

Sariska today refers to a tiger reserve of 866 sq. km, which includes areas officially under three categories of forest land: Wildlife Sanctuary, Reserved Forest, and Protected Forest. These categories, however, do not necessarily coincide with the core and buffer zones. The core area itself is divided into 3 parts: Core Area I, II, & III covering areas, respectively, of 400.14 sq. km, 126.50 sq. km, and 97.50 sq. km, which are not continuous with each other. Additionally, the buffer area of the reserve covers 241.86 sq. km (see Map).

While the declared buffer zone today has 16 villages, the core area contains 11 (Map; Table 1). The villages of Deori, Dabli, and Raikamala in the core area currently claim to be 'revenue villages'—villages that have agricultural land and formal land rights (*pattas*)—rather than 'forest villages'; the remaining 8 have no real legal status or land rights. Two other villages, Umri and Kiraska, used to be 'revenue

Table 1

Sampling Design Adopted for Household Surveys

Village	Total No. of HH*	Total HH Surveyed	Per cent HHs Surveyed
Bhagani	17	17	100
Dabli	68	15	22
Deori	73	15	21
Haripura	30	6	20
Kankwari	68	36	53
Kiraska	87	45	52
Kundalka	30	5	17
Lilunda	16	4	25
Raikamala	49	10	20
Sukola	22	4	18
Umri	33	33	100
All Villages	493	190	39

HH: Household

villages' when Sariska became a wildlife sanctuary. But in the 1980s the status of Kiraska village was officially mutated to Reserved Forest, and that of Umri earlier, in the 1960s.[24]

As far as informal rights of forest use are concerned, villagers are allowed to graze their livestock and collect forest produce within a certain arbitrary area (up to a radius of 1–2 km) around their villages. They are usually fined for grazing if their livestock stray beyond, particularly if they reach relatively better-guarded areas inside the tourism zones. Livestock are most often confiscated from tourist zones such as Pandupol, Kalighati, and Karnakawas. Local people report that grazing was allowed for a fee up to about ten years ago, but that system was withdrawn without notice. Villagers also have right of way through the reserve's gates so that they do not have to pay entry fees. Villagers believe that they have the right to collect timber for house construction and fuelwood for household use. However, there is some confusion about their exact rights and privileges. Even forest personnel admit that there is no clear instruction to them on what constitutes valid use by villagers.

Our interviews revealed that a committee had been set up for the settlement of rights in 1977 with the subdivisional magistrate of Alwar as its chair, as required by the Wildlife Protection Act.[25] A settlement of rights process requires an official notice asking the people to claim

[24] These dates are based on the timeline provided by the villagers. About Umri, a forester related how a past forest department director used false promises to trick people into transferring their revenue land into forest land. A villager of Deori, however, said that since Umri was under Deori's *lamberdaari*, the Deori lamberdaar, a Meena by caste, was told that if he gave up claims over Umri's revenue land, he could keep Deori. He accepted the offer and therefore kept Deori. If he had not done so, Deori too would have been converted to Reserved Forest.

[25] The settlement of rights is an administrative process that includes an initial declaration of change in land status from Reserved Forest to Wildlife Sanctuary, its local proclamation, the determination of existing rights to forest use in the specified area through an inquiry, their approval, and finally acquisition by the state of land rights or other rights after the relevant villagers have been provided an agreed compensation.

their rights within a specified period of time, which is followed by a verification process. Though the report was apparently made official in 1999, neither present-day forest officials nor local villagers knew about it. When questioned, the field director of Sariska said that the forest department is currently following the 1949 Rights Settlement report of Alwar State. The Constitution of India, the document defining Indian people's rights, came into effect from 26 January 1950; so the validity of a rights settlement document pre-dating the constitution, comes into question.

Living on the Edge: The People and Their History

Inside the core area of Sariska the villages tend to be small, with 15 to 100 households (Table 1).[26] The newest village among these is Bhagani.[27] Some of the villages, such as Kankwari, Raikamala, Dabli, and Deori, are much older. Kankwari, said to be at least a thousand years old, was inhabited by Bagrawats, Meenas, and Rajputs in the past. Deori too has temples dating back to 1820.[28] Other villages, however, refer their origin to the period of Maharaja Jaisingh of Alwar. There are also a few families that moved into Sariska during the twentieth century, from places as far as Jodhpur (470 km away), or as near as Dhwar Mala (barely 10 km from Sariska).[29]

[26] While there are 27 villages in all within the Sariska Tiger Reserve, our research was restricted to the 11 villages inside the core area. However, these are the villages that have always experienced the most conflict with reserve managers because the best wildlife was to be found around them.

[27] This estimate is based on a timeline as explained by some senior villagers of Bhagani.

[28] There is a Roopnath (Nath Sampraday) temple in Deori containing two statues. The newer one has a date of the 1880s (Vikram Samvat) engraved on it. The other statue is believed to be much older than this.

[29] Most of the Gujjars of this area say that they came from Dhwar Mala. Dhwar Mala is near Thanagazi, on top of a hillock. The legend is that during the Mughal period the ruler of Thanaghazi, a Muslim, tried to marry a Gujjar girl. Although the Gujjars agreed to the match, they subsequently killed him as well as the girl. Fearing reprisal, they then migrated to Sariska.

All the villages in the core area are inhabited primarily by Gujjars (87 per cent) who belong to the category of Other Backward Classes (OBC), designated as such for their relative socio-economic backwardness.[30] They are a community associated traditionally with pastoralism and dairy-farming. There are smaller numbers of Meenas (a Scheduled Tribe), as well as insignificant numbers of Meos, Brahmins, Rajputs, and Bairwa households in this area. Except for a few Meo households of Dabli that are Muslim, all the people in the area are Hindu. Despite being isolated from the outside world, people living inside the reserve do not worship a different pantheon of gods and goddesses.[31] The reserve is dotted with sites of Hindu religious significance. Villagers inhabiting the core zone worship at the Bandipul, Pandupol, and Bhartrihari temples (see Map). Religiosity akin to the world outside the reserve explains why, unlike many tribes, they do not have a distinct culture.

Outside the core area the villages are dominated by Meenas, both in terms of number as well as political power. Most of the old lamberdaar families are Meenas, as are the current representatives from the area to the Rajasthan state legislature. A Meena village on the southern boundary of Sariska is jocularly called the 'village of IAS' because of the large number of people from here who have joined the prestigious Indian Administrative Service. While in the eleven villages inside the core area Gujjars and Meenas live in relative harmony, outside there is considerable tension. (This became most apparent during the violent

[30] Other Backward Classes are a group of castes (as defined in Hindu society) that have been historically disadvantaged and therefore found deserving of affirmative action through reservations and protective legislation to try and bring about equality. However, they are ranked above Scheduled Tribes and Scheduled Castes in terms of their social advancement.

[31] The term 'outside world' is used here to designate the society, lifestyle, and patterns of socio-cultural and political behaviour outside the sanctuary. I wish to create this bifurcation in order to understand if they constitute distinct cultural worlds. Economics is not included here because of a visible distinction in the nature of economy—the production and distribution of commodities—between the world within the sanctuary and the one outside it. This distinction emerges because of the ban on agriculture in the sanctuary, apart from which integration into a commodified economic relation can be seen here as well.

protests across Rajasthan in 2007, when Gujjars demanded a change of their status to Scheduled Tribe.) Two villages where sizeable numbers of Meenas live at present are Deori and Kiraska. Both these villages were under Meena lamberdaari during the days of the Alwar state. Gujjars came in later, thereafter paying rent to the Meena lamberdaar.

As in most of rural Rajasthan, caste is socially the most important term of reference. In some accounts Gujjars are often depicted as a peaceful and contented people, never harming wild animals, particularly as they are lacto-vegetarians (Alves & Garcia-Perea 1998). When people were asked about poaching inside the area, locals almost always deny taking part and the common refrain was 'Gujjars don't eat meat or hunt.' There are several oral traditions about why Gujjars do not hunt. While talking about their existence in the reserve Gujjars often say: 'We Gujjars are very naïve. We don't understand the tricks and complexities of the outside world. If we are relocated, people outside would rob us . . . we are harmless people.' The most important aspect of caste dynamics, however, relates to local political activities. While political divisions exist mainly along caste lines, people's perceptions of politicians and local representatives also reflect caste concerns.[32] As in most of rural India, people usually take caste into account when voting. If there is more than one candidate from the same caste, the *gotra* (family tree) becomes the deciding factor.

Caste biases are also manifest in the villagers' historic and ongoing conflicts over forest use with the forest department. For example, the need for moving the villagers from Sariska was often articulated by forest personnel thus: 'These Gujjars don't want to work. Gujjars are lazy. Their women work while they eat *posht*'.[33] They don't want to move out. They want everything for free. They would never agree to leave this place because they wouldn't find free fodder and income without labour. Therefore they need to be evicted from the forest if this sanctuary has to be saved.' Interestingly, many of the guards and rangers in

[32] In Bandipul, when we referred to Kanti Meena's (a local MLA's) promise to get things in order, local villagers said, 'We know him very well. We are troubled by Meenas here and he is a Meena after all. He wins because Meenas vote for him. How can he favour us when our conflict is with the Meenas?'

[33] A derivative of opium used locally as a drug.

Sariska are Brahmins or Rajputs, traditionally the upper social strata in North India. Almost none are Gujjar. The casteist undertones employed by guards in their everyday dealings with local people further heighten the generally adversarial relationship between people and the forest department.

Decision-making processes within a village community are seemingly informal but are actually institutionalized locally. The older people in the community generally take the important decisions, such as those relating to elections when preferred candidates need to be decided on. When there are personal disputes amongst villagers, a group of elders generally meets to decide on the conflict. If there is a dispute over the decision, elders from five surrounding villages hear the case. This system, however, is not very effective where high stakes are involved. Such cases generally begin in the lower district courts. Women tend to be marginalized within the household and in village matters.

Left Out of Development

It would be safe to say that an uncertain existence inside a proposed national park has deprived local villagers of the basic development infrastructure that rural India can offer. Since the declaration of Sariska as a wildlife sanctuary, all developmental activity such as the building of permanent structures, including roads, wells, and schools, has been halted under the Wildlife Protection Act.

Contrary to urban perceptions about 'forest-dwellers', the local villagers depend totally on local markets for many of their daily requirements as well as their medical care, and depend on the forest only for fodder, fuelwood, and timber. So their distance from the market and accessibility is critical to their lives. The villagers in almost all cases need to travel a minimum of 10 km to reach the market, much of it on foot (Table 2). Basic healthcare, at a premium in much of rural India, is nearly absent here. The villagers need to walk anywhere between 2 and 14 km over fairly rough terrain just to reach a bus-stop from where they can get transport to a primary health centre (PHC). We often saw sick people being carried on a cot to the local PHC. For modern hospital facilities people need to cover a minimum distance of

Table 2: Basic Infrastructure in the Core Zone I Villages

Village	Fair Weather Road (km)	Nearest Market (km)	Post Office (km)	Bus Stop (km)	Bank (km)	Water Source	Annual Availability of Water*	Availability of Potable Water*
Bhagani	4	6	6	6	6	River	NO	NO
Dabli	4	10	4	4	10	Johad	NO	NO
Deori	11	16	10	15	16	Well, Johad	YES	YES
Haripura	1	10	2	2	10	Well, Johad	YES	YES
Kankwari	8	15	15	7	15	Well, Johad	YES	YES
Kiraska	5	20	10	7	20	Handpumps, Johad	YES	YES
Kundalka	2	12	2	2	12	Handpump, Well, Johad	YES	YES
Lilunda	3	13	5	3	12	Well, Johad	YES	YES
Raikamala	4	15	15	4	15	Johad, Kund	NO	NO
Sukola	4	15	4	4	15	Johad	NO	NO
Umri	3	25	25	14	35	Johad, Well	YES	YES

*Based on local perception of villagers.

30 km from anywhere in the core area. The only public health facilities that are available to all the villages are the polio drops vaccination and anti-malaria prevention programmes entailing pesticide spraying from time to time. Interestingly, local villagers did not report using wild plants for curing everyday ailments, as would be expected in a forest-dwelling community. The traditional knowledge base about the therapeutic values of plants, if ever it existed, exists no longer.

Another concern is the almost complete lack of educational facilities in the area. While the villagers do have access to government-run schools and those run by voluntary organizations, many children do not attend school because of the difficult terrain or the distances involved. Even when schools are accessible, the quality of teaching leaves much to be desired. Most of the government-appointed teachers come to work irregularly. Some of the teachers say they cannot teach because there are no proper school buildings. While money for school buildings was granted by the panchayat samiti in some of the villages, the funds cannot be utilized because of the prohibition on construction by the Forest Department.[34] Not surprisingly literacy rates are abysmally low. Our surveys revealed that the average literacy rate among the local people was only 32 per cent. Only about 1 per cent of the population above 6 years of age had completed their matriculation. One of the villages had no literate people at all while another had a literacy rate of 18 per cent. The backwardness of the villages is also reflected in the sex ratio in the study villages: we calculated it as 735 females to 1000 males, far lower than the national average of 933 (Table 3).

Many of the villagers do not have access to potable water for most of the year. They obtain it mainly from shallow wells, and sometimes forest streams, while livestock drink at *johads*—small man-made earthen reservoirs inside villages also used for irrigation.[35] In Bhagani, where there was no drinking water well, we saw people drawing water

[34] Panchayat samitis represent the local body for self-governance in villages. They are positioned between the district and village levels.

[35] The Tarun Bharat Sangh has been working in the area of water conservation in Rajasthan and one of its achievements has been to persuade people to build such water recharge and storage structures inside their villages (see also Bhatia 2000, Shrotiya undated).

Table 3

Demographic Details and Development Indicators of Sampled Households in the Sariska Tiger Reserve

Village	No. HH surveyed	Total population	Population (age <6)	Population (age 6 to 18)	Population adults (age >18)	Number of females	Number of males	Sex ratio	Per cent matriculated persons*	Per cent literacy **
Bhagani	17	72	18	10	44	30	42	714	5.56	22.22
Dabli	15	138	33	36	69	61	77	792	0.00	21.90
Deori	15	88	12	29	47	35	53	660	1.32	53.95
Haripura	6	46	5	18	23	24	22	1091	2.44	43.90
Kankwari	36	259	50	73	136	101	158	639	0.48	27.75
Kiraska	45	244	41	63	140	101	143	706	0.99	39.41
Kundalka	5	25	4	10	11	11	14	786	0.00	42.86
Lilunda	4	17	2	8	7	7	10	700	0.00	0.00
Raikamala	10	63	8	28	27	25	38	658	0.00	38.18
Sukola	4	45	8	15	22	19	26	731	0.00	18.92
Umri	33	226	46	75	105	104	122	852	1.11	25.56
All villages	190	1223	227	365	631	518	705	735	1.00	31.63

* *(no. of persons who have passed class 10 / total population > 6 years) × 100*

** *(no. of literate persons/ total population > 6 years) × 100*

HH: Household

from a stagnant pool in an open stream. People blame the water, universally reported to be polluted, for many of their health problems.

Most people in Sariska live in mud houses with thatched roofs while a small percentage have partially cemented structures. Most of the houses are bare-bones structures; they have windows without shutters and many have no doors at all. Almost all households had separate cattle-sheds attached to a small yard, however. By way of labour-saving equipment, a large number of households possess manually operated leaf-cutting machines which are essential for chopping tree leaves to obtain livestock fodder. A small number of households possess radios, cycles, and motorcycles. A few affluent households have invested in jeeps that are used by the entire village to transport milk to local markets.

Market Linkages

Most people sell their milk in the market and buy all their requirements there. Their economy is highly monetized and credit-based. Their major purchases, other than commercial fodder, are foodgrains and medicines. With a few exceptions, people buy their foodgrain from the towns nearby such as Thanagazi, Tehla, Akbarpur, Talab, Rajgarh, and Bhartrihari Tiraha. The purchase of grain is mainly on credit, with an interest rate of 2 to 3 per cent a month. In addition, villagers pay Re 1 per kg of milk transported if there is no all-weather approach road to their village. The transport of grains to a village for personal consumption costs Rs 10 for a 50-kg sack if it is connected by an all-weather road. In some of the remote villages, which are accessible only by fair-weather roads, people get together and hire a tractor to carry grain to the village. While a typical household possesses several ration cards and BPL (Below Poverty Line) cards, few report buying grain from such shops.

For some families posht is a regular component of market purchases. In some cases the posht budget exceeds that for household food. Cigarettes and bidis, too, are commonly purchased alongside clothing, shoes, utensils, torches, dry cells, ornaments, *khaat* (wooden cots), and *baan* (weaving rope for cots). Some use the wood of the dhok and kala khair trees in the forest to make these cots. Kerosene, for lighting, is among the essentials. Diesel and petrol are bought by very few—those that own jeeps for commercial transport of commodities or those who own motorcycles.

People in Sariska eat frugally. Most of the families eat vegetables only occasionally, mainly potatoes and cauliflower, which are locally inexpensive. During winter, *rabri* (a dessert made of thickened milk) and *chhaach* (buttermilk) are commonly consumed. Corn and oats are staple food in winter, wheat in the summer and monsoon. Ghee too forms an integral part of their daily meal. Without exception, people are completely dependent on wood for cooking, collected from inside the reserve.

Fever, malaria, jaundice, and frequent digestive problems were reported: understandable, given the generally low nutritional status and the lack of clean water.

Livelihood Options and Occupations

The villagers of Sariska depend almost entirely on the forest for their livelihood. Traditionally a pastoralist community, their main source of income is selling milk, *mawa* (a derivative of milk), and ghee. In 2004–5 a little over 89 per cent of our surveyed households reported milk- and mawa-selling as their primary occupation, which contributed to about 72 per cent of cash incomes. The share of total household income from milk sales was the highest in interior villages like Umri but relatively low in the outskirts of the core zone, as in Deori and Raikamala. Agriculture and daily-wage labour were reported as secondary occupations, by 45 per cent and 38 per cent of households respectively, together contributing to about 14 per cent of household cash income (Table 4). We estimated that another 6 per cent of the average household income came from the sale of livestock and 9 per cent from other sources such as pensions and army employment. Another possible source of income, from the selling of livestock dung, has been banned by the forest department. In villages with good road access people sometimes do sell dung clandestinely at a price of Rs 1000 to Rs 2000 per tractor-load.

Table 4
Contribution of Different Sources of Income to Gross Annual Household Income

Village	Per cent contribution from				
	Milk Sales	Agriculture	Daily Wage Labour	Other	Sale of Livestock
Bhagani	77.78	0.00	4.11	14.94	3.17
Dabli	81.35	7.54	0.74	4.60	5.78
Deori	47.56	35.24	10.87	0.00	6.34
Haripura	70.97	10.34	16.70	0.00	1.99
Kankwari	65.52	1.45	6.61	17.44	8.96
Kiraska	65.32	1.14	15.25	11.09	7.20
Kundalka	78.44	6.34	7.61	0.00	7.61
Lilunda	89.11	7.56	0.00	0.00	3.34
Raikamala	65.13	25.83	0.00	4.43	4.61
Sukola	79.94	3.13	9.40	0.00	7.52
Umri	90.07	1.77	0.47	4.80	2.88
All Villages	72.33	6.69	6.43	8.57	5.98

People in only a few villages—Dabli, Deori, and Raikamala—have agricultural land within the boundaries of the core area, being officially revenue villages. People here mainly grow wheat, corn, oat, mustard, and gram, much of it for household consumption. Some of the families in the other villages own property in buffer areas, on the outskirts of the reserve, or further away. For instance, the people of Umri, with few exceptions, have land in Losal. But overall only a negligible proportion of families (approximately 19 per cent) in the core area own any land outside, with most having less than 5 *bighas* each.[36]

As far as self-sufficiency in food is concerned, Deori tops the list. Though the average landholding is not very large in Deori, the irrigation facility provided by the johads enables them to harvest two crops a year. Some of the villagers even have wells and diesel-powered

[36] A bigha is the commonly used measure of land; it is roughly equal to one-fourth of a hectare, or a square plot of 165 ft on each side.

pump sets. Other villages depend principally on rain water for irrigation and therefore harvest only one crop a year. Villagers reported deficient rainfall during the five years preceding our study, because of which agricultural productivity was said to have declined. Considerable crop depredation by wild ungulates, such as the nilgai and the wild boar, takes place in the villages and buffer zone, losses which are uncompensated by the forest department (Sekhar 1998).

Given the level of dependence on milk in their cash economy, livestock is the villagers' primary asset. On the average each household among the 190 surveyed during 2004–5 owned 9 buffaloes, 1 cow, and 12 goats. The cows and buffaloes here, like cows and buffaloes anywhere in the poorer regions of pastoral India, do not yield much milk at the best of times and sometimes none. Goats comprised as much as 55 per cent and buffaloes 40 per cent of livestock holdings in the core zone; cows and sheep were rare.[37] The proportions of livestock types did not vary much across the villages despite differences in agricultural dependence and economic status.

Buffaloes are the most prized livestock in the area, particularly in the better-off households. From watching villagers tend their buffalo it was obvious to us that the villagers possess considerable expertise in buffalo-rearing and veterinary care. Each buffalo has a name and is treated like a member of the family. The children sing prayers to their gods to seek protection for their livestock from disease and to improve milk yields. It is commonly believed that the buffaloes suffer ill health if they are stall-fed and do not roam the forest.

Goats are reared mainly for sale. They are treated as a liquid asset because they are easily sold for a good price at any time. Goat herds commonly double or triple annually due to their hardiness and high rate of reproduction.[38] We found that poor households tend to rely more on goats as they require negligible investment of care, commercial fodder, and medical attention. The animal subsists on plants not

[37] Earlier there were significant holdings of cows but they were considerably decimated during droughts from 2001 to 2003.

[38] The average price at which goats are sold is Rs 400 to 600; but certain varieties of goat can be priced as high as Rs 6000.

digested by the buffalo and reaches vegetation inaccessible to larger livestock, such as that growing on steep slopes.

The economic status of the majority of local households is dependent upon the quantum of rain that, in turn, determines the quality and quantity of the available green fodder. It is the monsoon period, the time of plenty when milk production is the highest, during which the villagers save for the year and pay back loans. During normal monsoon years there is enough forest fodder available for about four months (July to October). The area within a radius of 3 to 7 km around the villages is generally used for the grazing of livestock, often crossing the permissible limits. Buffaloes are grazed closer to villages, but the goats are taken quite far, often across difficult terrain. Adults, and children of more than 8 years, accompany livestock on these grazing trips. While buffaloes mostly move without supervision, goats require constant attention because of the threat from leopards. At a rough estimate goats are grazed for about six to eight hours every day and buffaloes for eight to twelve. Buffaloes are often left overnight for grazing in the forest because the threat to them from carnivores is negligible: they are too large to be attacked by leopards, though tigers occasionally kill them.

Post-monsoon is hardship time in relation to fodder collection and storage. In November, when the grass in the forest begins to dry, people start storing it and spend several hours doing this every day. Every family member above 10 or 12 years helps in the fodder collection. The activity is of great importance as it saves a lot of money that would otherwise be spent on the purchase of commercial and farm fodder during the following summer. After October, other than the stored grass, leaves and branches are collected from trees and shrubs—raunj, baans, palash, cheela, dhok, chapaun (*Grewia spp.*), and jaal (*Capparis sepiaria*) being the preferred species—to feed livestock. Leaves are chopped up in leaf-cutting machines before being fed to the livestock. Unripe pods of the raunj are considered extremely nutritious and much sought after. This stored fodder is fed to livestock from the beginning of April, when there is little green vegetation left in the forest, right up to the beginning of the next rainy season in July. Naturally, the villagers try to feed their livestock as much green fodder in the forest as possible before using the stored quantity. Green leaves increase milk yield as well. But in times of drought even the rough leaves of the khajur, one of the least nutritious of plants, is used as livestock feed. And from April to July, when both the stored grass and the availability of forest fodder is at a premium, the villagers take their cattle out from the forest to feed them off farm fodder (mainly agricultural crop residue) bought from the farmers of villages nearby. Farm fodder is bought at about Rs 150 for a quintal; during drought years the price can go up to Rs 650.

Other than farm fodder, the cost of feeding buffaloes involves the purchase of *kankda* (seeds of the silk-cotton tree *Bombax ceiba*) and *khali* (oilcake residue), given to buffaloes, though generally only to the milch animals. Kankda and khali are important nutritional supplements for buffaloes, without which the milk yield is poor. These are mainly fed to buffaloes from September to March, or as long as they can be afforded by the family. One buffalo generally needs a minimum of 1 kg of kankda per day, which costs about Rs 15 (including the transport cost). But they also need to pay interest on their purchase of kankda at 3 per cent a month since they usually cannot pay cash. Those who buy khali also pay almost the same amount per day for it.

People usually sell their milk to a local dealer from their own village, who then sells at the next level. This middleman connects the local villagers to the larger market and earns a great deal out of it. Milk from various villages in Sariska is sold at dairies in Kushalgarh, Tehla, Sariska, and at Bhartrihari, all of which are located within a distance of 20 km. Milk is paid for at the rate of Rs 12 per litre from the better-connected villages and transported by jeep. Where the terrain is rough and there is only motorcycle access, the price paid for milk goes down by as much as 30 per cent. People in more inaccessible villages, however, sell mainly ghee and mawa made from their milk, items with a longer shelf-life. The price of mawa varies from Rs 35 to Rs 60 across these villages.

After *chaumasa* (monsoon), local villagers buy commodities on credit from shopkeepers and thereafter pay interest at the rate of 2 to

3 per cent per month. They pay back their loans out of their income the next monsoon. If incomes need supplementing, livestock is commonly sold off—mostly the goats.[39] There is hardly a time in the year when the household is not in debt. Among those we surveyed more than half had a debt of up to Rs 20,000. Another quarter of households owed between Rs 20,000 and Rs 40,000. As in much of rural India, most people take their loans from shopkeepers in the surrounding towns rather than from banks. These loans are taken not in the form of money but commodities, on which the interest is paid. The major component of local debt is commercial fodder. The purchase of grain and other household necessities keeps adding to this spiral of debt. When required, villagers help each other out with credit. Generally the person with the most buffaloes in a village and external sources of income functions as the local moneylender.

While livestock loss to leopards and tigers (until 2004) was commonly reported inside the core area, there are indications that these losses are very much a part of the calculations in a Gujjar's grazing economy. When asked about livestock losses to carnivores, a Gujjar man replied that 'Livestock kills are natural. It is the fate of the buffalo which is written by God.' Alves (1999) also reports local beliefs that 'The tiger and the cow must drink from the same pool' and that 'The buffalo is not sick too often because of the tiger', reflecting the perceived importance of the tiger in the grazing economy.[40] Rough estimates during 2004–5 indicate that up to 33 per cent of households reported loss of local livestock to large carnivores in the villages of the core area. Goats were most preyed upon, probably by leopards. While outlying villages such as Haripura and Kundalka did not report livestock loss during 2004–5, interior villages like Umri (33 per cent of households) and Lilunda (25 per cent of households) reported significant losses. In no household did we discover even partial compensation for livestock loss.

[39] Almost 6 per cent of the surveyed households' income comes from the selling of livestock. See Table 4.

[40] This saying perhaps refers to the possibility that tigers cull infirm individuals from the buffalo herd, thus indirectly contributing to the health of the herd.

There is a folktale in the area regarding Maharaja Jaisingh talking about two men in his state, Pahar Singh and Doongar Singh, who never asked for a penny but always gave him revenue.[41] In this tale Pahar Singh and Doongar Singh refer to people living in the Sariska area, who used to pay considerable land revenues and grazing fees to the princely states in the past. The economic significance of the area is proven by the astronomical revenues collected by the princely state of Alwar. According to one estimate a total of more than Rs 5.5 million was collected from the area during 1931, that went up from Rs 3 million in 1929 with the imposition of new grazing fees and land taxes (Mayaram 1997). Such economic prosperity, however, is a thing of the past. Villagers often lament their economic decline. The whole economic organization has changed and they are no longer an integral part of it. According to the older villagers the most striking change that has taken place in the last fifty years is that more than 70 per cent of the local households are now in debt, as compared to almost none at the time of Independence. Today, the average household economy, based on livestock-grazing, is subsisting on the edge. We calculated the gross annual income per household as approximately Rs 48,175 but the average household spends approximately Rs 18,000 every year on farm fodder and commercial fodder. Therefore the average annual disposable household income is approximately Rs 30,190. However, even this average figure is not an accurate portrayal of income levels because more than 60 per cent of the households have an income of less than Rs 25,000. Figure 1 shows patterns of expenditure and, indirectly, the precariousness of the household economy, which is subject to complete devastation in the event of natural disasters such as drought.

A typical Sariska household dependent on grazing buys farm fodder at Rs 150–175 per quintal after the monsoon. During times of drought the rate of farm fodder goes up to Rs 500–650 per quintal. According to this calculation, farm fodder costs Rs 600–1000 per buffalo per month. In the month of October, the average daily milk yield is only 2 litres per buffalo while milk sells at Rs 10 per litre, giving an income of Rs 600 per month from each buffalo. Thus, those who have five

[41] 'Pahar' refers to 'hill' in Hindi and 'doongar' to 'forests'.

Fig. 1: Proportion of Annual Household Expenditure in Different Categories

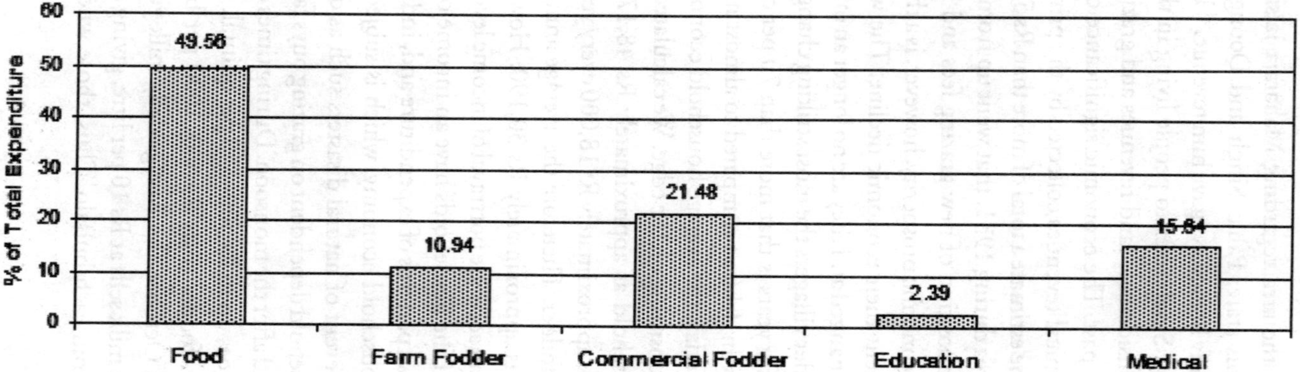

milch buffaloes earn a maximum of about Rs 3000 a month, and this in the period during which they have to save for an entire year.

At the time of our study the local people thought their area had suffered a steep decline in average rainfall over the past decade, resulting in a severe decline of fodder availability.[42] The reserve had faced a severe drought in 2002–3 which caused heavy livestock losses. Comparing the number of livestock lost in those two years with the numbers at the time of our study, we estimated that about 50 per cent of the buffaloes and about 70 per cent of the cows had probably perished, a loss nothing short of calamitous. Their distress became more acute when people sold some of the remaining livestock in order to survive the drought. While some villagers worked under the government-sponsored 'Akal Rahat Programme' (Drought Relief Programme) during this period, the general complaint about such programmes was that the forest department either employed outside people for the work meant for the villagers or used machines.

People said that though their income sources had lately diversified, their economic status had not changed much. The main reason for the diversification was that people had begun seeking employment outside. However, the number of people going out for work was still quite low in 2005. Among the 190 households surveyed, only 35 reported members leaving the reserve to work. Most of these workers were men who spent 4 to 6 months working in nearby cities—mainly Bhiwadi, Delhi, Jaipur, and Bharatpur. Leaving the reserve daily was not possible for most villagers because of transport constraints.

Some of the respondents felt that the employment opportunities that were available locally in the past had also declined. For instance, people in Kiraska practised agriculture till about 1995 but now were not allowed to do so by the forest department. This obviously had a devastating impact on the village's economy. The consistently deficient rainfall over the past few years was also blamed for adverse effects on agricultural incomes in villages such as Deori and Dabli. People also reported that the employment offered by the forest department,

[42] This is also borne out by the rainfall records kept by the Office of the Deputy Director of Agriculture (Extension), Alwar.

such as in road works and weed eradication, was limited: the jobs were often contracted out to external labour.[43] When the villagers were able to get these jobs, they frequently had to wait months for their wages. While there was a steep rise in tourism from 1990 to 2005, the villagers benefited only marginally. The Sariska Palace Hotel and Hotel Tiger Den employed a few villagers, but on daily wages, and often they were not paid for weeks together. Some of the villagers ran shops at Bhartrihari, 3 km from the reserve entrance. The few locals who were employed as jeep drivers by the owners said they were paid as little as Rs 1300 per month in 2005. The only recent development in terms of employment comes from labour works for the construction of johads built by the Tarun Bharat Sangh.

Discourses around Degradation

For several years now, ever since ecological research began in Sariska, warnings have been sounded by biologists about habitat degradation, particularly the impact of intensive biomass extraction such as firewood and fodder collection and livestock-grazing (Rodgers 1990, Johnsingh *et al.* 1997). Severe lack of tree regeneration was noted in Sariska almost fifteen years ago (Rodgers 1990). On a larger scale, studies based on remote sensing by the Forest Survey of India (1993) indicated a mixed picture of habitat change in Sariska between 1983 and 1989 whereby some open forests had 'improved' into dense forests. However, large sections of dense forest had also deteriorated to open forest during the same period. By 2004 tigers too were rarely seen, going by both biologists' and villagers' accounts. According to biologists no more than 10–20 adult tigers survived in the few patches of high quality habitat that still existed in Sariska in 1997 (Johnsingh *et al.* 1997). In 2004, at the end of which reports of the tiger's extinction were brought to light, the number was likely to be much lower, possibly 7–8. Around this time, some herbivores typical of semi-arid forest tracts, such as the four-horned antelope, had become extinct in Sariska (A.J.T. Johnsingh, pers. comm.).

[43] The general complaint of the people was that the works are contracted out mainly to people who are forest department employees.

Today, even to the untrained eye, the forest outside the designated core zone of 400 sq. km seems severely degraded, which implies that about 466 sq. km of Sariska has little value for conserving native biodiversity. Even within the core zone, based on rough visual estimates that are conservative, I estimate that up to 40 per cent of the total area is severely degraded and a large part of the remaining area moderately degraded. Only very few valleys, such as the Sariska–Kalighati–Slopka Valley, Pandupol, Nayapani Route, Bhaisota, and Governor's Route now have good quality forest. A more exact estimate of the degree and extent of habitat degradation can be made only with the help of quantitative digital mapping techniques.

At the time of our surveys there was widespread recognition of adverse changes in habitat condition among local people as well. In the course of the last ten years, large numbers of people had observed a marked decline in the quality and quantity of natural resources including grazing lands, forests, and water. While 97 per cent of people felt that the available area for grazing had significantly reduced during the last ten years, 85 per cent felt the same for forest area. Most of our respondents (93 per cent) felt that the time needed to collect biomass had significantly increased (Figure 2). While most people did not feel there had been any decline in tree species' diversity, reports of decline in some key species like guggal (*Sterculia urens*), kadakuda, and khaddu frequently came up in conversation. People felt strongly about the decline in the local tiger population, with nearly all agreeing that tiger numbers had declined. Madho Ram of Kankwari, 70 years old, recalled frequent sightings of the tiger, leopard, hyena, and sambar in his youth. He said that the Kankwari valley, which is now almost completely degraded, used to be densely forested in Maharaja Jai Singh's time when he worked as a game-beater at the massive tiger hunts being organized for royalty and British officers.

The documents of the forest department as well as most biologists' reports indicate a strong conviction that forest resource extraction in the form of grazing and wood collection by local villagers is the sole cause of biodiversity decline in Sariska. In fact there is unanimity on the cause-and-effect relationship between forest use and biodiversity decline (Government of Rajasthan 2004, Johnsingh *et al.* 1997).

Fig. 2: Perceptions of Local People on Changes in Living Conditions and Natural Resources (B: Better; W: Worse; S: Same)

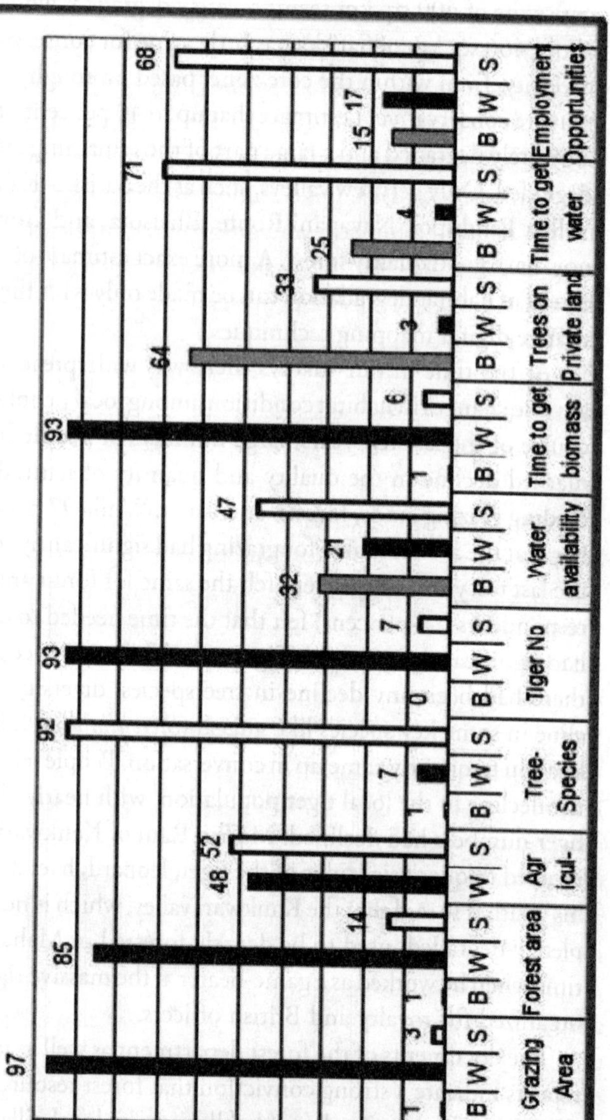

However, it is important to note that until recently most information on the human impact in Sariska was largely anecdotal. The first scientific study on the ecological effects of biomass extraction was carried out by our research team just before our village study, between 2003 and 2005 (Shahabuddin and Kumar 2006, Kumar and Shahabuddin 2005). At a casual glance there is ample proof of such a cause-and-effect linkage in Sariska. It is common to see women walking with axes in their hands, young boys and girls ripping off branches from dhok trees, and livestock grazing at any given time—not just near villages but also far away. The number of tree stumps and other signs of forest degradation decidedly increase as one approaches any of the villages. Grazing by buffaloes and goats is rampant despite the regulation (admittedly lax) by forest personnel.

Our ecological research has tended to corroborate such visual evidence of the impact of forest use upon biodiversity. We have found that intensive biomass extraction may cause significant changes in forest vegetation structure and species composition (Kumar and Shahabuddin 2005). When we compared areas where there had been intensive biomass extraction with those that were relatively undisturbed, we found that the canopy cover, the density of trees, the number of tree species, and the average height of trees were all significantly lower in the former. We also observed that extraction had stunted the trees in all the vegetation types: there were greater numbers of small trees and fewer large trees in intensively used areas. Tree species' composition also changed significantly in used areas because of the overexploitation of certain species that are preferred for fodder. For example, trees such as hingot (*Balanites aegyptiaca*) and *Capparis sepiaria*, that are not used for fodder, have increased in density around the forest near the villages. A number of exotic invasive species have become common in the used areas of the reserve, such as the annual herb chakunda (*Cassia tora*) and the short-statured tree vilayati kikar (*Prosopis juliflora*). Arusha (*Adhatoda vasica*), though a native understorey herb of the Aravallis, has become very common in disturbed and overgrazed areas, and appears to suppress grass and other native herbaceous species. Species diversity of shrubs and trees as well as basal areas were found to decline in proportion with the degree of human use over the last thirty years in another study (Yadav and Gupta 2006). Except in parts of the riparian zone, we observed extremely low regeneration, particularly of *Boswellia serrata* and *Phoenix sylvestris* (Rodgers 1990).

All the same, the linkages between human use and biodiversity decline are far more complex than our research indicates. Since low levels of regeneration are prevalent over habitats both intensively used and relatively undisturbed at present, we can deduce that patterns of utilization over the centuries have triggered changes in habitat that persist till today (see Johari 2007). There is other evidence of change in forest vegetation caused by commercial use over the decades, such as timbering and charcoal production: for example, the local rarity of several commercially extracted tree species—such as *Acacia catechu* (from whose wood charcoal was made). The lack of old dhok trees (more than thirty years old) in clear-cut areas also points to such changes.

In a related study on the impacts of biomass extraction on bird communities of Sariska from 2003 to 2005, we found that the overall diversity and abundance of bird species is not affected by intensive human use. However, there was a significant impact on the types of bird species inhabiting the forests. Several migrants and resident bird species, such as the grey-headed flycatcher (*Culicicapa ceylonensis*), the white-browed fantail flycatcher (*Rhipidura aureola*), Hume's warbler (*Phylloscopus humei*), Tickell's blue flycatcher (*Cyornis tickelliae*), the great tit (*Parus major*), the oriental white-eye (*Zosterops palpebrosa*), and the white-bellied drongo (*Dicrurus caerulescens*) occurred at much lower densities in used forests than in strictly protected sites. Being insectivorous, these species prefer taller and denser forests with a higher diversity of tree species. Bird species such as these may be in danger of becoming locally extinct given further habitat degradation in Sariska. Rare raptor species, and those restricted to scarce riparian habitats (such as the crested serpent-eagle, the brown fish owl, and the verditer flycatcher) seem particularly threatened. On the other hand there are also several bird species such as the Indian robin (*Saxicoloides fulicata*) and the black redstart (*Phoenicurus ochruros*) that are encouraged by habitat degradation. In general, changes in forest habitat in Sariska caused by intensive biomass extraction tend to favour birds that live in open habitats (and are therefore more adaptable to human disturbance) and adversely impact bird species that prefer closed forests.

While foresters and biologists have unequivocally linked anthropogenic influence with biodiversity decline, the local view of the causes of biodiversity decline in Sariska are quite different. Most people strongly believe that people's use has had no effect on biodiversity at all (83 per cent), while some believe that it has had a negative impact. In other cases the local people also feel a certain amount of biomass extraction is actually necessary for the health of the forest. For instance, they feel that restrictions on cutting fodder from ber trees in Kalighati valley has caused the widespread die-back (from an unknown disease) that can be seen today in that area. People believe that pruning actually encourages leaf-growth and density during the following growing season.[44] On the other hand many villagers believe that they have contributed significantly to the disappearance of trees over the years. Older villagers said that in earlier times only branches and leaves were lopped for fuelwood and fodder while the trunks were never harmed. From conversations with villagers it appears as if the traditional precautionary measures to stop the overexploitation of biomass and nurture tree growth have been all but abandoned in recent times.

While overgrazing and deforestation are admitted by some, local people feel that the arbitrary restrictions on forest use laid down by the forest department have also been responsible. For example, villagers pointed out that they often cut large branches rather than leaves, in haste, fearing discovery by forest personnel. People also feel a sense of confusion about the arbitrary changes in use rights that are effected from time to time. They pointed out that while in the past people were allowed to graze their cattle, now they are blamed for contributing to the decline in biodiversity. To give another example: the villagers of Kiraska say that many landed people bought goats because the ban on agriculture was strictly implemented in the core zone after the intention to declare the National Park was made (1982). Consequently,

[44] There may be some truth in this as it has been found that, to a certain extent, pruning encourages further growth. However, heavy pruning may reduce productivity or lead to mortality.

Illustr. 4: A forest guard in the Sariska Tiger Reserve at his tented camp, from where he radios his headquarters. Forest guards work under difficult field conditions and are insufficiently equipped to deal with both wildlife management and poachers.

ecological damage to the forest has probably been far more severe since the 1990s—because of the ban on agriculture, people have taken up goat-rearing on a large scale.

The villagers, in fact, expressed strong opinions on the way Sariska is managed and on the discourses that are constructed around the whole issue of biodiversity conservation (see Gupta 2005). Villagers and local activists felt that resource mismanagement has played a far greater role in deforestation than all the local village use put together. There are also stories of political pressure being frequently exerted on park management to allow illegal wood-extraction and even timber smuggling from the reserve. Villagers also commonly blame the forest personnel for poor management and for not protecting the reserve from outsiders. One villager said: 'The guards from Bharatpur don't do their job properly. They have no emotional attachment with the forest and wildlife whatsoever. Their only concern is to receive their monthly salaries.' Such statements refer to the fact that most of the guards serving in Sariska had earlier worked only in Bharatpur, having been recently transferred *en masse* from there. Since Bharatpur is a small wetland bird sanctuary, local people argue that the guards had little knowledge of a forest with large carnivores and were certainly not comfortable around them. Some of the guards said they had worked only in forest nurseries before being moved to Sariska.

Other observations similarly indicate that forest protection is inadequate in the reserve. Poaching and timber smuggling are both not uncommon. In the 1990s biologists reported instances of armed poachers killing tigers and sambar on the outskirts of the reserve (S. Mukherjee, pers. comm.). Guards also admitted to us that they were quite powerless to stop poaching by armed men. A guard told us that on one occasion, the flying squad formed for tackling poaching, comprising forty guards and a ranger, was not able to catch up with poachers who escaped with a dead sambar. During our study, people at Umri reported hearing frequent gunshots at night. The motivation among guards to patrol the forests and stop poachers or other intruders is low, which is understandable given their low pay-scales and lack of protection infrastructure and equipment, medical insurance, or physical training. The Tiger Task Force reported that over half of the forest guards in Sariska were between 45 and 50 years of age and therefore unable to cope with the rigours of field patrolling. No new field staff had been recruited for eighteen years because of a state-wide freeze on employment. Nor is there any system to keep younger staff on field duties and relegate older guards to administrative positions. Many guards admitted that the lack of arms, training, and inadequate field infrastructure crippled their efficiency and effectiveness. One senior forest guard confided to us: 'Two guards to a checkpost cannot do anything to prevent the cutting of trees and stop poaching. We do not get much help from our superiors either. Our allowances too are meagre; we have to organize our own food rations in the field and even pay for torch batteries out of that.' Our observations suggest that there is much biomass extraction pressure from outside the core zone that local forest personnel are unable to prevent. We found considerable clandestine grazing by camels, goats, and buffaloes, and fodder-collection. In 2004 we saw almost fifty camels being driven away by forest department staff from the Kalighati valley. In January 2005 a group of about forty women from near Tehla, a town on the southern edge of the reserve, were seen collecting cheela (*Butea monosperma*) leaves near Bhagani. Head-loading is also common, often taking place at night. It is not known from exactly where these pressures originate, but there is evidence of heavy firewood demand from neighbouring towns such as Tehla and Thanagazi, which are several km away from the boundary of the reserve. When we were going down the slopes from Kiraska village, within Sariska, we met people from outside the reserve, walking up towards the village with their buffaloes. They were going to a relative's house in Kiraska with their livestock. They planned to leave them there to graze in the forest while the grass was abundant in the monsoon. Local people say this is a common arrangement.

Apart from external extractive pressures, the emphasis on local forest dependency has historically obscured the fact that there are several other pressures originating from tourism and mining, the effects of which have not been studied at all, nor even considered in management planning (Government of Rajasthan 2004). Within the National Park there are two temples which are visited by large numbers of religious and other tourists, the Pandupol and Bandipul temples, while a few others have relatively few visitors, such as Tarunda and Algual. While Pandupol attracts the largest number of visitors, including huge numbers from the town of Alwar, Bandipul largely attracts people from villages in and around the reserve. Pandupol Mandir is located in prime wildlife habitat, near a perennial spring in the heart of the core zone. It has grown from a simple small structure to a two-storeyed, multi-roomed building over the past few years. An old villager from Haripura recollects that Pandupol had no shops or *dharamshala* twenty years ago, while today there are two shops and numerous enclosures for pilgrims to cook and rest in. A few people, including cooks and cleaners, have taken up permanent residence at the temple. The illegal expansion of the temple has been acknowledged in the report of the State Empowered Committee on Forest and Wildlife Management of Rajasthan Government (Government of Rajasthan 2005).

The tourism pressure, in general, is high. Interviews with guards reveal that, post-monsoon, the number of vehicles entering Core Area I via Sariska's main gate sometimes goes up to 600 a day, including buses, jeeps, motorbikes, and cars. Based on the number of tickets sold at the main gate and records of visitors on days when entry is free for religious reasons, it is estimated that the number of visitors at the Sariska Tiger Reserve was 2,60,651 in 2003 and 2,93,649 in 2004.[45] The number of vehicles (jeeps and buses) in 2003 was 14,306 and in 2004 it was 15,953.[46] Given that many people from surrounding areas enter on foot from two other gates (Siliberi and Tehla) and through a hill track from Bhartrihari, none of which are monitored, these figures probably fall far short of the actual number of visitors.

Forest guards say animals flee the prime wildlife habitats of Sariska for the surrounding hills during this season to escape the tourists. Bathing, the washing of clothes and cooking utensils, and the burning of plastic garbage at Pandupol severely pollutes the critical perennial spring which offers food, water, and shelter for animals during the harsh dry season and which waters a large part of the reserve. The practice of *sawai,* in which large amounts of cooked food are fed to pilgrims by devout people, has compounded the problem of water pollution. Pandupol Mandir has added a loudspeaker to its equipment during the last few years. In January 2004 a single harried forest guard was trying to control the several thousand tourists that visit the temple. A senior forest officer at Sariska admitted that 'Without doing something about the pilgrim traffic at Pandupol temple, there is little hope

[45] Forest department records.
[46] Ibid.

for wildlife in Sariska.' The reserve authorities plead they are helpless in curbing tourist traffic to Pandupol: it is a sensitive religious issue. The problem may get worse: at least four other small temples located near perennial springs in the core area could become important pilgrimage spots.

Mining for marble, limestone, and dolomite at the immediate periphery of the reserve has been a point of contention for at least twenty years (see Shrotiya, undated). The Tarun Bharat Sangh, which had initiated water conservation work in the local villages in 1985, filed a public interest litigation against the mining in the late 1980s. In its judgment in 1992 the Indian supreme court commanded the Rajasthan state government to stop all mining in the Aravalli hills, and as many as 470 mines in and around the reserve were shut down to prevent further environmental damage (Johari 2003). The Rajasthan state government took the stand that they were able to grant mining privileges because the legal boundaries both of the reserved forest as well as the proposed national park were not clear; the state government's nonchalant attitude towards wildlife conservation became painfully apparent from this. Today, although work at some of the mines near Sariska has come to a halt, several continue to operate around Malana, near Tehla, which is located on the periphery of the reserve. Apart from noise and dust pollution, the hydrological regime of the hills of Sariska is under grave threat from the pumping out of water from marble quarries that will likely affect local aquifers. The sound of dynamite blasts from mines in Malana can be heard even in the core area. However, despite the visible environmental impact, the issue of commercial mining is largely overlooked in all official documents on the management of Sariska.

Displacement: A Bitter History

Despite the visible impact of tourism, mining, and external extractive pressures on wildlife, it is the purported cause-and-link relationship between local people and ecological degradation that has dictated management policy in Sariska. This policy has focused on village relocation as possibly the only tool to secure biodiversity. The attitude of the forest bureaucracy was exemplified in the report of the Rajasthan State Empowered Committee on Forests that was set up in 2005 after the 'tiger crisis': 'In Sariska, all the reasons responsible for the disappearance of tigers *in toto* zero in on one single factor and that is the large number of villages inside the reserve, where no successful rehabilitation of villages has ever taken place. Therefore poachers could shelter in the villages of the area and kill tigers.' And: 'Tigers and people do not coexist. Wherever villages exist, the tigers in the vicinity have slowly perished.'

As we have seen earlier, the relocation of Sariska's villages is mentioned several times in documents from the early twentieth century (Johari 2003). In the 1970s from Karnakawas and Kiraska villages were relocated to Sirawas (near Silisere, Alwar District) and Bandipul (near Ajabgarh, Alwar District). It was on 25 November 1975 that the district magistrate at the time, Adarsh Kishore, issued a notification for the settlement of rights for the villages of Karnakawas, Kiraska, and Umri-Deori. People living in these villages were asked to inform the administration of their claims by 28 January 1976. On 21 April 1976 a Government of Rajasthan notification denotified the Rundh Bandipul and Rundh Dulawa Reserved Forest, changing them into revenue lands for purposes of relocation.[47] Similarly the land at Sirawas was also denotified from Reserved Forest status through a Government of Rajasthan order dated 23 March 1976. The area denotified was: 750 bighas in Rundh Sirawas, 251.19 bighas in Rundh Bandipul, and 244.4 bighas in Rundh Dulawa.[48]

The actual process of relocation of people from Kiraska and Karnakawas began in 1977. Apart from land allotments, cash compensations are recorded as having been paid to villagers. These cash compensations ranged from Rs 50 to Rs 9705. According to the Forest Department Status Report on relocation, 69 families of Kiraska were paid a total of Rs 1,20,975 as compensation. Of the 19 families which

[47] However, the Management Status Report for Sariska dated 2004 puts the date of forest land denotification as 21 April 1977.

[48] Rundh Bandipul and Rundh Dulawa are contiguous and together are often referred to as Bandipul-Dulawa.

had *pattas* (legal land entitlement) for the land they owned inside their old villages (67.18 bighas), 18 were allotted land at Sirawas. One family was allotted land at Rundh Bandipul. Kiraska was thereafter declared forest land and the villagers subsequently only given permission to perform religious activities at their *devsthan* (sacred site) and use the public road.

Most of the forest department officials we talked to see this incident as an exploitative mechanism by local villagers to benefit from both their newly allotted lands (by selling it off) while not giving up their rights inside the reserve. When confronted with these questions, villagers had a different perspective. They alleged that the promises made to them regarding the new site were not fulfilled by the forest department. For instance, they were not provided basic amenities at the site, such as electricity and a road. Nor was the land fit for cultivation when they arrived there. By all accounts they were simply evicted and compelled to accept whatever meagre compensation was being provided. In many cases they were given compensation and were then made to pay back the amount as pending 'fines' to the forest department.[49] Some villagers actually ended up paying out of their pockets at the time of their displacement. This incident of village displacement must also be seen in the larger political context. The relocation was undertaken during the countrywide 'Emergency' imposed by the Congress government of Indira Gandhi, between 1975 and 1977, when basic liberties such as the right to protest and gather publicly, had been withdrawn. Thus Sariska's villagers did not have even the opportunity to react publicly to their impending relocation in 1977. It is not surprising that forced eviction still terrifies villagers and colours their perceptions of the latest relocation plan (Johari 2003).

Where does the truth lie? To evaluate the situation for ourselves we decided to visit two of the three relocation sites. It was 2005, almost three decades after people had been relocated there. Our visit to the Sirawas site revealed the stark contrast between promises made and the reality of the situation in these two villages. Originally an area covered

[49] The villagers said that they were not given any reasons for the fines. There was no clearly laid out or transparent process for the payment of these fines.

by the exotic tree species vilayati kikar and surrounded by steep hills on three sides, Sirawas is now inhabited by people who bought land from the original allottees of Kiraska village. The trees were cleared by the villagers themselves, though they had been promised cleared land by the department. The land is fertile and even the water table is satisfactory. However, there is no road to the site from Silisere and one needs to walk about 25 km to reach the site. The other approach is by boat across the Silisere lake that most villagers cannot afford: the site thus remains to this day, approachable with difficulty. There is no school at Sirawas, except a Rajiv Gandhi Pathshala that was sanctioned in 2002 but awaits inauguration. Nor are there any health facilities or access to electricity. While electric transmission wires pass through villagers' fields to a farm house that belongs to the relative of a leading Indian politician, the villagers themselves have no electricity. It was alleged by the villagers that the farmhouse of around 300 bighas was built on land illegally allotted to the owner from the originally denotified portion of Reserved Forest land.

Old forest department personnel revealed to us cases of mismanagement on the part of the forest department in allotting land during the earlier relocation.[50] Their view was that most of the land provided to the Sirawas people was uncultivable. Maps of the revenue department, if coordinated with topographical maps, indicate that in Sirawas the area actually allotted to relocated people is a hillock not cultivable because of its rocky character. Additionally, if one looks at the map of the area one finds that a large portion of land has not yet been allotted, despite being de-reserved, even three decades after relocation. It was this situation which led most villagers to give up their allotted lands. While nine families sold off their land, ten others returned to Sariska without doing so.

The second site, Rundh Bandipul, presented a picturesque view in April, with flame-of-the-forest trees (*Butea monosperma*) in full bloom: its red flowers blazed across the forests during our visit in 2005. Rundh

[50] The forest department officials said the responsibility of marking and allocating the land after its denotification was that of the revenue department, so if any lacunae remained it was not their fault.

Bandipul is mainly occupied by original allottee families from Karnakawas. In this area, where a rivulet runs past the village towards Ajabgarh, is also located a recently built seven-star hotel which has virtually blocked off the villagers' access to river water. When villagers were relocated here from Karnakawas in 1977 the forest department had not cleared the dense vilayati kikar trees here. The villagers themselves cleared the area and began cultivation. The land is reported to be fertile and the water table is satisfactory. But other more serious problems persist so many years after the relocation. The lands are not marked clearly and distributed among the beneficiary households. Most of the villagers cultivate the lands according to their own boundary markings, which was acknowledged by officials from the district administration. During a meeting on 27 April 1992, involving the project director of Sariska, the additional district magistrate, the tehsildar of Rajgarh and Thanagazi and other officials, a camp was organized on 9 May 1992 at Bandipul Dulawa to mark the lands allotted to people from Karnakawas and pattas to those who had not received them. But to our knowledge no action has been taken on this front so far. The thirty-five families settled here fear that if their lands are not marked properly they may lose their lands and homes once again.

A more serious social problem revealed itself at the relocation site in Bandipul during our visit. The area surrounding the new settlement is dominated by people of the locally powerful Meena caste living in twenty-seven Meena villages/hamlets (also called Sattais Vaas). The Gujjars who have shifted to the area from Karnakawas in 1975–7 face constant threats to their lives from these surrounding Meenas. Men from one of the relocated families showed us injury marks from physical fights with the Meenas and told us that the Meenas once brought along a bulldozer to destroy their crops and threw their agricultural implements into a well. According to villagers, a farmer from Pratapgarh who illegally bought 3 bighas of forest land, occupied another vast chunk adjoining the river and constructed a wall along it, cutting off the Gujjars' access to river water. The villagers relocated from Karnakawas thus continue a harsh existence in terms of access to water, basic security, and development infrastructure. No wonder then that several of the families returned to Sariska from this site; their descendants now live in Chhota Kundalka, which is located at the edge of the Sariska core area.

Relocation Planning and Policy: A New Era?

Despite the failed attempt of 1975–7, plans to relocate the eleven villages inside Sariska persisted. The process for denotification of an area in the buffer zone near Dabkan, in the southern part of the reserve, was initiated in the 1990s. Soon after there was much confusion over the exact boundaries of the reserve. It later turned out that the proposed resettlement site was technically a part of the Sariska Wildlife Sanctuary. The Supreme Court judgment in Tarun Bharat Sangh vs. Union of India, filed by the Sangh against miners operating at the boundaries of the National Park (order was passed on 29 July 1997) disallowed even the union government from denotifying land in the 490 sq. km of the reserve proposed as National Park. The forest department was therefore forced to drop the plan for denotification of Dabkan. A new site at Badhod Rundh, 75 km from Sariska in the adjoining district, was selected for relocating people from Sariska. On 24 December 2002 the forest department submitted a relocation package to the high court for four of the eleven villages—Bhagani, Umri, Kankwari, and Kiraska.

During our field surveys we turned our attention to the process of relocation planning in terms of how participatory and democratic it had been. The evidence from displacements at other development sites, such as dams, indicates that resettlement has usually been highly unsatisfactory often resulting in impoverishment of the oustees. The relocation policy of Rajasthan says that the 'willingness of people' is an important factor and that villages will be shifted out only with their consent.[51] It also states that the assistance of a local voluntary organization, namely the Tarun Bharat Sangh, will be taken to obtain popular

[51] The Indian constitution's 73rd and 74th amendments make it mandatory for the Indian government to adopt a decentralized mode of governance by involving local institutions such as village panchayats in both policy-making and implementation.

consensus for such a plan. The proposed relocation package was to be disseminated in well-publicized public meetings and workshops to be organized by the forest department (or the mediating voluntary group), after which negotiations would follow with individual families.

The information that we obtained from local villagers during our surveys revealed a completely different picture. The process adopted seemed to be a repetition of the 1970s incidents. Our household surveys revealed that the forest department had not held planned or publicized meetings in any of the four villages from where the relocation was planned in the first phase, either before or after submission of the relocation plan for approval to the union government. A few unplanned meetings were held, however. In the four villages that were to be relocated in the first phase, 55 per cent of our respondents said that they had not heard of any meetings with the forest department, while 41 per cent had heard that such meetings were being held but had not attended them. Some of the local households had been informally told about the impending relocation by forest guards, who are often the only official source of information for villagers.[52] Others obtained information on the proposed relocation only when the forest guards initiated surveys to identify beneficiary households and began measuring their lands in order to calculate the compensation. A large section of the population (37 per cent) came to know about the proposed relocation by word of mouth from other people or forest personnel (40 per cent), and 23 per cent of the respondents did not know about the plans even at the time we contacted them.

In the course of developments leading to the preparation of a relocation package, not only were there no negotiations on the issue of relocation, most of the villagers were not shown the proposed new site. Through 2002–3, on just one occasion, the forest department took about thirty-five villagers from Kankwari, Umri, Kiraska, and Bhagani (male elders, as is the tradition) to the new site in two vehicles. When asked, 71 per cent of the people said they had not seen the new site

[52] It is important to note that even the forest guards themselves lacked details of the relocation package and process, and so could not convey the details to the villagers.

while 26 per cent had seen it. What social situation would they find at the new site? Most people (59 per cent) responded that they did not know about the caste or occupation of people living around the proposed site, while 41 per cent did. As with much of the information relating to relocation planning, this information too came to them from informal sources.

As for the compensatory package itself, 50 per cent of the respondents said that they had some knowledge of it while 49 per cent had no idea. Of the people who knew about the package, only 28 per cent were satisfied with it. The satisfied people came from Bhagani, which they were very keen to leave because of their particularly harsh living conditions. It is important to note here that even those people who claimed to know what the relocation package contained, had little knowledge of the details of the package in terms of the break-up of the compensatory amount. They did not know that the compensation of Rs 1 lakh per family promised in the package included the common village-wise expenditure on community infrastructure in addition to compensation for trees, wells, crop compensation, disturbance allowance, transportation allowance, and land development. Many thought that they would receive Rs 1 lakh in cash in addition to the other benefits of land and infrastructure. Most of the villagers (72 per cent) had not formally agreed to the relocation as of 2005, such as indicating willingness to move or acceptance of the package, despite plans having been finalized by the reserve management.

Other principles laid down in Rajasthan's state policy, such as the involvement of NGOs in developing the relocation plan and package, had obviously not been followed. A Tarun Bharat Sangh worker at Gopalpura denied that his organization had been part of the relocation process to motivate people to move, as described in the reserve management's relocation document. He said that the Sangh has traditionally been against such displacement from forests. Their focus instead has always been on nurturing a development process that would harmonize local people's livelihoods with wildlife (see also Shrotiya undated, Bhatia 2000).

Even by late 2005 no official at Sariska had knowledge of an implementation committee having been formed, which, according to the state policy, is a prerequisite for final displacement of villagers. There was no evidence that rural development schemes, which are supposed to be implemented on priority for resettled people, were being co-ordinated with the forest department's plans to ensure a smoother livelihood transition. The nonchalance with which the district authorities were handling the relocation became starkly clear during a public protest in Sariska in response to a sadhu being removed from Tarunda by the forest department in February 2005. It was, ironically, this mobilization that forced the district magistrate to come to Sariska and talk to the villagers about their problems. During this public meeting it was obvious that neither the district magistrate nor the local district forest officer knew about problems relating to land rights and allotments during previous relocations from the Sariska core zone.[53] The absence of people's participation in relocation planning had obviously led to insufficient understanding of the basic needs and aspirations of local people—an essential precondition for a successful relocation programme.

According to the relocation package for Bhagani village (the only one we could get access to), a cash compensation of Rs 16,000 and a 'disturbance allowance' of Rs 7000 was allotted to each household of about six members to tide over the transition period. These allotments were rather meagre, considering that the local people would have been forced to change their primary occupation from livestock-grazing to cultivation in a new environment (see Table 5). For the construction of a house, a cattle-shed, and fences, each homestead was allotted a sum of Rs 40,000 to Rs 54,000 per family, which too seemed insufficient. Our appraisal of the formal relocation package suggested that all the compensatory items, including personal costs and community works, were being squeezed into a sum of Rs 100,000 per household. There is little justification for this allocation, given the wide diversity in needs

[53] Secrecy has shrouded the entire process of relocation ever since the 'tiger crisis' of 2005. The district magistrate of Alwar refused to entertain questions from us unless we brought a recommendation letter from the forest minister of Rajasthan. We were refused copies of the relocation plan for three of the four villages that were planned to be moved during the first phase of village displacements.

Table 5

Relocation Package for Bhagani Village (19 HH) of the Sariska Tiger Reserve and State Guidelines for Compensation

A. Bhagani Village	
Individual HH Land Compensation	
Agricultural land per household	1.6 ha
Land for house construction	0.5 ha
Individual HH Cash Compensation	
House construction	Rs 40,000 to 54,000
Cash compensation	Rs 16,000
Disturbance allowance	Rs 7,000
Land development	Rs 8,000
Transport of belongings to new site	Rs 3,000
Miscellaneous	Rs 1,800
Extra for well, if already present on the land (only 1 in Bhagani)	Rs 50,000
Community Works (on per-village basis)	
Approach road	Rs 1,50,000
Electricity	Rs 1,50,000
Other	Rs 4,000
Total planned compensation package for Bhagani	**Rs 18,38,200**
Required package (@ Rs 1 lakh per family)	**Rs 19,00,000**
B. State Guidelines	
(a) INDIVIDUAL COMPENSATION	
House compensation	Rs 51000 for average construction area-85 sq.m
Crop compensation (To be given to compensate for lost crop and/or less production in the first year at new site)	Rs 6000
Private well	Rs 5000
Tree compensation	Rs 200
Disturbance allowance	Rs 7000

Table 5 (*contd.*)

Transportation allowance	Rs 3000
Land development	Rs 10000
Miscellaneous	Rs 1800
Total (a)	**Rs 84,000**
(b) COMMUNITY WORKS	
Approach road	Rs 2000
Drinking water	Rs 1500
Cattle pond	Rs 1000
Community hall	Rs 2000
Dispensary	Rs 4000
School	Rs 4000
Electricity	Rs 1500
Total (b)	**Rs 16,000**

and aspirations of different communities in different geographic contexts even within Rajasthan. Further, there were no allotments for women who were widowed or unmarried (and more than 18 years of age).

In 2005 our visit to the new relocation site of 222 hectares, Badhod Rundh, located 75 km from Sariska, almost convinced us that this was an ideal agricultural site. In terms of land allotment, the proposed relocation was progressive in historical terms, with each household receiving land titles of 2.1 hectares each even though they did not possess formal land titles inside the reserve.[54] But the total land available at the site was much less than the required amount for the villages to be moved. The land calculations were done without any provision for community facilities, such as a school, a hall, and cattle-ponds, as required by the state guidelines.

During our visit in winter, agricultural fields all around the site, (then covered by vilayati kikar) glowed with mustard flowers, lush green wheat and vegetable fields. People in the surrounding village reported satisfactory crops of wheat, mustard, maize, gram and bajra.

[54] 'Centre Agrees to Relocate 11 Villages Near Sariska', *Hindustan Times*, New Delhi, 19 July 2005.

School and health facilities were available in Badhod, barely 5 km away. The site is located on the state highway to Jaipur (about 8 km from the national highway), offering easy access to markets, wage labour, and other facilities. Some of the existing homesteads around the site were a picture of prosperity, possessing modern agricultural machinery, borewells, diesel pump-sets, cemented houses, and livestock shelters.

However, our conversations with the local villagers revealed that expensive borewell facilities would be required in this area to irrigate fields because the water table had receded as deep as 400 ft, possibly because of water-intensive cultivation of wheat and mustard in this low-rainfall area. As an example, a family in the village adjoining Badhod Rundh reported having just spent Rs 2 lakhs to put up a submersible pump. The relocation package had not budgeted any such irrigation facilities for the two villages proposed to be moved here. Worries over irrigation facilities and drinking water are specially serious in the low-rainfall zone in which Sariska is located, where surface water availability is limited to the short wet season from July to September.

Other investments required for agriculture—seeds, fertilizers, and pesticides—had not been considered in the compensation package either. Neither had other communal facilities such as halls and schools. While the relocation plan made brief mention of utilizing existing governmental schemes to develop infrastructure at the new site, there was no budget for such items. Cooking gas connections and alternative sources of fuel had not been considered and financial provisions for electrical connections (Rs 1.5 lakhs) and for the construction of the approach road (Rs 1.5 lakhs) seemed inadequate too. Conversations with senior forest personnel revealed that there was no guarantee that basic village amenities would be in place *before* the villagers were relocated, a condition that is obviously critical for successful rehabilitation.

We envisaged that the lack of forests and pastures close to the relocation site could become another serious concern if agriculture was not successful in the area and the relocated people required fodder to sustain their milk-based livelihoods. The proposed relocation site is adjacent to the village of Kakwa, which is dominated by the Jat community. As mentioned earlier, Gujjars are traditionally looked down upon by Jats in the existing caste hierarchy in this part of Rajasthan. Conflicts relating to livelihoods, water, grazing pastures, and fuelwood were therefore likely to arise in future.

The biggest lacuna in the official relocation plan was the lack of provision for income compensation during the transition period when this semi-nomadic grazing community shifted to an agriculture-based livelihood in the marginal semi-arid agricultural lands of Rajasthan (see also Sharma and Kabra 2007, and Mehra *et al.* 2004). Without some income compensation, the relocated villagers would be even less inclined to give up forest-dependency and explore employment opportunities. In 2005, therefore, the plan for relocating two villages from Sariska was riddled with innumerable problems. While the average villager inside Sariska was already living on the edge, with an annual

Illustr. 5: Villagers from the erstwhile Bhagani village in the Sariska Tiger Reserve who have been relocated outside it. Previously landless, they are optimistic about their future as they now possess agricultural land and are better connected than they were inside the reserve. However, they still face challenges in relation to re-creating secure livelihoods.

household disposable income of Rs 30,000, at least he/she had free access to water, fuelwood, and livestock fodder inside the reserve. The issue at hand was to provide all this, and more, if the displacement plan was to be attractive to the locals.

Reclaiming the Wilderness

Based on the series of events that played out during the three years after the disappearance of the tiger from Sariska, several interesting observations can be made on biodiversity governance. As it turned out, many of the recommendations of the Tiger Task Force made in July 2005 which related to village displacement, the deployment of protection forces, and the re-censusing of tigers have been taken up in earnest.[55] However, as of 2008, the forest bureaucracy has still not indicated any intention of concurrently taking the other steps relating to institutional reform, participatory management, or infrastructural improvement in Sariska, or in any other tiger reserve. The apathy towards greater public participation in decision-making related to wildlife conservation in the country has never been greater. The state governments' response to the tiger crisis continues to be simplistic. They aim to create a 'people-free zone' inside Rajasthan's tiger reserves without having a clear idea of how this will save the tiger.

What is striking about the current conservation crisis in Sariska is the virtual absence of a sense of ecological history in the administrative response of the reserve management. The historical legacy of commercial forest use, tourism, and mining on local ecology and tiger numbers has been continually ignored in the national discourse on conservation. From the start, the relocation of villages was made a priority in PA management, as though local forest use and locally abetted tiger poaching were the *sole* obstacles to effective conservation. While there do exist significant linkages between forest resource use and habitat degradation, what is overlooked by most is that a large proportion of this extractive pressure on the reserve is exerted by external towns and villages, sometimes as far as 20 km away, rather than merely by villages

[55] 'India to Spend $13.15 mn to Protect Tigers', *Times of India*, New Delhi, 2 March (online edition).

inside the core area. The need for initiatives to improve buffer zone management and provide legal avenues for economic benefit to the surrounding villages has been completely overshadowed by the bureaucratic obsession with creating 'inviolate space'. The tiger has been reintroduced in a bid, as it were, to reclaim the wilderness, however reduced and fragmented that wilderness might currently be. The fact that the original threats to the big cat still remain has been overlooked, perhaps to save the tiger reserve itself from extinction.

It is clear that there is a need for significant change not only in the way government perceives the role of the people living in and around Indian forests, but also the role of the managers themselves. What exactly needs to be reconsidered, perhaps radically, in our forests and wetlands is elaborated in the coming chapters, particularly the way village displacement, natural resource use, and PA management are undertaken all across India's wilderness.

2

Displacement Nemesis: Creating People-Free Spaces

As we drove through acres of tree stumps and degraded forest on a back-breaking dirt road, I spotted the resettlement colony through the dust haze. It was a pretty picture from afar. The cluster of white houses looked striking against the thick forests that had been left standing on the other side. Each house was white with a red-tiled roof, fenced in with bamboo, and had a small kitchen garden at the back. There was even a water tap in the front yard. I had come with the researchers Deepshikha Mehra and Kim Beazley to meet people recently displaced from the Tadoba-Andhari Tiger Reserve in Maharashtra, in late 2007.[1]

Tadoba–Andhari is a lush and large (625.40 sq. km) tiger reserve in one of the most backward- and tribal-dominated parts of Maharashtra, the Vidarbha region. Surrounded by agricultural tribal villages, Tadoba is much larger than most protected areas in India and boasts of high biological diversity. It has rolling hills and plains covered with a mix of moist and dry deciduous forest. It was constituted in 1995 by adding land to a game reserve dating from British times. Tadoba harbours a healthy population of tigers, for whom the habitat is considered ideal, being partly open and interspersed with grasslands.[2]

[1] Mehra was affiliated to SHODH, a research-based NGO in Nagpur, Beazley to the University of Cambridge.

[2] National Tiger Conservation Authority & Wildlife Institute of India 2008.

Tadoba also has a diverse assortment of other carnivores such as leopards, wild dogs, and smaller cats, in addition to high ungulate densities and over 200 bird species. The resettlement colony we were visiting, named Bhagwanpur or New Botezari, was made up of Gond tribal people who had been moved from the village of Botezari in the heart of Tadoba in the summer of 2007. Botezari was the first of the six forest villages that were proposed to be shifted out from the reserve during the next few years, with the aim of creating unfragmented habitat for its rich wildlife.

Rebuilding Lives

A closer look at the houses revealed the poor quality of materials they were made of. The cheapest kind of tile had been used for the roof, which seemed to be clinging vulnerably to the wooden beams—until the next heavy shower. A single layer of bricks made up the walls of the two-room tenement that we found ourselves in. The beams of the house were made of unfinished timber poles. Not being constructed from good quality material, several houses had developed cracks in their roofs soon after the families moved in, when the monsoon had broken in all its fury.

Discussions further revealed the sorry state the villagers found themselves in. Unusually heavy rains had washed away most of what had been planted by way of crops for the year. Given the highly seasonal nature of agriculture in this region, crop failure had left the people in a precarious position. The inputs for agriculture, such as seeds and fertilizers that were provided the first year, had proven inadequate. Some of the start-up agricultural inputs had, in fact, been donated by a local voluntary group, the Sahyadri Foundation.

The villagers had been moved to Bhagwanpur just before the monsoons, against the pleas of local NGOs such as SHODH of Nagpur, as well as village representatives. The NGOs had tried to persuade the forest officers to wait for the infrastructure to be completed before shifting people here. They pointed out that the irrigation pond had not yet been completed, nor had the allotted fields been fully ploughed. The access road to the state highway, about 3 km away, had not yet materialized. Most importantly, no arrangements had been made to substitute the fuelwood and fodder needs of the villagers, who had been completely dependent upon the lush forests of Tadoba for such goods, till just a few months ago.

Though a new overhead reservoir had been constructed for household purposes, the pressure of the water was too weak to reach the houses and the taps often ran dry. A large well provided potable water for the entire colony but it was difficult to say to what level the water level would dip during the next dry season in the event of a drought. The construction of the health centre and primary school was incomplete and, so far, had no staff. Now that the monsoon was over, there was no irrigation water as the promised irrigation pond—to be created by damming a small tributary—had been left half-finished.

Worst of all, there was hardly any employment available for the new settlers. Lacking the educational level required for even low-paid jobs in the nearby city, people were limited to living off daily-wage labour on road construction. Our informant, an enterprising young woman called Shantabai who was helping Kim Beazley with her research, told us that most people were getting, at most, eight days of wage labour each month. Paid at the rate of Rs 68 per day, for working on the connecting roads to the village, each family could barely make Rs 2000 per month. They did not have enough money to buy food but were managing to survive on the additional rations provided to each family through a government scheme which ensured a certain amount of cereal grain at very low cost to families certified to be living below the poverty line (BPL families).

Soon other men and women joined our conversation. Some said that their incomes were so low that they were constantly having to make choices between medical help and food. People were falling ill more frequently due to poor nutrition. There was obviously not enough income now to substitute for the enormous range of products they were earlier obtaining free from the forest, including nutritious food items, medicines, fibre, fuelwood, and fodder. According to detailed studies by Deepshikha Mehra and her colleagues, the average annual monetary income of a forest household from commercially sold forest and agricultural products and daily-wage labour had amounted to Rs 8870 when they were inside Tadoba. In addition they had been consuming forest and agricultural products (in the form of fodder, food, paddy), whose monetary value was estimated at as much as Rs 314,241 annually per household (Mehra *et al.* 2004). Obviously the government rehabilitation team had not taken these benefits from the forest or their commercial value into account while planning the rehabilitation process. The total amount allocated per family for rehabilitation was only Rs 100,000, including land filling, house construction, and communal infrastructure development. Within this budget the only cash being received by the villagers was a meagre Rs 1000.

Some young men of the village, educated through middle and high school, had applied for jobs as forest guards in the area, since such a government job could assure long-term security of income. However, most applications had been rejected on the basis of inadequate educational qualifications. Of the few qualified applicants within the village, just one had made it to the recent interview.

The villagers faced a severe shortage of fuelwood and were having to resort to digging out roots and stumps of trees surrounding the colony. They were also 'stealing' at night from the nearby forests, which were legally out of bounds for them, being demarcated by the government for commercial forestry operations in the future. Ironically, the government had deforested the entire tract of land (approximately 500 ha) that had been demarcated for resettlement of the six villages prior to shifting, despite the fact that only a portion of it was to be used for house construction during the first year. Pastures were supposed to have been demarcated for the villagers out of the existing forest land through provision of grazing licenses, but so far none had been received. The villagers had informal access to some pastures but these were unproductive and inadequate. As a consequence, the livestock, comprising a few buffaloes and goats owned by each family, was not yielding much milk.

It was clear to me that unless some immediate measures were taken by government agencies, there would soon be deaths from hunger. It seemed likely that soon some villagers would decide to violate the law and attempt to move back to their original place of residence. Forest villagers have no insurance against disaster, disease, or crop failure: in times of acute distress there is no option except to move to another location, preferably a known one, and hope for the best.

Yet this was without doubt a better relocation than India's development refugees have historically been provided. For instance, each of the village households, including the landless, would soon be receiving full legal rights to agricultural and homestead land, something that they had been denied inside the tiger reserve, given the restrictions of the Wildlife Protection Act of 1972.[3] They were also physically closer to the government's health, transport, and educational infrastructure. Their daily movements were no longer restricted by heavy rain or wildlife attacks, nor were their crops threatened by deer and wild boar. Much governmental investment had also gone into the development of the new resettlement site. Committed forest officers had worked hard, within the constraints of a scanty financial allocation and limited expertise, to try and settle the villagers into their new location as best they could. The government of Maharashtra had even formed an independent advisory panel with well-known experts and administrative officers, so that discrepancies in rehabilitation measures might be detected and rectified. Maharashtra was, in fact, one of the few Indian states that actually had a law on the resettlement of 'development victims'. The tragedy was that even after all these efforts the rehabilitation could be doomed to failure simply because of faulty planning and implementation.

The Nemesis of Conservation

There is no other policy issue that evokes as much passion and debate among Indian conservationists as people's displacement from national parks and wildlife sanctuaries. At a conference in February 2006 on

[3] The process of legalizing landownership had, however, not been completed at the time of our visit. The villagers did not yet have agricultural land ownership documents, but only a house plot occupancy certificate and an agricultural land plot number. Kim Beazley informed me that the ownership could be transferred only once the reserved forest was finally converted to revenue land.

Illustr. 6: A house in the resettlement site called Bhagwanpur, or New Botezari, where oustees from the Tadoba Tiger Reserve, Maharashtra, were relocated in 2007. The villagers face hardships on account of poor house construction, uncertain irrigation, and other infrastructural problems.

conservation issues in Delhi the ideological divide between biologists on the one hand and social activists on the other was stark.[4] This conference was attended by conservationists of all hues, many young biologists, social scientists, representatives of non-profit organizations, and forest managers, most of whom are known to be eager to break the escalating divide between the 'two sides'.

The social activists, some of whom had been working with marginalized tribal groups in remote forest areas for several years, felt that

[4] 'Future of Conservation in India (FoC)' is an Indian network of ecological and social organizations and individuals committed to effective and equitable conservation of biodiversity. Its aim is to foster dialogue and engagement in complex conservation issues, and help tackle the increasing threats that both biodiversity and people's livelihoods face. FoC has been active since 2006 on issues relating to the implementation of the Scheduled Tribes and other Traditional Forest Dwellers (Recognition of Forest Rights) Act 2007 and the declaration of Critical Wildlife Habitats.

displacement was largely unjustified and even unnecessary for wildlife conservation. The unjust manner in which forest peoples have been pushed around to make way for large irrigation projects, game reserves, and commercial plantations foreclosed—as far as they were concerned—the option of displacement from PAs. In many cases, they said, villagers had historically been moved into the same forests by the government to work as labour on plantations and timber extraction. The pathetically poor record of the government in independent India in successfully rehabilitating oustees had also convinced social activists that rehabilitation could never be successful under the existing laws and therefore should not be attempted in future. They stressed the role of people's traditional knowledge and cultural linkages with the forest in future forest conservation models, particularly as the forest department had not shown itself capable of protecting forests from large-scale 'development' in post-Independence India (see also Sekhsaria 2007).

On the other hand, the biologists attending the meeting were convinced that the aims of wildlife conservation could be fulfilled only if large 'inviolate' and unfragmented areas of forests were secured by moving out resident people and restricting human uses of the forest. They justified their concerns by evidence of declining animal populations in human-modified ecosystems and intensifying competition between human biomass needs and those of wild fauna and flora at the interface between villages and PAs (see also Madhusudan 2005a, K.U. Karanth *et al.* 2005, Kumar and Shahabuddin 2005). Innumerable animal species, particularly mammals, have become restricted to tiny parcels of their past habitat due to the spread of the agricultural frontier, rapid urbanization, and pollution. The one-horned rhino survives precariously in a tiny fraction of its historical range (Dinerstein 2003) while the Bengal tiger is literally on the verge of extinction (National Tiger Conservation Authority & Wildlife Institute of India 2008). They argued that there are numerous reports of successful regeneration of previously degraded forest after the eviction of even small tribal hamlets from protected areas (see K.U. Karanth 2006, Johnsingh 2006). Biologists at the meeting felt strongly that since a mere 5 per cent of land area has been set aside for protecting biodiversity in protected areas, there was moral justification for leaving this rather small area to nature. To achieve this they suggested the just and sensitive relocation of forest dwellers, and rehabilitation measures that involved serious attempts to develop livelihood security for displaced people. They also suggested overcompensating such people for their losses during the transition period.

Not unexpectedly, by the end of the conference little had been agreed on amongst this motley group of conservationists. Initially the organizers had attempted to get a joint public statement signed. They soon gave up as the participants fought tooth and nail over almost every phrase in the proposed statement.[5]

The deliberations of the conference were a stark reminder for me that the 'people vs. parks' debate has only intensified since early 2005, when it was officially acknowledged that the tiger had disappeared from the Sariska Tiger Reserve and declined to extremely low numbers in several other tiger reserves. At that time, as we saw in the previous chapter, the majority of forest managers and wildlife experts, barring a few, had pushed for people-free zones, the villages inside reserves being seen as the primary cause for high levels of poaching and habitat degradation (Rangarajan and Shahabuddin 2006). The continuing high priority currently accorded to village displacement is indicated by the fact that in 2008 the National Tiger Conservation Authority allocated as much as $1.024 billion for the purposes of relocation, planning to relocate as many as 40,000 villages from 29 tiger reserves during the eleventh Five-Year Plan period.[6]

A Historical Perspective

Till a few years ago, little was known about when, where, and how many people were moved out from forests by the Indian government,

[5] Subsequently, however, some of the conference participants came together to edit a set of experiences in conservation-induced displacement from different countries in a special issue of the academic journal *Conservation & Society* (vol. 4, no. 3) which gave an impetus to further studies and documentation of the problem in India by biologists and social scientists.

[6] 'India to Spend $13.15 Million to Protect Tigers', *Times of India Online*, 2 March 2008.

whether pre- or post-Independence. In colonial times the reservation of a fifth of the land area of British India as government forest between 1878 and 1900 aimed principally to increase revenues and upgrade the growing stock of marketable timber (Rangarajan and Shahabuddin 2006). Early in the twentieth century, especially in southern and western India, botanists had come up with the argument that controlling hill people was essential to save the forests from them (ibid.). In some cases, this was with the intention of enhancing wildlife populations: during the 1860s the evictions of villages from the banks of the Ramganga river in what is now the Corbett Tiger Reserve created 'people-free' zones where grasslands on the old village sites provide valuable habitat for deer, elephants, and other mammals today. It seems likely that many more forest-dwelling people were shifted from forests and game reserves without attracting much attention by the urban intelligentsia in the early twentieth century.

Village displacement for wildlife conservation became the norm in India in the early 1970s. For the first time there was a co-ordinated relocation drive to secure the habitat of endangered mammals, in response to international calls (ibid.). In the Kanha National Park in Madhya Pradesh, the village of Supkhar was relocated to open up living space for the central Indian barasingha deer (Holloway 1978). During 1972–87 nearly 500 families of buffalo-herding Maldharis were moved out of the core zone of the Gir PA with the aim of reducing the levels of lion predation on domestic stock (Choudhary 2000). Displacement has since become an important objective of park managers in several states. It was often funded by the union government under schemes like Project Tiger, launched in 1973. Displacement in India had its counterpart in other parts of Asia during this period, such as at the Chitwan National Park in Nepal, where it has been well documented (Ghimire 1999). There are also several cases in Vietnam (McElwee 2006), as well as numerous parks in Africa (Rangarajan 2003, Brockington 2002).

Until very recently there was very little published information on the numbers of people involved in displacements from PAs. From about 1972, when relatively improved documentation began, the total number of people estimated to have been displaced from PAs is rather low. The Tiger Task Force Report (Ministry of Environment and Forests 2005) estimates 2904 families (or approximately 14,520 people) having been moved from twelve tiger reserves and three other PAs. This is very likely a gross underestimation. My own calculations, based on a comprehensive review of newspaper and journal reports, seminar proceedings, research papers, forest department accounts, and unpublished data suggest a much higher figure, roughly 49,000 people from as many as 37 PAs (including wildlife sanctuaries and national parks).[7] Another recent review by the environmental organization Kalpavriksh suggests 20,000 families (approximately 120,000 people) from 23 PAs (Kalpavriksh 2007). These widely varying estimates of dislocated people result from the extremely scattered data on PA-related displacements, data which is mostly buried away in Forest Department records. These records can, in most cases, be unearthed only through field visits since there are none available with the union or state governments. Even in the field offices of PAs, records relating to displacement are difficult to find, in part because the issue is so controversial.

Relative to displacements caused by developmental projects, such as industry and hydro-electric dams, PA-related displacements have tended to affect smaller communities within each instance. This is because PAs are often set up in relatively remote sites where human population densities naturally tend to be rather low. However, displacements from Indian PAs are now being planned on a much larger scale, involving several villages at a time. A case in point is the Kuno Wildlife Sanctuary, from where 24 villages involving 5000 people were displaced between 1998 and 2003 (Sharma and Kabra 2007).

The Social and Economic Impact of Displacement and Relocation

One might suppose that in terms of the relatively small number of people displaced from PAs—'oustees' is the term generally used now

[7] Unpublished data are taken from the questionnaire survey of protected areas undertaken by the Indian Institute of Public Administration from 1999 to 2002.

to describe such people—the challenge of rehabilitation is supposedly easier to handle than in the case of larger development projects. But this is not so, for almost every instance of conservation-induced displacement involves for the individual oustee an abrupt occupational and cultural change. Often the enforced transition is from forest-dwelling, hunting-gathering occupations to a settled agricultural existence. Forest-dwelling people tend to be more vulnerable to impoverishment after their dislocation from forest-based livelihoods: very often they simply do not possess the education, language skills, and exposure to markets that is required. And this within an economic environment that is far from easy even for people who possess those skills. Conservation-induced displacements also disproportionately affect marginalized tribal groups—though there have been several cases of non-tribal relocation, such as in the Corbett Tiger Reserve (see Negi 2003) and the Bhadra Tiger Reserve where PA residents were relatively recent migrants (K. Karanth 2007). Given these conditions, the rehabilitation of forest-dependent peoples requires a very different approach. A great deal of sensitivity to ethnicity and history, and careful attention to the development of new livelihood skills as well as to the deployment of existing traditional knowledge are imperatives if relocations are to have even a remote chance of success.

The likely impact of displacement should, for a start, be seen in the context of the existing development status of villages located inside forests. Development has been denied to numerous villages located inside notified national parks and sanctuaries because there are laws prohibiting developmental activities for 'non-forest purposes' such as the construction of roads, clinics, schools, and wells. While livestock-grazing, agricultural activity, and fuelwood-use are usually restricted soon after the initial notification of a PA, local residents are rarely provided alternatives for such biomass requirements or resettled successfully. The relocation plans for such villages (which are usually faulty and inadequate) stay in the files for years, either on account of local opposition or bureaucratic red tape. Consequently, those villagers live in a state of uncertainty and deprivation with little access to the basic amenities of life, and in severe conflict with managements, for years together (Mehra *et al.* 2004): as we saw in the previous chapter, villagers inside the core zone of the Sariska Tiger Reserve have been living under the threat of eviction for nearly thirty years, with highly restricted access to both forest resources and developmental infrastructure.

Anecdotal accounts by activists of the social impact of village relocation have not usually been backed up by detailed studies, though a notable exception to this is the doctoral work of Asmita Kabra (2007) which tracks the socio-economic impact of displacement for oustees from the Kuno Wildlife Sanctuary. This study is remarkable for the fact that it comprehensively compares the socio-economic status of households that have been relocated outside the sanctuary with those that still exist inside it. A number of newspaper reports, popular articles, and press releases by NGOs—such as SHODH in the Tadoba-Andhari Tiger Reserve that have intervened in specific recent relocation cases—also allow room for some analysis. Based on these few available reports and papers I attempt below to arrive at certain generalities.

It is very clear that in most cases of displacement involving forest villages the dependence of people on forest resources for energy, nutritional, construction, medical, and commercial purposes is overlooked during the planning stage. I was a witness to this in Tadoba. The significant cash income obtained by forest villagers through sales of NTFP in local markets is never properly estimated. Even when the comprehensive nature of forest dependence is recognized by planners, their basic assumption is that the new sources of income in the resettlement site—usually settled agriculture—will adequately compensate and enable the purchase of the goods and services previously available free from the forest. In fact, it has been found in almost every case that agricultural productivity in resettlement sites tends to be low and therefore inadequate as a substitute for buying previously available forest goods (Sharma and Kabra 2007).

Most pastoral/semi-pastoral people who are forest-dependent survive within an intricate livelihood mosaic of livestock-rearing, small-scale agriculture, NTFP collection, and daily-wage labour (Kabra 2008). In the few cases that have been closely observed, relocation has resulted in the decoupling of these survival mechanisms (ibid.) and the effect has been pauperization. Kabra also notes that the effort and drudgery involved in NTFP collection, sales, and fuelwood collection increase significantly after displacement, while the number of NTFP items collected goes down, particularly the high value items (Kabra 2007). Another conspicuous trend is that for oustees the proportion of income from daily-wage labour rises substantially after displacement (ibid.).

Such loss of livelihoods has been consistently noted in all the cases of completed or proposed PA displacements that have been studied: the Satpura Tiger Reserve, the Sariska Tiger Reserve (Shahabuddin *et al.* 2007), the Tadoba-Andhari Tiger Reserve (Mehra *et al.* 2004), the Kuno Wildlife Sanctuary (Kabra 2007).[8] Loss of livelihoods also takes its toll on human nutrition and health, whereas displacement planning gives no room to this. Kabra (ibid.) found that nutrition based on hunting and fishing had gone down drastically among the displaced hunting community of Sahariyas. The net result of such problems is that oustee families, facing severe food and water shortages, fodder scarcity, and nutritional difficulties try to make their way back to their earlier habitat. Many of the oustees from Kuno, for instance, attempted to return to the sanctuary after facing a starvation crisis in 2004 folowing successive years of drought (Bunsha 2005, Sharma and Kabra 2007).

It is often assumed that relocating villages from PAs will result in improved access to development and communication infrastructure, and health and educational services, since the oustees are generally moved closer to existing highways and towns. Such promises, in fact, are very commonly made during displacement planning. The actual experience has been rather variable: it has not been positive in some villages of Kuno because the access of resettled villagers to modern infrastructure depends not only on the location of the new resettlement site but also on the quality of existing and new government-sponsored facilities at the site of relocation. Yet it is not as if there are

[8] For the Satpura Tiger Reserve, documentation exists in the shape of a letter from Kalpavriksh Environmental Action Group to Chief Wildlife Warden, Madhya Pradesh, 16 March 2006.

no positive instances: the relocation of oustees from the outskirts of the Corbett Tiger Reserve to the town of Kashipur is reported to have brought some of them closer to roads, health, and educational facilities previously unavailable to them (Negi 2003). This is reported also for Gaindikhata, to which oustees from the Rajaji National Park (Uttaranchal) have been moved (Johnsingh 2006).

Faulty Planning Processes and Inadequate Relocation Packages

The ineffective village rehabilitation process has its genesis in the planning stage. An adequate relocation can happen only if the mechanism adopted takes popular aspirations, needs, and constraints into consideration and rationally evaluates all the requirements beforehand. This is principally due to the fact that the oustees are hardly ever met or consulted before the plans are drawn up; nor are adequately knowledgeable social and economic experts involved (Shahabuddin *et al.* 2007). Therefore, baseline surveys which can assess the livelihood status of the proposed oustees are rarely carried out before displacements are made.

Far from discussing their possible needs during rehabilitation with the people being summarily ousted, the process of informing people, obtaining consent, and drawing up of lists of beneficiary families has in most cases been found to be faulty and lackadaisical. In the Kuno Wildlife Sanctuary, beneficiary lists were drawn up in a slipshod manner, leaving out the names of many oustee families; later such problems had to be rectified because of the intervention of local NGOs (Sharma and Kabra 2007). In Sariska, as we saw earlier, several families had not even heard of their impending displacement—not even after the official relocation plan and package had been finalized and sent for clearance to the union government (Shahabuddin *et al.* 2005).

While the focus of most rehabilitation packages so far has been monetary compensation and land allotment, the necessity of skill development, social adjustment, and the establishment of accompanying infrastructure continues to be ignored. Numerous accounts show the lack of basic development infrastructure at resettlement sites even decades after displacement (Ministry of Environment and Forests 2005, Shahabuddin *et al.* 2005). The fact that most oustees belong to marginalized Scheduled Caste or tribal communities, and therefore possess limited skills to fight for better conditions makes matters even worse.

Most forest and PA resettlements have worked on the principle of 'land-to-the-landless', making these resettlements relatively progressive in comparison with development-induced displacements. A total of two hectares of land is allotted to all oustees, irrespective of whether they owned land previously. Therefore, in one sense, the successful allotment of good quality agricultural land is likely to result in a localized 'land reforms' exercise (Sharma and Kabra 2007). However, the quality of agricultural land allotted to oustees is what really determines how successfully they are able to re-establish secure livelihoods in the resettlement sites. The resettlement of primarily agricultural households from the Bhadra Tiger Reserve is instructive in this regard (K. Karanth 2007). Displacement from this tiger reserve has been reported to be far more successful in restoring oustees' livelihoods—and in the relatively short period of a year—than most other cases in the country. This happened because the necessary attention was given to the identification and allocation of good agricultural land (Kabra 2008). In contrast, in Kuno, many villagers still complain of barren land where they were moved without its proper development (Bunsha 2005). In the absence of a support system that could help develop land quality, along with irrigation facilities, families are unable to extract much from these allotted lands, a problem evident in the Chandaka Wildlife Sanctuary (Asher and Kothari 2005) and the Sariska Tiger Reserve (Shahabuddin *et al.* 2005).

Land compensation apart, financial commitments to rehabilitation badly need to be reconsidered. Recent analysis indicates that the existing allocation for rehabilitation of PA villages needs considerable enhancement to make it viable for oustees. According to the centrally-sponsored Beneficiary-Oriented Tribal Development Scheme (BoTD), Rs 100,000 has been kept as the upper limit on per-household expenditure on relocation, including personal costs and community works (but excluding the cost of land). There is little justification for this flat allocation given the wide diversity in needs and aspirations of different communities in varying geographic contexts. The Tiger Task Force (Ministry of Environment and Forests 2005) has recommended at least Rs 250,000 per household, apart from land costs.

The suggestion for increased allocation of resources to village resettlement can be justified by observing a number of gaps. For instance, an important lacuna in rehabilitation packages is the lack of income compensation for the transition period, during which oustees are expected to carve out a new livelihood for themselves in a new environment. When people are required to shift to an entirely new way of life—agriculture-based livelihood instead of nomadic pastoralism, for example—settling in is likely to take at least a few years and comes, as we have seen, along with huge psychological and related health costs to the people who have been shifted out. During this period, it is critical that their incomes are more than adequately compensated; income insecurity among oustees is a systemic outcome of most relocation plans in the country. There seems little doubt that the existing class and caste hierarchies—manifest in the disparities of power between those who do the planning and those who are, literally, at the receiving end of these plans—play a large part in the skewed conception and execution of resettlement.

Hurdles in the Implementation Process

Even ample rehabilitation packages may not be sufficient when the implementation process lacks transparency and local participation. Importantly, when a relocation is decided on, there is no legal binding mechanism that places the onus for effective rehabilitation either on the forest officer responsible for relocation or on the district administration. It is usually up to the individual commitment of local forest officers and/or district officers to carry out a just resettlement programme. In such a situation the participation of oustees and NGOs can be an important driving force for effective rehabilitation.

Generous allotments for 'community works' or 'fuelwood and pasture development' do not in themselves guarantee its satisfactory usage. For instance, in the Kuno case as much as Rs 8000 was allocated per household for fuelwood plantations, Rs 8000 for pasture development, and Rs 9000 for community works; but many of these goals were not realized on the ground (Sharma and Kabra 2007). The involvement of existing village panchayats and gram sabhas at the initial stages could have led to much more effective programmes in the relocation sites. The original relocation plan for the Kuno Wildlife Sanctuary had envisaged the formation of village development committees (VDCs) that would act as the nodal agency at every step (ibid.). These would have helped in information dissemination and problem-solving, possibly minimizing the grievances of the community. In practice, the involvement of these committees was arbitrary, ad hoc, and minimal, leaving the community with no effective mechanism for grievance-redressal and making it vulnerable to exploitation by the lower-level sanctuary staff as well as by powerful members of the community itself (ibid.).

A Positive Experience: Relocation in the Bhadra Tiger Reserve

For all this there are reasons to believe that it is possible to undertake resettlement more humanely. The relocation of 419 households from the Bhadra Tiger Reserve in 2002 is a case in point. The resettlement has been far from perfect, with households in one of the two relocation sites still facing problems of livelihood security (K. Karanth 2007). Most households feel that the compensation amount paid in cash at the time of shifting was insufficient given the long period of time taken to establish new livelihoods. However, the overall satisfaction level among the oustees is much higher than in previous cases of displacement in the country. All of the resettled households now have ownership of good agricultural land and access to electricity, health services, running water, schools, and transport (Kabra 2008). Access to modern assets such as phones and bicycles is reported to have significantly increased from 2002 to 2006, suggesting higher disposable incomes among many households (K. Karanth 2007).

Part of the reason for improved resettlement from Bhadra has been the presence of committed forest officers and the involvement of local

NGOs in the process of alternative land identification and allotment, all of which helped the oustees negotiate their rights. The financial package made available to them also amounted to four times that of the standard used elsewhere in India, and the compensatory payments were made in time.[9] Another important factor was that connecting roads, schools, primary health centres, and panchayat buildings were put in place *before* the oustees moved in, so that they could develop their new livelihood within a shorter span of time (ibid.). In the Bhadra resettlement sites, oustees have also found themselves with better access to alternative jobs—this on account of their greater educational qualifications to start with (ibid.). While the role of greater governmental accountability and efficiency in states such as Karnataka cannot be negated, the oustee community was in this case made up of social groups that have a prominent place in state politics. They could consequently much better negotiate their rights during the planning process than forest-dependent tribal peoples with little access to outside information (Kabra 2008).

Looking for a Balance

It is clear that a balanced approach can be adopted to the contentious issue of displacement. This is possible through paying greater attention to site-specific details rather than by getting trapped in semantics. There is no profiting from extreme positions, such as on the impossibility of coexistence of human settlements with wildlife, or on the necessity of community participation in wildlife management, without qualifying either perspective with cultural, ecological, and socio-economic specificities.[10] There is a general consensus among ecologists that many wildlife areas would profit from being free of human habitation. There is anecdotal evidence of this from the Rajaji National Park, the Sariska Tiger Reserve, and the Tadoba-Andhari Tiger Reserve where wildlife populations have visibly bounced back in old village sites with the help of appropriate management

[9] Ministry of Environment and Forests 2005.

[10] Report of the State Empowered Committee on Forest and Wildlife Management 2005.

Illustr. 7: Large mammals such as the one-horned rhinoceros require large and continuous stretches of suitable habitat to survive—the reason why they are now restricted to a few national parks in India. (*Photo: Jawed Ashraf*)

strategies. In many cases village people are, in fact, keen to move out of PAs given that many more educational, development, and employment opportunities exist outside these remote areas than inside them. The fact that the WLPA constrains the development of basic infrastructure such as concrete houses, permanent wells, and proper schools certainly encourages *younger* people to explore employment outside (Ghate and Beazley 2008). The government could well turn such aspirations into effective relocation opportunities through well-designed and well-financed rehabilitation schemes.

The Tiger Task Force recommends minimizing conservation-induced displacement or treating it as 'the last resort' for protecting habitats and species, citing the unsatisfactory track record of the government in effective relocation (Ministry of Environment and Forests 2005). However, biologists would find it difficult to agree with such a recommendation. As a society, Indians need to agree on a certain minimum natural area that should be managed for biodiversity, this being largely left to the forces of ecology and evolution. There is increasing evidence that without such allocation it may be impossible to save many of our vulnerable species—those that require large areas or are endemic, or habitat-restricted—from extinction in the long run. Following a commitment to set aside space for nature, financial resources and public support for displacement need to be created. The displacement option should not be foreclosed only because it has been difficult or badly managed thus far, as suggested by the TTF.

At the same time, it would be counterproductive to force relocation in areas where it is not practicable or where traditional sustainable ecosystem management already exists. There are innumerable instances of ecosystems managed by local villagers, including sacred forests, grasslands, and coastal fishing areas that currently harbour much more biodiversity than a suburban apartment complex in Pune or a private beach resort in Goa.[11] Many of these management systems are based on considerable local knowledge of plant regeneration, ecological relationships, and animal behaviour. There is also a revival of old systems of agriculture that foster biodiversity and that have effectively done away with pollution from pesticides and fertilizers, a serious problem across the country.

The way forward, then, would be to actively supply economic and other incentives for such voluntary community conservation, rather than discourage it—as wildlife policy currently does in India. This option can be applied to categories of protected areas in India such as community reserves and conservation reserves that are already mandated by law but have yet to see effective implementation. The important thing is to recognize that there is more than one category of protection possible, and that these varying management regimes can effectively complement each other in the larger landscape. Public recognition of the possible diverse forms of conservation, by biologists and foresters, can also help mould public opinion in favour of biodiversity among tribal representatives and social activists, and win their support in cases where there are few options to village displacement.

[11] In fact there are numerous cases of villagers fighting off large-scale development interests in India today, in order to preserve their nature-based livelihoods, and in the process saving habitats important for wildlife.

It remains difficult even for diehard wildlife biologists to ignore the larger politics of village displacement in India which has, understandably, alienated many social activists from the very concept of wildlife conservation. In most PAs, management plans tend to prioritize the displacement of resident villages, while other external habitat pressures are habitually ignored. In numerous Indian PAs, the damaging effects of hydro-electric projects, industry, commercial tourism, mining, and quarrying, often of a serious nature, are overlooked even as the authorities come down heavily on local subsistence-level uses (Sekhsaria 2007). The case of the Narayan Sarovar Sanctuary in coastal Gujarat, where 90 per cent of the PA (originally 765 sq. km in area) was denotified by the state government in 1993 to make way for mining, is a case in point. The deleterious effects of unrestricted commercial tourism, mostly operated by city-based interests, have already been well documented in places like the Ranthambhore Tiger Reserve. Yet few restrictions have been placed on the numbers of vehicles or tourists that can utilise the reserve. A well-studied example comes from the Great Himalayan National Park in Himachal Pradesh, where the fate of the globally endangered western tragopan, a pheasant species, was pitted for several years against the grazing and plant collection activities of local people. In 1999 a part of the park was carved out to make way for a hydroelectric project. Ironically, the accompanying road and dam construction are certain to wipe out forests in a section of the park that had earlier been considered critical for the pheasant species (Chhatre and Saberwal 2006). The PA Update documents many cases of larger industrial and development interests threatening the existence of wild species in protected areas.[12] Support by biologists of public struggles against large-scale takeover of forest lands for development projects, which benefit only a small section of India's people, would go a long way in building a broader support for equitable conservation in the country.

We left Bhagwanpur in the late afternoon and drove fast on the state highway to reach the reserve gates before sundown. As we re-entered

[12] Website: http://www.kalpavriksh.org/f1/f1.2/pa_update/index_html.

Tadoba in the growing twilight, refreshing forest smells enveloped us. Soon we stopped to watch a pair of wild dogs silently tussling in the grass by the side of the road. The nightjars had begun their twilight vigil, swooping low over our jeep as we disturbed them from the rough tracks. The biological benefits of protected areas seemed all too real.

But I found myself asking a question: in a democratic society, should one have to make a choice between wildlife and poor people? Does the process of rehabilitation of villages have to be so difficult? If an affluent family is asked to move from an elite neighbourhood for the construction of a new road, is the approach as lackadaisical? And if the well-off are displaced, would the process for developing alternative livelihoods be so half-hearted and incomplete for them?

I corrected my self-questioning: an elite family in a typical Indian city is unlikely to be asked to move at all. New infrastructure in India is increasingly being created over powerless slum colonies and the agricultural landholdings of poor people. Other vulnerable sites are also being targeted, like pavements, parks, green areas, and, more recently, priceless heritage structures. The inequities in protected area management seem to closely mirror not only the deep inequities in Indian society but also, ironically, the pathetically low values that urban Indians typically associate with common spaces and the common good.

It follows, then, that not much can be done for conservation in India unless it is paralleled by moves towards greater equity and a more effective democracy.

3

The Endangered Tribe of the Wildlife Biologist

High-quality biological research is one of the primary needs for managing wild habitats, particularly protected areas. Most of India's protected areas are surrounded by landscapes modified by people—such as agricultural fields, degraded forests, orchards, and mines. While each of these land uses has an impact on adjoining wildernesses in often intangible ways, the PAs themselves extract costs from the surrounding human settlements, costs that usually go unaccounted. How to harmonize ever-changing demands on India's wild areas with the protection of wild species is an issue that, therefore, requires continuous biological research, particularly research that is sensitive to other facets of human development as well.

Despite the recent expansion of the protected area network in India, there is a glaring lack of relevant research that can help direct their management. A recent documentation of the forty-one PAs in the state of Maharashtra reveals that most of these PAs hosted very little research, apart from the annual census of carnivores and ungulates by the park managers themselves and the occasional biological inventorying by university researchers (Pande 2005). There is therefore little basis for evaluating how well a conservation strategy is working. Are there improvements in forest biomass and diversity after protection began? How much grass can be extracted for human use and in which seasons should it be cut? What is the extent of compensation required by a village family to offset the costs incurred by crop-raiding wildlife? Apart from applied research that seeks to address specific management issues, many PAs do not even have a comprehensive inventory of the organisms within them. So their managers often do not even adequately comprehend what they are trying to protect.

There are several reasons for this dismal state of affairs. State forest departments and PAs have neither adequate infrastructure for ecological research nor trained personnel. Nor are there any channels for forest managers to tap ongoing research at universities and research institutions. The situation is not helped by the sheer paucity of qualified researchers in the ecological sciences. The fact is that field biology is not the preferred career option for the typical biology graduate in India. Compared to the abundant and lucrative opportunities in the areas of biotechnology and cell biology—given their applications in the medical world—the field biologist is faced with relatively low-paid job options restricted to universities and research institutes. Once positioned within a government-run setting, most field biologists have little incentive to excel in research or publish papers. It is therefore easy to understand why there are so few successful field biologists in India and why they tend to be those who work in research NGOs.[1] Several biologists have established their own research programmes while others work as independent researchers and consultants.

The problems of field biology do not end here. One of the more serious problems facing Indian biologists today is the difficulty they face in simply getting access to their objects of study—wild species of flora and fauna and the ecosystems they inhabit.[2]

Research Permits

Because of the declining forest cover and quality of habitat outside Indian PAs (that is, wildlife sanctuaries and national parks), sites that are sufficiently protected from human use, and therefore suitable for

[1] Examples include the Nature Conservation Foundation, the Ashoka Trust for Research in Ecology and the Environment, and the Centre for Wildlife Studies: these aim to build a scientific foundation for wildlife policy and management in India.

[2] See also Madhusudan *et al.* 2006 for a critical review of this trend.

biological studies, are scarce. For instance, to study aspects of rainforest ecosystems a researcher would need to travel to either the Kalakad-Mundanthurai Wildlife Sanctuary in Tamil Nadu or the Silent Valley National Park in Kerala. Most biologists thus need to work at least partially in PAs, and for such work formal permits are required from both union and state governments.

It has never been easy to get research permits to work inside PAs. Researchers have had to write to the chief wildlife warden of the state in which his/her study area lies. This official then asks the approval of the forest officer in charge of the relevant protected area before granting, and sometimes refusing, the required permit. Though the procedure for application is rather straightforward, a permit can take several months to be sanctioned. It is of course all the more difficult to obtain permits for wildlife research if the research involves the capture of animals, manipulation of the habitat, or nocturnal observation.

To make things yet more difficult, new guidelines on the regulation of wildlife research have been promulgated by the union Ministry of Environment and Forests in August 2006.[3] These new guidelines have been formulated without much consultation with scientists and scientific institutions, and through a rather secretive process, despite several representations by biologists (Madhusudan *et al.* 2006). Though these guidelines have not yet been enacted into law or put into practice, they have already made the issuing of permits even more complicated and time-consuming than before, in most Indian states. When these guidelines are finally implemented, each application for a research permit will need to go through an additional expert committee which is expected to meet every four months: another obvious instance of India's bureaucracy creating difficulties for its citizens. In cases of research requiring the capture of animal species listed in Schedules I and II, separate authorizations are now required from two other divisions in the ministry of environment and forests, apart from the relevant state's chief wildlife warden. Bureaucracy remains oblivious of the fact that ecological research is often subject to stringent seasonal and annual schedules requiring observations at specific times of the year.

[3] http://www.envfor.nic.in/divisions/wildlife/guidelines_scientific.htm

Therefore, delays in research projects for even a few months can result in loss of data for the entire year. Instead of instituting a process which in the financial sector is known as 'due diligence', i.e. ascertaining case by case the merits of each application and deciding whether or not a permit should be issued, a wall of bureaucracy is erected to sabotage valuable research.

Such restrictions effectively exclude some types of research that sometimes are the only way to validate certain ecological hypotheses. For instance, an accurate estimation of the population density of any animal species requires capture, marking, subsequent release of the animals, and finally, recaptures of the animals. Since researchers rarely manage to get permits for capture, they have to be satisfied with purely observational methodologies involving the visual counting of individual animals. The state's denial of permits is understandable if such marking techniques are to be used on endangered species; the problem is that these are blanket rules which apply equally to species whose populations are unlikely to be affected by accidental deaths or injuries. Another example: studying the effects of annual fires on forest trees and shrubs might involve setting fire to small plots of forest/grassland and examining the effects after some months through the observation and measurement of plants. Such experiments require repetition for at least a few years if statistically viable samples are to be obtained. It is almost impossible to get permits for such manipulation of habitat, even over very small patches of forest habitat, inside PAs. Yet such manipulation is often undertaken by the PA managers themselves, for other purposes.

In the rare instance where field experiments have been allowed, they have led to important insights for management. For instance, a long-term study was carried out in the Kalakad-Mundanthurai Tiger Reserve to study how fire control affects the spread of a grass species (*Cymbopogon spp.*), one that is not eaten by wild deer and which therefore reduces the suitability of grassland habitat. Only after sustained observation over a three-year period was it found that the existing fire control practices were actually encouraging the growth of *Cymbopogon* rather than decimating it (Sankaran 2005). A similar study in the reserved forests of central India revealed that the use of fire for facilitating the collection of commercial forest produce—such as mahua flowers and tendu leaves—can significantly decrease the growth rates and increase the death rates of tree saplings (Saha and Howe 2006). Further, individual marking of plants showed that different species were affected differently by fire (Saha and Howe 2003), which explained why some species were becoming more abundant over the years. Yet another well-known instance of unresearched management efforts that boomeranged on wildlife was the banning of buffalo-grazing inside Keoladeo Ghana when it was converted to a national park in 1981. Buffaloes from the surrounding villages had helped reduce the plant biomass inside the wetland areas, effectively stalling the gradual progression of this world-famous wetland to a scrub forest. Within a few years of the ban, weeds and grasses began growing uncontrollably, reducing the wetland habitat for fish and waterfowl, a process that was uncovered only by a ten-year-long ecological study by the Bombay Natural History Society (Vijayan 1991, Lewis 2003).

Even when permits are obtained, they can sometimes be withdrawn by the government without sufficient reason. One instance was the withdrawal of a research permit to the well-known herpetologist Romulus Whitaker in April 2007, to study king cobras using radio telemetry. Though the permit was restored after a formal enquiry established that no rules were broken during the study, the scientist and his team went through much trauma apart from losing an entire year in their project schedule. Other cases of the termination of research permits given to eminent scientists and graduate students have been documented by the Tiger Task Force (Ministry of Environment & Forests 2005). Many of these scientists believe their permits were withdrawn in response to their criticism of the management by the forest department, and their reporting of the worsening forest conditions that they had observed.

In short, restrictions on research methods to be used have constrained the types of research questions that can be asked by wildlife researchers, making them dependent on decisions taken by bureaucrats and managers of sanctuaries and national parks (Madhusudan *et al.* 2006). In a knowledge-based society it is absurd that the work of scientists—to decide research questions, formulate hypotheses, and develop methodologies best suited for asking specific research questions—has been sabotaged by bureaucrats.

Foreign Collaborations

If one looks at the achievements in wildlife research in other countries, an inescapably distinct feature is the involvement of foreign collaborators and international peer-review. Developing countries such as Nepal and Uganda have hosted several wildlife research projects that have been designed and implemented in collaboration with foreign universities and research institutions. In Nepal the twenty-year-old involvement of the Smithsonian Institution, the United States National Zoological Park, and the Worldwide Fund for Nature in the ecological study and conservation of the one-horned rhinoceros has significantly enhanced understanding of the ecological needs of this highly endangered mammal. The study led to the reintroduction of the rhinoceros in its old habitats.[4] The long-term collaboration also helped to develop capacity among local biologists and park managers for science-based conservation (Dinerstein 2003).

In Uganda, Thomas Struhsaker, a primatologist from the United States, enlisted scores of Ugandan and foreign students to undertake research on a wide variety of subjects, ranging from insect diversity to the behaviour of primate species in the country's rainforests. In this process, between 1970 and 1988, Struhsaker helped create a cadre of biologists and foresters who are now independently carrying forward the long-term research programme initiated by him (Struhsaker 1997). His interventions led, among other things, to the establishment of the 766 sq. km Kibale National Park by the Ugandan government. Indian biologists, however, face considerable restrictions if they wish to collaborate with foreign scientists. Up to eleven different clearances need to be obtained from several different government departments

[4] See also Seidensticker 2008 for a discussion of how scientific studies have helped establish baselines for ecosystem restoration and management in the Chitwan National Park.

Illustr. 8: The spread of invasive species such as the herbaceous *Cassia tora* in the Sariska Tiger Reserve reduce food availability for deer and other wild animals: this is on account of the unpalatibility of its leaves, flowers, and seeds. Field research can yield solutions to such problems in protected areas.

before a foreign researcher can be issued a research visa for field studies: including the departments of environment, human resources (education), home affairs, defence, and external affairs. Such clearances are known to take months, often pre-empting the collaboration or causing its abandonment. Currently, there are no more than a handful of projects involving a foreign collaborator in India. The documentation of management in the PAs within Maharashtra mentioned earlier, reveals that not one of them had ever hosted any research with foreign collaboration (Pande 2005).

India's xenophobia goes back a long way. Detailed study of correspondence between the Indian wildlife establishment and foreign institutions reveals that the government made a conscious decision to limit the access of United States biologists and research institutions, purely with the purpose of asserting greater governmental control over the then booming conservation movement in India (Lewis 2005). In the 1970s Kailash Sankhala, erstwhile chief wildlife warden of Rajasthan and famous naturalist, refused a valuable chance to establish scientific field stations in three wildlife sanctuaries in India in collaboration with the Smithsonian Institution for fear of allowing unfettered access to foreign biologists. The antiquated Nehruvian rhetoric of the government was that they were ensuring Indians developed their own scientific expertise and were freed from their dependence on foreign biologists. It is possible that in refusing permission to the Smithsonian, the Indian government actually took a deliberate step in moving against Indian biologists who were attempting to collaborate with various universities and research institutions in the United States at the time (Lewis 2005).

The recently passed Biological Diversity Act (2002) is an additional obstacle to field-based taxonomic studies, a domain heavily dependent upon foreign collaboration (Prathapan *et al.* 2006, Prathapan *et al.* 2008). The act was intended to protect the biodiversity of developing countries and confer rights to local people over their own traditional knowledge.[5] Lately, however, the act has instead become an impediment to serious taxonomic work. Advances in taxonomy require the free exchange of specimens amongst collectors, museums, and international research institutions located in various countries. Indian taxonomists, particularly, depend on international collections for identification since very few collections within India are up-to-date and well curated. Frequently, comparisons with more than one collection are required when it is suspected that a specimen may represent a new species. The Biological Diversity Act mandates that a large fee be collected on every specimen sent out of the country, and that permits be obtained from the union government. Earlier, no such rules existed and scientists freely sent specimens abroad, as long as they could certify that the aim was not commercial. These new rules are being seen by Indian taxonomists as literally sounding the death-knell for taxonomic research in India, since these requirements are unlikely to be met by an average scientist in India (Prathapan *et al.* 2008). They point out that many of the fears of the government on illegal patenting and biopiracy in relation to museum specimens have little logical

[5] Under the agreement with the United Nations Convention on Biodiversity (UNCBD).

basis. The quantity of biological material required for such patenting is much larger than can be provided by a few specimens.

Government restrictions are not confined to environmental research. Difficulties are also faced by foreign researchers working in the social sciences. Getting clearances from a host of government departments is difficult for them simply because of the supposedly 'sensitive' nature of their planned study. Consequently Indian researchers are reciprocally deprived of valuable scholarly exchanges and collaboration of the kind vital for improving quality of research and competing with the best in the world. Research by the science historian Michael Lewis shows that the Indian government's exclusion of US funds and scientists in the 1970s had, in the long run, a deleterious impact not only on the training of Indian biologists and forest officers but also on progress in ecological research (Lewis 2005).

Management Applicability

Ecologists and field biologists have recently been called upon by the Indian government to explain how their research can be applied to the management of the protected area that they are working in. Even before the new guidelines began to be formulated, more than one ecologist was faced with the question: what good is your research for the management of this sanctuary? What purpose is served by documenting the species of butterflies found in a forest? Is it not a waste of time tracking herds of wild bison for hours together with no other purpose than to record their feeding habits? Researchers are increasingly asked these questions, indicating that the issue of applicability has become of considerable importance in decisions regarding research permits. The new research guidelines of 2006 also emphasize that preference will be given to research that has visible and immediate implications for the management of Indian PAs.

In asking such questions India's forest history is ignored. There are innumerable examples of seemingly irrelevant research turning out to be valuable for management much after it was undertaken. For instance, observations on the occurrence of trees, mammals, birds, and amphibians in the Western Ghats, by numerous biologists over more than fifty years, is today allowing an assessment of the protected area network in this area which is a global biodiversity hotspot (Das *et al.* 2006). Another example: research on the relationship between tigers and ungulate density, established through years of focused study, has established benchmarks for evaluating the effectiveness of tiger reserves (see K.U. Karanth *et al.* 2004). There is at the minimum a need to study the ecology, behaviour, and evolution of various animal species, if one is to understand how best to conserve them in their natural habitat.

Clearly many management-oriented questions cannot be addressed without access to well-protected ecosystems that need to be used as 'control' sites. For instance, long-term studies on rainforest birds in the mosaic of coffee plantations and protected rainforest fragments in the Annamalai Hills helped derive specific management recommendations for how to manage coffee for maximal biodiversity (Shankar Raman 2006). In this study, three types of alternative bird habitat, namely coffee plantations, forest fragments, and cardamom plantations, were systematically studied for bird diversity. Comparisons with continuous forest habitat indicated that the similarity of bird species with those of native forest is much higher in coffee plantations which had native tree species for shade cover rather than those with exotic ones. This was also true for fragments that were adjacent to forest habitats rather than to open areas or plantations. The study shows that mimicking natural tree species composition and habitat structure could considerably increase the value of coffee plantations for forest birds.

Another key debate in conservation that is being addressed by new studies is the comparative importance of community-conserved areas and strictly-protected areas for biodiversity. To study community conservation, Garcia and Pascal (2005) studied the diversity of trees and shrubs in sixteen different sacred groves protected by local villagers. The data on plant diversity was then compared with that obtained from comparable forest from the nearby Brahmagiri Wildlife Sanctuary in the Western Ghats. Analysis showed that while sacred groves do protect a large proportion of wild plant species, they lack one-third to one-half of the species that are endemic to the Western Ghats, that is, those not found anywhere else in India. The absence of many endemic species was attributed to the fact that sacred groves tend to be small fragments that suffer from higher degrees of human disturbance both physical and that caused by extraction. Clearly, sacred groves, at least in this case, are not an effective substitute for long-term strict protection, though they do harbour significant diversity. Neither of these studies on conservation in human-modified landscapes could have been undertaken without the availability of a control site for comparison, protected from human disturbance for relatively long periods. They provided valuable information on how to maximize conservation even inside used habitats. Such research, if encouraged by the forest department, can be extremely useful for guiding policy on community reserves and community conservation areas, the two new types of PAs that are now mandated by the Wildlife Protection Act, and to monitor the impact of investment in Joint Forest Management and the India Ecodevelopment Project.

There are possible models in other developing countries. Tanzania is one of the countries where management plans for all major protected areas are now developed with formal input from researchers (Thirgood *et al.* 2007). Research, jointly undertaken by local and foreign scientists, has helped to develop viable wildlife disease control methods and sustainable harvesting practices for forest products, and to understand the effects of protection on large ungulates. One of the major contributions of long-term research has been to discern the effects of major perturbations, such as droughts, floods, and elephant decline, thus helping scientists get an insight into variability in ecosystems, an understanding that is vital in setting up management goals for PAs in India.

Independent and Government-Sponsored Research

While obtaining access to PAs is not an easy task for any Indian researcher, things do get smoother if one is working for a government-sponsored research institute or project. Till recently, this preferential approach to government-sponsored research was just a rumour, though felt strongly by biologists. But the new guidelines for granting research permits actually institutionalize these double standards by stating that scientists working on projects funded by the ministry of environment and forests or other government departments, such as the Botanical Survey of India, will enjoy priority in obtaining research permits. Researchers from government institutions more frequently receive permission for manipulative and nocturnal research techniques. Often, researchers from governmental research institutions get preferential treatment over other matters that may seem mundane, such as access to accommodation inside a protected area. The guidelines state:

> However a research project which has been approved by Deptt. of Science and Technology, Ministry of Environment & Forests, Department of Biotechnology, and other scientific Deptt. of the State/Central Government would not be required to be reviewed by the committee. Chief Wildlife Warden/Director, Wildlife Preservation may pass necessary orders in such cases to grant access.

There is no obvious basis for differentiating between government-sponsored research and independent research. If the scientific credentials of independent researchers are suspect, one only has to scan the internet to assess research productivity—by looking at publication records in peer-reviewed international journals, lists of research grants obtained, and participation in academic conferences. Several research NGOs are undertaking high-quality research of relevance to management and are involved in hands-on implementation (for instances of these, see Shahabuddin and Rangarajan 2007). In a democratic society, there is an important role for independent research along with government-sponsored research; the former can act as a counterbalance to vested interests in the environmental sector.

The TTF, set up in 2005 to investigate the causes of visible tiger decline in India, also recommended involving a larger range of disciplines and institutions in wildlife management. It proposed a country-wide tiger re-census to be undertaken in 2006 using the latest methods. Of the proposed new tiger census the TTF said:

> This extensive effort cannot be undertaken solely by the in-house agencies of forest departments. In fact, the positions of research officers have lain vacant in a majority of tiger reserves and little relevant scientific work has

> been accomplished. Nor can the Wildlife Institute of India be made the sole agency responsible for the entire spectrum of scientific work for that would mean failing to take advantage of the enormous potential in a multitude of other Indian agencies.

The TTF also recommended establishing an external scientific expert group to advise the tiger census that was to be undertaken by the Wildlife Institute as well as a multi-disciplinary reserve-level management committee to prepare the new management plan for each tiger reserve.

Yet India's forest managers, barring a few, have failed to recognize that independent researchers inside forests can be useful and should not be seen as a hindrance to management. Frequently, such researchers report on poaching, illegal timber smuggling, weedy invasive species, and rare wildlife. There is quite obviously a need to foster dialogue and interaction between forest managers and researchers. It is ironical that in an age of globalization when there is instantaneous transfer of data from one corner of the globe to the other, one can discern a disturbing trend to marginalize researchers and even make them subservient to the needs of the government. It is as if science-based perspectives are viewed as a mortal threat by a forest department that believes it has a monopoly on knowledge of the forest.

The Capacity of the Indian Forest Department

There is a strong case for curbing irresponsible, destructive research in protected areas, given their fragile status and the intense human pressure that they face. It is also necessary to check the illegal transfer of genetic diversity outside the country through effective enforcement mechanisms. However, for this to happen it is necessary to build the capacity within the forest department to be able to judge scientists and their research output fairly, as well as to monitor the movement of genetic material. It is necessary to inculcate a more scientific mindset among the guardians of India's forests and wildlife.

Unfortunately, the training given to forest officers at the start of their career is inadequate, particularly for those that do not even have a graduate degree in biology. The government sought to rectify this lacuna in biology training by initiating a diploma course in wildlife management at the Wildlife Institute of India for in-service officers. However, the fact that most of the teachers are themselves from the forest service detracts from the purpose of scientific training and creative thinking among the managers. Further, only a small percentage of serving officers can undergo training at the Wildlife Institute of India because of the limited possibility of placement. Most of the serving personnel do not have much exposure to scientific techniques. My conversations with forest guards inside tiger reserves indicate that they have next to no training inputs even in crucial areas such as legal amendments and forest laws. Besides the need to improve scientific training, Saberwal and Kothari (1996) discuss the need for incorporating course material related to understanding politico-economic and cultural origins of resource use, so that foresters can be made more sensitive to people living in and utilizing parks. Such an orientation is missing not only from training materials used for the forest department but also from curricula for graduate students in wildlife conservation. It is important to note that lack of exposure to social issues could be part of the reason why many relevant management questions are not being asked by researchers.

One of the in-house solutions implemented by the forest department, though only in tiger reserves, is to institute a research officer to implement management-oriented research and monitor external research projects. Investigations by the TTF indicate that the instituting of such research officers has made little difference to the quality of management research (Ministry of Environment and Forests 2005). There are several reasons: many research officer posts remain vacant on account of insufficient personnel at the required expertise level. Research officers that do exist, work under the constraint of having to produce results that the managements want, thereby eliminating the independence necessary for research. Above all, most of the appointed research officers do not have the training required, nor sufficient funds to carry out relevant research inside their PAs. Park managements thus remain unequipped to undertake the types of research required for their proper management.

The basic training course for field officers has also to be revamped to include new and emerging issues of basic ecological science, economics, and sociology—which need to be taught by the right academics. Much more needs to be invested in the basic training of state-level officers and those in the Indian Forest Service. Apart from improving scientific capacity within the forest service, a solution could be to encourage the forest department to fund research by academic institutions, research NGOs, and independent researchers through an open and transparent scientific review system. Individuals, universities (both foreign and Indian), and research institutions (both private and government) could compete for these funds and for the right to do research inside specific PAs as suggested by the wildlife biologist Abi Tamim. The competitive process is bound to weed out low-quality research. Universities, voluntary bodies, and research organizations could then enter into official agreements with state governments that would give them access to specific PAs for research for a defined period. Such agreements can then be revised periodically, depending on the performance of the institution.

Researching Inside PAs

Even if permits and grants are finally obtained, sometimes after much delay, it is often a challenge for wildlife researchers to implement rigorous research given the lack of basic facilities in most PAs. In some cases not even a functional rest-house or dormitory is available for researchers. The smaller PAs are even less equipped for research: researchers often have to move from their rooms at short notice to accommodate a visiting VIP. Most researchers work on a shoestring budget that does not allow for prolonged stay in tourist resorts and hotels. Resorts are often located at a distance from PA boundaries, making regular field observations difficult. The rules for working in PAs need to be properly publicized and uniformly implemented. Day-to-day 'policing' of researchers has to be stopped: the recent requirement to report on which areas of a reserve are being visited on a given day is certainly not required.[6] Even government scientists, who today undertake much of the research inside PAs, require much more autonomy to be able to

[6] However, to the credit of most park managers, this rule is rarely implemented and many exceptions are made for accredited scientists.

carry out research and monitoring tasks with credibility and transparency. The tiger crisis of 2005 was a direct result of secretive attitudes among field managers. For years the pugmark method had been used to census tigers inside tiger reserves (Ministry of Environment and Forests 2005), despite scientific evidence that it was inadequate for either detecting population decline or for counting exact numbers (K.U. Karanth *et al.* 2004). As we saw earlier, tigers had declined in most reserves whereas reports from the field continued to be optimistic. The process of modifying the census techniques was done under tremendous pressure from the public and the media.

The new tiger census was planned as a far more technically sound exercise that would take into account the results of an international peer-review process to be undertaken by two wildlife biologists from the USA in 2007. However, the process of designing the new tiger census was fraught with confidentiality as well, causing its international reviewers to critique it (Maraj and Seidensticker 2006). There was no peer-review at the critical stages of the project being undertaken by the Wildlife Institute of India. Because of this the review comments of the US-based scientists could not be incorporated into the final field design of the project, leading to several discrepancies in data analysis and interpretation. Several possible sources of error in sampling design, implementation of field protocols, and analysis were noted by the reviewers. The international review process therefore turned out to be of little consequence in determining the final field approach in the tiger census. For instance, the two reviewers wrote in their evaluation report of the initial field exercise: 'It is reported that "The spatial and apatial data that are likely to influence tiger occupancy of a landscape will be used for modelling in a GIS domain." Most details of how this is to be done are yet to be made explicit, transparent and peer-reviewed.'

Secrecy is the antithesis of science; all results and methodologies adopted by the government have to be exposed to public scrutiny and debate. By the same token, scientists working inside PAs should be required to present their research to park managers on a regular basis. To enable sharing of knowledge, state forest departments need to organize annual research seminars where researchers present their findings and also be involved in open discussions on the important management and socio-economic questions facing PAs. I have personally attended such a workshop in the Kalakad-Mundanthurai Wildlife Sanctuary, where I was convinced that there could be productive exchange of expertise and information between managers and scientists.

Opening up Minds, Sharing Knowledge

There are some encouraging signs. Indian universities and research institutes are becoming more open to foreign capital, foreign ideas, and knowledge than in the past. Collaborations are being fostered between Indian and foreign universities for developing curricula and courses in science. These developments are welcome: they are likely to increase the cross-fertilization of ideas and bring in foreign expertise. One must hope that this openness will extend sufficiently to ecology and wildlife biology as well, for the Indian government badly needs to encourage collaboration with foreign universities and institutions to improve and upgrade the quality of wildlife research in India. Several countries require that a foreign researcher work with a native counterpart at their university or research institute, and that all publication emerging out of the research be undertaken jointly. These are effective ways to ensure that the benefits of research reach the country in question. But for this to happen, the process of issuing research visas has to be simplified. A ceiling can be imposed on the number of foreign collaborative projects to be allowed in a given state during a given year, if there are limited personnel for monitoring projects and enforcement of rules. The TTF also suggests a single-window clearing process for all matters relating to wildlife research so that the process of granting permits can be streamlined and the 'layers' of decision-making on each proposal be reduced.

The enterprise of conserving India's wild areas is by no means an easy one. The task is likely to become even more difficult with new developments such as global warming. But the task of biodiversity conservation can be made substantially easier by taking on board a more diverse set of concerned citizens, particularly the increasingly marginalized biologist.

4

The Promise of Community-Based Conservation

I have tried to show until now that Indian wildlife conservation has followed a principally exclusionary paradigm, based on strict nature protection, with little room for public participation or benefit. So far, rather perfunctory attempts have been made to develop partnerships with people living in and around PAs or to compensate them effectively for economic losses caused by wildlife. To make things worse, the inadequate rehabilitation of displaced villages has contributed to the building up of hostility at the periphery of wildlife reserves. It would be safe to say that, together with poor governance and lack of good science, India's wildlife policies have led to a near-collapse of the conservation machinery all across the country.

At this point it would be instructive to discuss the possible alternatives to the existing system of nature conservation in India. The view that wild areas partially or largely managed by local residents—lately named community conserved areas or CCAs—can be effective in saving species and ecosystems from extinction is rapidly gaining ground.[1] The reasoning is that once people are conferred charge of ecosystem resources from which they can legitimately benefit, they will have far stronger stakes in conservation than they currently have. Further, people living in and around forests are believed to have a natural proclivity for ecosystem conservation due to their adaptation

[1] See for instance Bray *et al.* 2003, and Schwartzman *et al.* 2000.

to local ecological conditions, and their traditional harvesting and agricultural techniques which tend to minimize damage.[2] Forest-dwellers often have animist religious beliefs in nature-based cosmologies that are intrinsically tied to forests and their forest-based livelihoods. So social activists tend to see community-based conservation not just as the most effective way to preserve nature but also as a significant means of empowerment for local tribals who have hitherto lived at the margins of society.

Today, instances of community conservation can be witnessed globally, ranging from extractive reserves in Brazil and forest reserves in Tanzania to community forests in Nepal and forests under JFM in India. In each of these variations of community-managed landscapes, considerable progress has been made in rejuvenating forest ecosystems, to the extent that community-based conservation is today seen as a long-term solution to the problem of protecting natural diversity. But are community-conserved areas by themselves an adequate substitute for strict nature protection? To what extent and under what circumstances can local communities successfully protect biodiversity? These questions have fuelled debates in conservation for well over two decades, but only very recently has the issue begun to be seriously researched by scientists. I take recourse to the expanding literature on people–forest linkages—from the ecological, sociological, and socio-economic perspectives—to answer these important questions.

The Science of it All: 'Sustainable' Extraction

A critical component of community-based conservation is the 'sustainable use' of species and ecosystems, since the incentive for local people is usually the guarantee to let them extract biological resources for either commercial purposes or for satisfying local needs.[3] Sustainable use is theoretically based on the calculation of 'sustainable extraction limits' for the animal or plant species that are hunted or collected.

[2] See for instance Gadgil and Guha 1995.

[3] Such as NTFP, controlled grazing, and controlled timber sales.

Such a limit needs to be calculated with the help of the basic principles of population ecology. For instance: 'how many deer, and of what ages, can one cull for a trophy-hunting conservation programme without causing a decline in the local population?' And: 'how much fruit can be harvested from a native tree species without affecting its future regeneration?' These are the questions that need to be answered while designing a typical use-based conservation programme.

A comprehensive review of the published research on CCAs shows, however, that such questions are rarely posed in real life, and, even less, answered. There are extremely few instances of community conservation programmes that take into account calculated extraction limits, or that regularly monitor the ecological impact of forest use so that undesirable changes can be stalled in time.

This is not surprising. The concept of sustainability is a slippery one. For one thing, there is the difficulty of defining the 'ideal ecosystem' that would be acceptable to the largest number of interest groups (see Lele and Norgaard 1996, Middleton 2003). For instance, to a wildlife biologist the ideal ecosystem may be one that harbours maximal biodiversity. On the other hand a forester would prefer to see a stand of tall trees of large girth and height so that timber production can be maximized.[4] Without a consensus on the ideal ecosystem it is difficult to ascertain the sustainable-use level for any resource. There is also a large group of conservationists who feel that the intrinsic dynamism of ecosystems does not allow clear definitions of the ideal ecosystem (Saberwal *et al.* 2000). Records show that ecosystems can change tremendously in their properties over time due to catastrophic events, past human use history, and other external factors—such as land use in their surroundings, or climate change.

Even if conservationists of different persuasions do agree on which properties of ecosystems are to be conserved, serious difficulties then crop up in the calculation of extraction limits. The calculation of these extraction limits is crucially dependent upon knowledge of both mortality and fertility rates of various age-classes of the local

[4] This issue has been addressed by several historians of forestry in Asia, for instance Guha 1985, Rangarajan 1996, and Sivaramakrishnan 1999.

population. These, in turn, require meticulous observation. The matter is complicated by the considerable variation of all these population parameters, not just from year to year but also across sub-populations[5] of the same species that exist in different regions.[6] These variations across both time and space are extremely difficult to capture by numbers on account of the short-term nature and small scale of most field studies. The inadequacy in calculations of sustainable extraction means that nothing more accurate than ballpark estimates can be obtained for most of the required population parameters. Further, most practitioners agree that the sustainability of most use-based conservation programmes is contingent upon an effective biological monitoring mechanism that can detect adverse impacts, if any, in time for mitigation measures. Such monitoring depends on comparisons of the relevant ecosystem properties between used and protected areas. Unfortunately, in many human-dominated landscapes it has proven difficult to find control sites that can be used as baseline monitoring zones for biodiversity (Freese 1997).

Given the difficulties of delineating sustainable extraction limits, it is understandable that most existing sustainable use programmes still lack rigorous evaluation from an ecological perspective. A close look reveals that even cases of overtly sustainable use, such as the JFM scheme in India and community forest management in Nepal, are dogged by biological difficulties (Rodgers *et al.* 2003, Shahabuddin and Prasad 2004, Nagendra *et al.* 2005).[7] As another instance: little is yet known about the long-term genetic and ecological impact of village-based trophy-hunting upon mountain sheep populations in

[5] Separate smaller populations that do not have linkages with other such populations of the same species—and thus have population growth rates that are more or less independent of each other.

[6] The actual effects of harvesting of various plant parts can be quite complex, depending on ecological conditions, as seen in the case of *Khaya senegalensis* in Benin. Here, pruning leaves caused reduced fruit production to a larger extent in drier regions and in larger trees than in wetter areas and smaller trees: see Gaoue and Ticktin 2008.

[7] The issue of biological sustainability in JFM is dealt with in detail in chapter 6.

the northern mountains of Pakistan (Shackleton 2001). These concerns are specially serious given that only rough estimates are available of the population of mountain sheep existing in this remote area, many parts of which are inaccessible. The fact that the males with the largest horns are shot in these trophy-hunting programmes is also likely to impact the future population trends of the species.[8] The Community Forest Enterprises in Mexico, again, is termed an unequivocal success (Bray *et al.* 2003) in terms of area covered and motivation of communities. Yet there is little evaluation of its long-term conservation benefits specifically based on biological attributes.

Biologists also fear that while it may be possible to assess extraction levels for given species that are sustainable, it would be almost impossible to quantify the 'indirect' effects of forest product extraction on dependent animal species. Many of these dependent species are fruit-eaters that disperse seeds away from parent trees and shrubs, helping them to regenerate. Many other animals are pollinators without whose services seeds cannot be produced (see Shahabuddin and Prasad 2004). Still others are specialized herbivores that require a continuous supply of the leaves of specific plant species. Many of these dispersers and pollinators may, in fact, be critical for the continuing existence of several plant and animal species in the forest. The fact is that the indirect effects of fruit or flower extraction on dependent fauna may not be visible immediately. The exact impact of such use may be seen only after several years, when frugivore populations begin to decline in response to chronic scarcity of a particular plant species (Terborgh 1998).

Even if the extraction of a single species is designed to be sustainable, the overall effects of ecosystem use may not be. Typically, in developing countries, people use forests for a number of activities that take place simultaneously: such as grazing, NTFP collection, fuelwood gathering, and the setting of ground fires to facilitate NTFP collection. A set of such activities when carried out simultaneously sets in motion a number of adverse changes that reinforce each other and ultimately

[8] Larger male mountain sheep with larger horns are likely to produce larger numbers of offspring that will survive to maturity. Thus the preferential elimination of larger sheep could have a long-term impact upon the population.

affect the survival of both plants and animals (Shahabuddin and Prasad 2004). Such a situation can also be envisioned when there is harvesting of leaves or fruit from a number of tree species, which leads to more extensive damage than if only a single tree species was exploited. In fact, such situations are quite commonly seen in the intensively used forests of India.

In short, 'sustainability' in the context of used ecosystems is a rather fuzzy concept, not only theoretically but also practically. Interestingly, few proponents of the sustainable-use paradigm have attempted to analyse it from the perspective of possible ecological impact.

What about Traditional Knowledge?

If science is currently playing a marginal role in devising and maintaining the sustainable-use paradigm, could local communities possess and implement their own knowledge of ecology to prevent negative impacts on plants and animals? The role of local traditional knowledge of plants in devising and perpetuating sustainable harvest methods is important in the sustainable use of a habitat. Local communities use a variety of ingenious techniques to preserve the diversity of organisms that have been developed over generations of trial and error. Cutting fruit directly rather than lopping whole branches of trees, harvesting fewer culms at a time from a bamboo clump, and harvesting only a portion of an underground tuber rather than the entire tuber are practices commonly followed by forest-dependent people.[9] The traditional knowledge of ecology seems to go along with a deeper conservation ethic that is intertwined with religious taboos. For instance, studies have found that conservation behaviour among indigenous herbalists in Rajasthan is closely linked to their understanding that humans and animals are closely 'interdependent family members who share substance, interests and obligations to each other' (Snodgrass *et al.* 2007). Sacred groves are commonly preserved for a given deity but result in protecting a number of animal and plant species.

[9] See chapter 5 for an in-depth study of traditional knowledge used for conservation in a Gond tribal community in central India.

However, there is evidence that increasing modernity, the growing dependence on the cash economy, and technological innovation frequently lead to a loss of traditional knowledge and conservation behaviour among local residents. Some evidence of this comes from an interesting study of fishing communities in coastal Papua New Guinea. In this study, Cinner *et al.* (2007) looked at the influence of markets and modernity, measured by quantitative indices, on the use of customary conservation methods used by fishermen. In particular, the practice of closing fishing grounds for a part of the year is known to be deployed as a resource conservation measure. The researchers found that levels of material wealth and the distance of each village to the market significantly altered local conservation behaviour. Communities that regularly imposed seasonal bans on fishing tended to be more remote and less modernized than those that did not. Agrawal's comprehensive review (2001) of the factors influencing common property management institutions also indicates the importance of markets, technological innovation, and strength of linkage with the cash economy. Agrawal says that social scientists more often than not tend to ignore these issues while evaluating community resource management institutions.

Where Economics and Ecology Meet

One of the inherent assumptions in a community-centred approach to conservation is that the economic and in-kind benefits flowing to local communities provide sufficient incentive for them to conserve nature. Low-level extractive uses such as sales of NTFP have long been envisioned as the cornerstone of community-based conservation. In 1989 a landmark paper in the journal *Nature* (Peters *et al.* 1989) calculated the NTFP-based commercial value of a single hectare of tropical rainforest to be as much as $6330, which was quite substantial compared to economic returns from timber evaluated over the same period. The finding that monetary returns from NTFP production may surpass even those from timber-extraction led to significant changes in the way international donor agencies and conservation groups saw the role of people in forest conservation. Use-based conservation suddenly appeared likely to present a viable alternative to strict nature protection, given the possibility of local benefit-sharing without a significant impact on natural ecosystems.

Today, however, the ambitious financial estimates of NTFP-based livelihoods are increasingly being called into question. A critical review of the NTFP paradigm (Sheil and Wunder 2002) pointed out that neither Peters *et al.* (1989) nor succeeding analyses of NTFP-based income estimates had taken into account the tremendous variability in the fruiting and flowering of forest trees from year to year. For instance, a tree that produces a hundred kilograms of fruit one year may produce as little as ten during the next fruiting season. Further, the costs of transportation and marketing of NTFP could be substantial but were often ignored in the calculations, leading to overestimates of the economic returns from NTFP collection and sales (Sheil and Wunder 2002). Regional variability in plant growth and productivity were found to further reduce the predictability of revenues from NTFP.

The well-studied cases of brazil-nuts (see Silvertown 2004) and andiroba (*Carapa guianensis*; Plowden 2004) in the Amazon basin are instructive in this regard. Plowden's micro-study of the process of extraction, processing, and marketing of andiroba seeds in eastern Amazonia revealed minimal financial rewards from the seeds, whose oil is extracted and sold, because of the low density of this tree species in the forest. Brazil-nuts are valuable but occur as a highly variable resource both in time and space, as the trees fruit *en masse* after long periods of dormancy, forcing dependent people to constantly shift their occupations and foraging areas. In case after case NTFP is being found to be an unstable source of income, not just for biological reasons but also due to highly fluid market situations for forest products and shifting global prices (see Endress *et al.* 2004). In an interesting study of NTFP collectors in the Periyar Tiger Reserve in India, it was found that NTFP collection was resorted to by people who had few other livelihood options—by those lacking agricultural land or other productive assets—and yielded poor returns to the collectors in comparison with earnings from wage labour (Gubbi and MacMillan 2008). Biomass extraction and sale appears to be the last resort rather than a preferred occupational option among marginalized communities.

Ecotourism is another livelihood option that may be overrated with respect to its potential for sustaining people living in and at the margins of protected areas. A non-consumptive use, such as ecotourism, was thought to be the perfect solution to inadequate employment and lack of conservation initiatives in remote areas—a way to channel park-generated revenues to local villagers. However, a number of recent empirical studies indicate that revenues from ecotourism are dependent upon a large number of factors, ranging from the attractiveness of the site, the degree of tourism specialization, the distribution of variously priced tourism options at the site, and the level of local organization and development. Considerable variability in these features from place to place results in uneven returns from locally managed ecotourism. Further, revenues usually reach only a small subset of local people, given that tourism volumes need to be reduced to a minimum if ecological impact has to be minimized. Prices also need to rise considerably before ecotourism can make a substantial contribution to the local economy (Chase *et al.* 1998). In a detailed study of the Cuyabeno Wildlife Reserve in Ecuador, a popular rainforest reserve, it was found that even in this relatively successful ecotourism operation local incomes are not of the scale required to change land and labour allocation decisions by villagers in favour of ecotourism (Wunder 2000).

The effectiveness of ecotourism is further reduced by the fact that in most cases ecotourism ventures are financially and technically supported by external city-based investors without whose support the necessary tourism infrastructure cannot normally be built. While their capital is welcome in such situations, the presence of such external investors tends to marginalize local decision-making bodies and reduce their effectiveness in controlling the adverse impact of development. Such a situation was evident in Costa Rica's Monteverde National Park, one of the world's well-known rainforest reserves with well-developed ecotourism infrastructure, where locals now have little political power in decision-making on economic benefit-sharing and local development alternatives (Weinberg *et al.* 2002). Partly as a result of this, runaway growth in tourism outside the national park is causing pollution and waste management problems which remain neglected and are very likely to affect future tourist traffic.

Does Security of Tenure Lead to Better Management?

It has been proven adequately that used ecosystems can be managed sustainably only when local people have security of tenure over the area's resources, and therefore have a strong stake in its long-term management.[10] Apart from land tenure, social capital, social cohesion, and democratic governance are now proven to lead to improved resource management by village institutions.[11] Social capital feeds directly into the strength of local village institutions and governance, which, in turn, determine how well an ecosystem is managed. For instance, in the Kayapo Indian Reserves of Brazil robust common pool institutions and satisfactory biological criteria, that were initially agreed upon, resulted in the the flow of direct benefits to all members and led to effective conservation (Schwartzman and Zimmerman 2005). Other key variables likely to influence the ecological outcome of community-based resource management are clarity and consensus on the rules of ecosystem use and the degree of local authority and accountability to the community (Poteete and Ostrom 2004). Clearly, the degree of empowerment, the extent of local participation in decision-making, and efficient forest monitoring mechanisms (Nagendra 2007) are three of the key variables that decide success of community-based initiatives. There now exist several examples of such cohesive and well-managed community-based institutions all over the world.

Yet there is growing evidence that even in forests where local communities enjoy full decision-making powers over forest management, habitat degradation sometimes follows. In some cases the continuous

[10] However, it is increasingly being found that in many cases legal tenure is not as important as the perception of the people about security over the resource in question. This, to a large extent, is dependent on the behaviour of the state agency which enforces the arrangements.

[11] The term 'social capital' refers to the extent and quality of social cohesion and bonding within and across different groups, and which is known to enhance all aspects of public well being.

Illustr. 9: A man making plates out of the large leaves of the creeper *Bauhinia vahlii*. It is not clear if unpredictable and scanty financial returns from NTFP such as these can form a sustainable basis for community-based conservation.

extractive use of community-managed forests gradually leads to the conversion of native forests to monocultures of the commercially extracted plant species. Weinstein and Moegenburg (2004) studied the process of extraction and marketing of fruit and palmito from the acai palm tree (*Euterpe oleracea*) in eastern Amazonia. This valuable tree species occurs in river floodplain forests where local people possess full rights over use. It was found that the increasing demand for acai fruit led to intensification of forest management practices that favour the growth of this palm species, resulting in the conversion of diverse floodplain forest into acai-dominated forest, resembling plantations. Similarly, large swathes of forest under the JFM programme in eastern India, though regenerated by people themselves, now resemble plantations of native sal trees (*Shorea robusta*) due to intensive use of the habitat for fodder and NTFP collection. Consequently, the other species are nearly eliminated due to overexploitation and adverse changes in soil conditions. The sal trees are preserved because of their immense coppicing ability, and because only their leaves are collected manually by the local people for making disposable plates, the main source of their cash income (Shahabuddin 2003).[12] Low-statured forests with open canopies, poor species diversity, and tree density have become the norm in this region, particularly in areas under heavy use (ibid.). In the community forests of Nepal, too, the majority of NTFP species are undergoing rapid decline due to lack of sufficient knowledge and concern among local residents (Pandit and Thapa 2003). In yet another instance, changes were found in species composition over time even in an autonomous community-managed reserve (Saha and Howe 2003). In contrast, in the Indian Western Ghats, Rai and Uhl (2004) show that security of tenure over forests is the primary factor affecting the attitude of extractors towards sustainability of extraction of uppage (*Garcinia gummi-gutta*) fruit. They found far more tree damage (caused by the lopping of branches during fruit collection) and reduced regeneration of trees in open access forests than in the privately owned forests of this region. However, even in this case the long-term impact of collecting fallen fruit on local fruit-eating birds and mammals, and the effect of forest management practices on the local diversity of forest trees, have not been considered, so it is difficult to draw more general conclusions.

Two large-scale studies of community forestry carried out recently in South Asia support the view that in places where there is heavy demand on natural resources, economic imperatives may eventually override ecological ones. In a detailed examination of the Annapurna Conservation Area Project in the high mountains of Nepal, Baral *et al.* (2007) found that livelihood issues generally won over conservation priorities, particularly during the early years of the project. It was only after several years of the project period that conservation issues began to be addressed directly. Even now, biodiversity and degradation issues are not confronted directly. Nagendra (2007) also found in a country-wide analysis of community forestry in Nepal that the extent of human dependence—as manifest in the size of the registered 'user group'

[12] See chapter 6 for a comprehensive study of JFM in West Bengal, where it has been officially under way since 1990.

dependent on a given forest patch—played an important role in the success of forest regeneration efforts: forests experiencing a moderate degree of extraction are more likely to regenerate successfully than those facing heavy pressure.[13]

Another large-scale study of community forestry in the van panchayat forests of Uttarakhand, which are managed autonomously by people, corroborates some of Nagendra's findings in adjoining Nepal. This study (Sarkar 2008) was unique in its large sample size of forty-five villages and in being able to relate socio-economic characteristics with ecological indicators. Van panchayats are considered to be at the vanguard of biodiversity conservation in this region due to the close management by villages for usufruct needs and considerable autonomy in decision-making. Their management can be contrasted with that of government-managed reserved forests that for all practical purposes represent an open-access situation. Comparisons of basal area, canopy cover, and regeneration status showed that van panchayat forests have undergone considerable degradation during recent years, having fared no better than open-access forests under government control. Interviews with local communities revealed that increasing extractive pressure on the forests due to increasing population and weak vigilance mechanisms are primarily responsible for forest degradation. Attitudinal surveys further showed that while local people were clearly aware of the degradation of their forest resources, they were not concerned enough to initiate ameliorative measures. Sarkar also found that while there were vigilance mechanisms in place to control the types and levels of extraction, in most of these sites the vigilance was ineffective. This study shows that even in the presence of secure tenurial rights there are other social factors at work that determine the efficacy of community conservation.

Local communities also exhibit considerable variation in their governance qualities due to differing histories and ecologies. The sustenance of good governance in village institutions often requires

[13] However, interestingly she also found that when user-groups were too small, it affected the effectiveness of reforestation measures as the communities were constrained in their ability to provide appropriate physical inputs and monitoring.

continued engagement by external actors over time, such as by voluntary groups and funding organizations, particularly in situations where the needs of economic development threaten forests. It has been suggested that the total devolution of management to local communities without the necessary co-ordination by state-sponsored institutions can lead to fragmented ecosystem management, which is far less effective in conserving biological diversity (Murphree 2004).

Other factors external to communities that impinge upon the stability of local resource management institutions and enforcement of rules include population growth. The population of user groups is likely an important factor in determining the intensity of particular uses of the forest and, in turn, it determines the ecological impact upon various components of the ecosystem (see Agrawal 2001). For instance, the most plausible reason for the relative success of the vast extractive reserves in the Amazon, such as the Alto Jurua, is the extremely low extractive pressure on the ecosystem: less than six persons inhabit a square kilometre in the reserve (Ruiz-Perez *et al.* 2005). Over fifteen years of observation the forest cover in the reserve remained stable and the local population even declined slightly. The reason for stability of the population was traced to the diversification of income sources. These included outside opportunities in addition to existing extractive activities.

Biodiversity Thriving

The ultimate test of effectiveness of community-based conservation efforts can only be a quantitative comparison of the conservation values of used and protected areas within the same eco-region. This is because the presence of distinct suites of species in different ecosystems can confound any study of human impact which requires comparisons between used and undisturbed habitats. Very few scientists have actually compared community-managed and strictly protected areas in terms of biodiversity patterns and survival of species, partly because such protected habitats are becoming rarer by the day.

One of the rare instances where such a comparison has been made comes from a comprehensive study of sacred groves and strictly protected forests in the Western Ghats of Karnataka. Sacred groves are patches of forests that have been preserved by local communities for religious reasons, sometimes over many years. Many are sites of old temples and host large numbers of religious pilgrims each year; they are also used by local people to satisfy some of their biomass needs. Garcia and Pascal (2005) compared the occurrence of tree and shrub species in seventeen sacred groves with equivalent-sized plots in the adjacent Brahmagiri Wildlife Sanctuary which has enjoyed a strictly protected status for several years. The surveys showed that on the average both density and basal area of trees and shrubs was much lower in sacred groves than in protected forests, indicating that human use tends to reduce overall biomass. In terms of diversity, the total number of species protected by sacred groves was higher than that protected by the wildlife sanctuary if comparable habitat areas were examined. However, the number of tree species that are endemic to the Western Ghats and that are protected by the sanctuary was more than 50 per cent greater than that protected by sacred groves. The researchers also found that the species of trees in the two differently managed forest types were quite different. For instance, the most abundant species of tree found in natural forests had completely disappeared from sacred groves. One can conclude from this study that while the network of sacred groves did protect a large number of local tree and shrub species, they did not offer comprehensive protection to the species that are most sensitive to habitat change. The small size of sacred groves, along with high levels of use and exposure to 'edge effects',[14] detracted from their effectiveness in conserving the entire range of woody species diversity. Edge effects tend to amplify in smaller forest patches due to a greater exposure to outside conditions. This has been found to result in reduced germination and a lowered survival of sensitive species.

There are a few other examples of explicit scientific comparisons of community-managed and strictly protected areas in terms of their biodiversity conservation value, and these enable more general conclusions. One of these is a very large landscape study of differently

[14] 'Edge effects' refers to the suite of changes in micro-climatic and biological characteristics that occur in the portion of the forest close to the forest edge (such as the forest habitat adjoining a pasture). Typical changes that have been found are increases in the daily range of temperatures encountered (it is both hotter and colder than in the interior of the forest), greater parasitism of bird nests, and reduction in soil moisture.

managed habitats in Tanzania, where forty-one sites located along a four-step gradient of increasing human activity—from national park to a forest-village mosaic—were studied for a variety of taxa. It is interesting to note that while the total number of species did not vary much along this human-use gradient, suites of species were completely altered, that is, each land-use category was discovered to host rather distinct categories of each taxon. An interesting statistic uncovered was that the abundance of trees was only 34 per cent, the abundance of amphibians 23 per cent, and that of birds 50 per cent of that measured inside the national park. Further, large mammal species were largely non-existent in the used ecosystem categories, in contrast to the rich assemblages inside the strictly protected national park. In contrast, small mammals and butterflies seemed to be encouraged by the conversion of forest to forest reserves (Gardner *et al.* 2007).

A similar set of results was obtained by biologists in another large-scale study in the moist forests of the Western Ghats, where 25 sacred groves, 10 reserved forests, and 23 coffee plantations were studied (Bhagwat *et al.* 2005). It was found that evergreen trees and forest-preferring bird species increased in density with decreasing intensity of land use, that is, they were most abundant in strictly protected landscapes followed by sacred groves and coffee plantations, in that order. Conversely, deciduous tree species and open-area bird species increased with the intensification of land use.

Clearly, used ecosystems tend to harbour sets of species that are different from those found in non-used forests within the same ecosystem. This is principally due to the fact that there are groups of species that are more vulnerable to forest disturbance than others, and the upshot is that different taxa respond rather differently to land-use change. As seen in the case of the sacred groves of Karnataka, endemics, habitat-restricted, and area-sensitive species are most vulnerable to local extinction.[15] Even a casual survey of large mammal populations in South Asia would indicate that most endangered mammalian species today, such as the elephant, the tiger, and the rhinoceros, exist only

[15] Habitat-restricted species tend to choose some micro-habitats over others while area-sensitive species are those that require large areas and therefore easily go extinct in habitat fragments below a certain size.

within strictly protected areas rather than in forests used by indigenous populations (Terborgh and van Schaik 2002). The reason is that large mammals require large amounts of biomass—whether animal prey or vegetation—and also a diversity of juxtaposed habitat types. These can be met only within large continuous patches of natural habitat.

Additionally, species that are narrowly specialized on a given resource tend to lose ground in human-used landscapes. In a landmark study that tracked the recovery of bird species in plots abandoned after being used for shifting cultivation in the north-eastern Himalayas, it was found that certain specialized bird species that survive only in unused primary rainforest are not able to reinhabit the secondary forest that develops after the abandonment of shifting cultivation plots—not even after a hundred years of forest recovery (Raman *et al.* 1998). Elsewhere too, some bird species are affected even by a minimal management of forest ecosystems. For instance, in South African riverine forests, bird species such as woodpeckers and barbets depending on deadwood for cavity-nesting are adversely impacted by chronic fuelwood collection (Du Plessis 1995). In pine forests in the south-eastern United States, cavity users such as flycatchers, wrens, and woodpeckers are affected by the removal of snags even in minimally managed forests (Lohr *et al.* 2002).[16] More adaptable, geographically widespread, and opportunistic fauna, as well as those that are commensal to humans, tend to flourish in human-altered landscapes (see Garcia and Pascal 2005, Raman *et al.* 1998).[17]

Species Refuges

The importance of strictly protected habitats also lies in the important role they play as 'source habitats' or refugia where the increased productivity of vulnerable plant and animal resources enhances their

[16] Snags are standing dead trees that provide nest-holes for animals such as snakes, civets, squirrels, owls, and woodpeckers. Cavities are more easily made by these animals in dead trees because of the rotting wood.

[17] A commensal relationship between two organisms denotes one that is of use to one species but does not harm or benefit the other species. An instance would be the relationship between racoons and humans. While the racoon

survival potential in adjoining habitats and safeguards them from local extinction (Gell and Roberts 2003). Inviolate areas improve resource status in their surrounding areas through a spillover effect. In fact, the maintenance of forest refugia in a mosaic of human-modified agro-forestry landscapes was undertaken commonly by forest dwellers in the past, possibly as a means of resource conservation. Landscape-level approaches combining strictly-protected refugia with multiple-use areas have, in fact, being considered seriously as an option by modern conservationists as well (see Joshi and Gadgil 1991, Bray *et al.* 2003).

A striking example of how even small inviolate areas can dramatically improve resource status in surrounding areas can be seen in Fiji. A recent revival of the traditional practice of fishing closures in Fiji, initiated jointly by academic researchers and local communities, led to dramatic improvements in the catch and catch-size of the endangered clam species *Anadara sp*. which is commercially sold (Gell and Roberts 2003). After forty months of such closure of a 24 ha. area near a fishing village, clams increased in abundance by thirteen times in the closed area and five times in the surrounding fishing area. The success of a single fishing village in thus rejuvenating its fishing economy has, in fact, spurred numerous others in Fiji to return to the practice of closing areas for fishing.

The protection of micro-habitats that are rare in the landscape is another function served by strictly protected areas. Riparian corridors, marshy swamps, perennial streams, rocky outcrops, and cliffs are examples of such rare micro-habitats that often support habitat-restricted species. Some of these micro-habitats may not exist in forest areas used by people on account of their exploitation for particular economic needs, and consequently they are lost along with their suites of species. For instance, the water pollution and disturbance caused by tourism and grazing at the few perennial streams in the Sariska Tiger Reserve may have led to the decline of the rare

---

feeds off the domestic trash generated by people, people are neither benefited nor harmed by racoons.

four-horned antelope, which was thought to be utilizing this habitat intensively (Rodgers 1990). Dependent people and wildlife compete for green fodder at these streams during the harsh summer, when there is little forage available in the upland forest—and religious pilgrimage sites are preferentially located at such streams as well.

Where Does India Stand?

Without a doubt, community-based conservation has played an important role in preserving and often regenerating native biodiversity in India, as in many parts of the world. Multiple-use forest ecosystems with appropriate institutional mechanisms tend to maintain green cover and serve as important sources of biomass for dependent people, sometimes deflecting extractive pressures from PAs. Today, the regeneration of thousands of hectares of forest under JFM, and self-initiated management in India and other developing countries, testifies to the power of community-based conservation. Multiple-use areas also provide population sinks and corridors for dispersing animals and often form much-needed buffer zones between strictly protected areas and human settlements, whether suburban or rural.

Yet, on closer examination it is often found that habitats under some form of extraction, even subsistence-level use, may not harbour the full range of species that are found in strictly protected areas. Part of the reason is the considerably fragmented nature of most community-managed systems, apart from the fact that extraction is often only loosely monitored in these areas, posing the danger of altering habitats for sensitive wild organisms. There is considerable evidence now that the conservation value of managed ecosystems is highly dependent both on the extent and intensity of human use, and the numerous factors that control the effectiveness of the local institutions that manage common property resources. Further, the economic and in-kind values from natural ecosystems under current conditions often do not represent sufficient incentive for keeping land-use intact under natural habitat, whether forest, desert, or wetland. Even robust social institutions banking on a traditional conservation ethic may not be a guarantee against land-use change in the current situation of rapid population growth, modernization, and the monetization of forest livelihoods, all of which impose considerable strain on natural resources. So it would be safe to say that CCAs, while they can effectively complement the existing network of strictly protected areas, cannot be a stand-alone solution for comprehensive nature conservation.

How has India fared in terms of the success of community conservation? The vast country is home to myriad forms of people-based conservation, some initiated by the government, and many others that arose spontaneously in the past as a response to resource scarcity or socio-economic marginalization. In the next three chapters I examine three different forms of community-based conservation that have taken root on the Indian subcontinent: state-sponsored programmes such as JFM and ecodevelopment on the one hand, and self-initiated community conservation on the other. Each of these forms of people-based management vary in their degrees of participation and benefit-sharing, as well as the extent of economic benefits that local residents derive from them. Each has had rather different results on the ground as far as biodiversity is concerned. I attempt to show why these initiatives vary in terms of their effectiveness and also explore the question of how the potential of these developing models can be enhanced so that the aim of nature conservation can be met more substantially in the long term.

5

Does the Community Care? Forest Management in Mendha (Lekha)

One day I accompanied a group of men going out to cut a tree for a very special purpose: to carve a totem for an upcoming marriage. The reigning deity of the clan into which the bride marries is carved on a tree-trunk and placed in the centre of the new house.

It was already 10 a.m. on a blazing hot April day when I left with the group for the tree-cutting ceremony. We walked to a part of the forest that I had not visited earlier. We stopped to find a suitable tree about half a kilometre from the edge of the village. There was apparently a choice of three possible trees and there was quite a discussion before the men decided on one of the trees, a handsome fifteen-metre-tall shiwan tree.[1] A brief religious ceremony was carried out in front of the tree. The men seemed to be asking forgiveness for cutting it. It did not take long to fell the tree. As it came crashing down slowly, I suddenly felt moved not only by the death of the impressive tree but also the tremendous respect that these local villagers seemed to have for it. But my mind was a whirl of other contradictory thoughts. I pondered on the sheer wastefulness of the ritual! How long could this small patch of forest sustain traditions such as these?—**Field Notes, April 2000**

In 2000 I was freshly out of my doctoral programme in conservation biology in the United States. I had just returned to India and was keen to use my freshly acquired knowledge for 'real-life'

[1] Marathi name for *Gmelina arborea*, a hardy timber tree: Pathak and Gour-Broome 2001.

conservation, as I called it. It seemed an opportune time for me to link up with conservationists who were trying to achieve something on the ground.

Today there are many grassroots conservationists working with forest-dependent people in India, trying to revive and sustain the precarious forest resources that rural livelihoods critically depend on.[2] Yet I had found that there was little scientific research to guide forest use, whether local or commercial, which demonstrated the impact of such use on forests, grasslands, water bodies, and oceans. A comprehensive review that I carried out with a colleague revealed, for instance, that there were extremely few studies assessing the population status of commercially important tree species in India, many of which are suspected to be declining. Most of the species assessments that we did find were anecdotal at best.[3]

There was another reason for my eagerness to explore more carefully the biological implications of resource use. The traditional divide between the votaries of people-based conservation and those advocating strict nature protection was only deepening in the absence of quantitative biological data. My own limited experience had led me to believe that many local communities do have sophisticated ecosystem management practices and they frequently understand some aspects of biology better than trained scientists. Yet it was also clear to me that valuable biodiversity continued to be threatened by intensive rural biomass extraction in many sites, even in areas where people had secure tenurial and managerial rights. Could it be possible to find a meeting ground between the advocates of traditional forest management and those of modern science, to arrive at a more inclusive and more sustainable form of conservation? Some of these questions could really only be answered with a systematic study of a real-life conservation effort that attempted to utilize both streams of knowledge.

I approached Ashish Kothari of the environmental organization Kalpavriksh for ideas about where such a community-based conservation effort could be studied or, better still, advanced with quantitative

[2] See, for example, Gadgil 2001, which describes a number of such instances, in some of which he has been involved for several decades.

[3] Shahabuddin and Prasad 2004.

science. Kalpavriksh had, for two decades, been working with a number of grassroots groups on environmental conservation issues. Kothari pointed me to an intriguing little village of tribals in the heart of India—Mendha (Lekha), located in Gadchiroli district of Maharashtra. Gadchiroli lies in one of Maharashtra's most backward areas, with tribals constituting 39 per cent of its population.

Mendha (Lekha) promised to be an intriguing place in more ways than one. Around that time the people of Mendha had been in the news for taking on a powerful adversary—the Maharashtra state forest department. Apparently they had 'declared independence' from the forest department after a minor rebellion! Further, activists, social scientists, and biologists met in Mendha regularly to design and plan conservation in association with local villagers. Lately the villagers had been looking for inputs from scientists to address the problem of dwindling NTFP resources in the forest whose responsibility of protection they had taken on themselves.

Mendha turned out to be just the right place to tackle my questions. Over the past nine years I have visited the village several times, interacting with people of various age groups and both sexes, attending local workshops, and exploring the forest with the aim of understanding community conservation. At the centre of my investigation were the questions: what makes a 'poor' village community conserve forests? How effective are they?

Mendha (Lekha): The Heart of Hope

Almost as soon as I entered Mendha I was impressed with the general level of awareness about natural resources and conservation. A sense of confidence and empowerment, rarely seen in a typical Indian tribal village, was palpable. The children seemed well nourished and most of them attended a primary school inside the village. Several attended a middle school in Dhanora town, three km away. The women were vocal and hardly shy of talking to strangers. The village itself was clean and the houses, though tiled, were designed in the traditional style. These were definitely a people in charge of their own destiny, relatively speaking at least.

In 1998 Mendha was a small village of just 70-odd families and had a total population of 324. The people of Mendha belong to the Gond tribe that is widespread in Central India—in parts of Orissa, Madhya Pradesh, Chhattisgarh, Andhra Pradesh, and Maharashtra. Before 1950 the local people had *nistar* rights on forests, which were controlled by feudal landlords.[4] They commonly practised shifting cultivation and were highly forest-dependent. In 1950 all the forests in this region were nationalized and handed over to the Maharashtra state forest department to manage. The forests on which Mendha depended were officially declared Protected Forests (PF).[5] These were within the circumscribed village area, covering about 1900 ha. (Pathak and Gour-Broome 2001).[6] In 1992 the PF was converted to Reserved Forests (RF), but without the complete legal procedure for settlement of rights, leaving just 350 ha. for the benefit of the village. The basis of declaring them RF had been contested by the villagers at the time, and they had laid claim to a much larger area of 1829.79 ha., of which the RF cover was 1806.49 ha. (Ghate 2004).

The people of Mendha have always been highly dependent on forests, with their only cash income coming from commercial sales of NTFP such as dried tendu leaves, mahua flowers (*Madhuca indica*), chironji seeds (*Buchanania lanzan*), and the amla (*Phyllanthus emblica*) fruit. A lot of their household needs are met from their forests, including food items, medicines, timber, and fuelwood. Their mainstay, however, is the cultivation of small parcels of agricultural land for rice, vegetables, and lentils, mostly consumed within the household. In 2007 it was estimated that 53 of 84 (63 per cent) families grew sufficient grain for their annual consumption, owning between 1 and 15 acres. Only 5 (6 per cent) families were landless at the time (Tofa

[4] *Nistar* refers to bona fide rights of the people to collect biomass for subsistence purposes.

[5] Protected Forests (PF) allow more local rights for local villagers than do Reserved Forests (RF). Rights of villagers are generally 'extinguished' in RFs but only through a well-defined legal process. These are categories defined in the Indian Forest Act of 1927.

[6] A detailed administrative history of the region exists in Pathak and Gour-Broome 2001.

and Hiralal undated). Education levels were low, as would be expected in a remote village in one of Maharashtra's least developed regions. Only 30 per cent of the locals had ever been to school; most had attended only a few years of primary school (Pathak and Gour-Broome 2001). However, most of the people speak fluent Gondi and Hindi, and many can write Hindi.

For years, like thousands of other forest dwellers in India who do not have legal rights, the locals had been subject to harassment at the hands of forest department officials. Though they historically had nistar rights in the forest, the officials had begun denying them access after the drastic delimitation of their forests as PF in 1950. It had become common for locals to bribe forest officers to allow fulfilment of their basic needs, such as fuelwood and grazing. There were frequent conflicts between forest contractors sent by the forest department for commercial operations and the local villagers who attempted to drive them off. In 1989, emboldened by a regional movement against a large dam project that was led by a local Gond leader, the popular discontent among the locals finally exploded.

Teak timber was one of the forest products that had been placed out of bounds to locals due to its commercial value. In defiance of the department's rules, the local people decided to re-establish their village *gotul* using teak timber.[7] This gotul was broken up by the forest department officials with the help of the police. The villagers responded by rebuilding the gotul and courting mass arrest. Faced by firm, though non-violent, opposition, the forest department finally gave up and informally allowed the villagers access to their forest resources (Tofa and Hiralal, undated). This event turned out to be a turning point in village history.

Ever since the gotul-building incident, the unity of the villagers has been maintained by a unique process of consensual decision-making on most village issues, including development and forest conservation.

[7] '*Gotul*' refers to an institution among Gonds which resembles a school, guesthouse, and meeting place all rolled into one. (A monograph by the anthropologist Verrier Elwin is titled *The Muria and their Ghotul* [1947].) Young people interact, socialize, and undertake cultural activities in a gotul. The gotul has become a symbol of social and cultural revival for Gond tribals, particularly after the gotul-breaking incident in Mendha.

The villagers realize that good governance is the only way to achieve effective conservation of their forests, which in turn will lead to security of livelihood. Since 1989 their relationship with the forest department has also improved considerably. In 1998 the forest was placed under the JFM scheme after another long agitation by the villagers.[8] Under the JFM agreement the responsibility for forest protection is held jointly by the villagers and the forest department in return for cash and in-kind benefits to local people. While the forest department is yet to fulfil its responsibilities towards benefit-sharing of commercial returns under JFM, the local villagers continue with their extraction and forest protection activities as they did before the signing of the JFM agreement. A JFM committee (JFMC) has been constituted comprising a male and a female member from each household. Forest management decisions relating to restoration, planting, and harvesting are now made jointly by the department and the JFMC, though the villagers' decisions on forest management are usually accepted. The villagers co-operatively resist illegal extraction by outsiders and encroachments with help from the forest department. Today, the villagers are effectively in control of their patch of forest and also control access to it by forest department officials, researchers, and villagers from elsewhere. The forest department is forced to submit to their decisions on the methods and means to manage forests. The new status of empowerment of the tribals *vis-à-vis* the forest department is expressed in this way: 'Earlier the villagers would flee to the forest or hide themselves in their homes at the sight of any urban man wearing trousers or any auto vehicle. They would be frightened to come out. Now they are no longer afraid of them. The inferiority complex in them has been greatly reduced and they now deal with outsiders on an equal footing' (Tofa and Hiralal undated).

Another major victory the village has achieved over the years is curtailment of the operations of the Ballarpur Paper Mills in the area.

[8] While the villagers wanted to formalize their relationship with the forest through a JFM agreement, the forest department initially did not want to bring the forests under JFM. This was because the Mendha forests did not meet the definition of 'degraded forest' mandated by the act. Only after further agitation was JFM formally adopted.

Illustr. 10: Devaji Tofa, the elected chief of Mendha village in Central India, whose people have 'declared' and retained their autonomy in governing their local forest resources since 1989. The banner says: '*In Our Village, We are the Government.*'

This industry had earlier been awarded contracts by the forest department. The local villagers were resentful of this arrangement for several reasons. What incensed them most was that Ballarpur was getting bamboo at throwaway prices from the government, much below the market rate at the time. What made things worse was that the mill operations were highly unsustainable—entire bamboo plants were destroyed permanently because of the practice of cutting all of the individual bamboo stems in a clump. This ultimately leads to the withering of the entire plant. Large forest patches were destroyed thus and laid to waste. Because of popular protests, harvesting by the paper mill was stopped, as was all other commercial extraction. Now, controlled bamboo harvesting is done jointly by the JFMC and the forest department, with the bamboo being supplied to local farmers and artisans on a priority basis. Only the bamboo remaining after local purchases is sold to traders. Through their united efforts the villagers have also managed to set higher prices for their extracted NTFP, such as mahua flowers and chironji seeds, than anywhere else in the region.

Interestingly, the struggle for power over forest resources has been intertwined with socio-cultural revival in Mendha. Historically, like many other tribal communities, Gonds possessed sophisticated systems of governance that emphasized self-reliance. This helped them in reviving their socio-cultural values more successfully than many other marginalized tribal groups in India. The revival of the *gram sabha*,[9] the village body that includes every adult in the village and that decides local issues consensually, has been an important part of their movement. Lately, the Mendha villagers have joined other Gond villages and leaders in Andhra Pradesh, Chhattisgarh, and Bihar within a larger movement to regain stewardship of natural resources and land.

The consensual decision-making practised within the village as a part of gram sabha procedures is a deliberate move away from mainstream democracy as practised in India at large. Majority-based decision-making is recognized to be fraught with the danger of creating interest groups in any community (Tofa and Hiralal undated). Consensus development on any issue is infinitely more time-consuming than a fast-paced voting system in which the majority wins. However, such decisions based on consensus turn out to be far more stable and sustainable, since every individual is persuaded of the usefulness of the decision. For instance, discussions on whether the villagers should jointly invest in a tractor lasted more than a year, but now the tractor is intensively used to profit and is well maintained (Hiralal pers. comm.).

There have been other important developments in the village as an offshoot of improved local governance. For instance, Mendha has been able to tap into numerous government development schemes, such as for watershed management, drains and well construction, and desiltation of tanks. The funds that come to the village are more effectively utilized as well because of participation in the work

[9] Also called *gaon-samaj-sabha* locally (Hiralal and Tofa undated).

by village members. By the simple expedient of registering the gram sabha as a voluntary organization, the money is received directly in the gram sabha's account rather than filtered through the district administration—a process that inevitably leads to leakages. As many as 1000 gully-plugs (to stall erosion), 17 farm ponds, 1 forest tank, and 1 community well have been constructed co-operatively by the villagers, utilizing various government schemes and by the effective contribution of their own labour. In fact, no development work by government officials, contractors, traders, or NGOs can be undertaken inside the village without the permission of the gram sabha.

The village has been further empowered through the establishment of a village fund that has largely freed the villagers from the clutches of exploitative moneylenders, the bane of the rural economy all over the country. Each family in Mendha contributes 10 per cent of its income in the form of cash or farm produce to the village fund. Villagers are free to borrow from the fund for their large expenses, such as weddings, education, or medical treatment, at a very low rate of interest (Rs 2 per annum), with a constraint on the net amount that can be borrowed. The fund is also utilized for community works in addition to individual loans. Any village-level corruption in the utilization of development funds or locally generated village funds has been tackled through a transparent process of fund disbursement and account-keeping (Tofa and Hiralal undated). Two persons are authorized to operate the account as joint accountholders and a third keeps the passbook; these positions rotate annually. Those authorized to withdraw cash are not authorized to disburse it, leading to even more transparency.

The participation of women has been closely linked with the effectiveness of the gram sabha in the village. While participation levels of women in the gram sabha are not very high, they show a definite improvement over earlier times, when women were not even allowed to come to meetings. Now, women speak up assertively when there is a serious problem needing attention. Women have been responsible for the ban on liquor production, sale, and consumption inside the village: liquor having been identified by the women as largely responsible for hampering decision-making and women's participation in meetings. No one locally has challenged this ban so far, though some clandestine home-based brewing goes on in the village.

Many other agrarian practices that promote sustainability have been revived, such as the establishment of a common village granary to which each household contributes each year.[10] This granary acts as a security net in years of famine, which is not infrequent in this largely rainfed zone. With the help of a matching government scheme the villagers even managed to double the quantum of grain that the villagers had collected. The practice of *tulurmutha* has also been revived whereby village priests collect a fistful of grain from each household after the annual harvest, mix up the collection, and then redistribute them to households in a pre-sowing ceremony, a practice that could be important in maintaining genetic diversity of crops (Ghate 2004).

An important factor in local empowerment and participatory forest management has been the support of an innovative scholar-cum-activist named Mohan Hirabai Hiralal and his Chandrapur-based voluntary group Vrikshamitra. Mohan Hiralal had actively participated in the tribal movements of the 1970s and later undertook a PhD on Gond tribal anthropology. Over his initial years at Mendha he provided an important interface between local villagers and district/forest administration until the villagers had developed the confidence and skills necessary to manage their affairs more or less independently. Hiralal has been frequently consulted by the villagers regarding government policies, development programmes, and forest laws through the last twenty years or more (Ghate 2004). His training as an anthropologist and engagement as a social activist have helped him connect deeply with the social structure and problems of the village. He has been equally comfortable networking with external experts in various fields.

Today, the pride of every villager in their unique gram sabha and the cohesion amongst them is inescapable. Men and women, young and old, are unanimous in their view that the control of the gram sabha on the forest had led to significant benefits for everyone, particularly

[10] This *dhankosh* contains 150–200 quintals of rice at any given time, dispersed over all the households within the village.

for overcoming fuelwood and grazing shortages and improving local water availability. A banner outside the village meeting hall reflects the new attitude:

> **The government in Mumbai and Delhi is ours; but in our village we are the government.**

Treasures of Local Knowledge

Even a few days in Mendha enabled me to understand the deep relationship of the people with their forest. The ordinary person there was a walking encyclopedia of knowledge on the uses of plants, whether of a grand *Boswellia* tree or just a humble weed growing on the forest path. According to the People's Biodiversity Register compiled for Mendha, as many as 550 plant species have been recorded as being used for some purpose, including medicine, food, fuelwood, fish poison, agricultural instruments, gum, and rope fibre.[11]

Yet, despite this tremendous local knowledge, the locals were also reaching out to outside experts to learn more about how to conserve their forest. I first happened to reach Mendha on a day when a workshop had been organized inviting a diverse group of experts in watershed management, forest ecology, medicinal plants, and rural technology, to discuss future interventions for better ecosystem management. At this workshop we discussed topics such as the productivity, pollination, and seed dispersal of the mahua (*Madhuca indica*) trees. The villagers were worried about its decline in productivity and lack of regeneration. The possible reasons for an observed decline in karu (*Sterculia urens*), tendu (*Diospyros melanoxylon*), and salai (*Boswellia serrata*) were also talked about. Even the possible reasons for decline in tree diversity and productivity were discussed—such as the use of fire for NTFP collection, the lack of seed dispersers, and the destruction of seed crops by wild boar. Alongside, techniques for germination of

[11] People's Biodiversity Register, Mendha (Lekha), 2005, has been compiled jointly by the voluntary group Vrikshamitra, the Gram Sabha of Mendha (Lekha), and the Centre for Ecological Sciences of the Indian Institute of Sciences in Bangalore, through a long process of local discussions and research.

commercially used species, cultivation on farms, and improved local extraction of some tree produce consumed their minds. There were discussions regarding the modalities to exhaustively document use of living organisms and study the causes of the decline in local ecosystem diversity.

The discussions at the workshop revealed the surprisingly robust knowledge of ecological relationships that the villagers possessed. I realized that the revitalization of village intellectual traditions is as central to forest conservation as anything else. Here I saw a freshness and vigour in thought which is not often encountered in rural India. The language barrier did not seem to be a problem at this workshop, despite the fact that most of the locals spoke only Gondi and the visitors were from Delhi, Bombay, and a number of other towns in Maharashtra. This confluence of traditional knowledge with new developments in modern science seems to strengthen Mendha's forest conservation movement rather than weaken it.

I was most interested, however, in understanding the methods being employed to ensure sustainability of forest use as well as their long-term efficacy. Discussions revealed that forest use is subject to rules that have been consensually decided in the gram sabha over the years. These rules are not inflexible but are subject to change, depending on changing circumstances. For instance, the cutting of entire trees for any forest product, such as fruit, seeds, or leaves is strictly prohibited. For any unusually large extraction, such as for house repair/construction, or the making of agricultural instruments, the gram sabha's approval has to be obtained. The rules on forest harvest are imposed through forest patrolling, and fines for violations. A group of young men takes care of forest protection activities from 10 a.m. to 5 p.m. each day. Households take it in turn to send members as watchmen each day. Violaters are often caught and later fined at the next gram sabha meeting. An offender is reprimanded verbally for the first violation; if he repeats the violation he has to put in extra labour as a payback to the village. Practical measures are also in place to support forest conservation, such as the widespread use of biogas for cooking. Almost every house has a biogas plant which is used for cooking purposes, thereby saving hundreds of trees from being cut for firewood each year.

Firewood needed for heating (and sometimes cooking) is collected co-operatively a few times each year and delivered to each household equitably.

There are other rules, such as a ban on using synthetic poisons for fishing: these had begun to cause large-scale fish mortality in the river. Now, only plant-derived poisons are used to temporarily stun the fish, which are then caught in a net. To control the harvest, fishing is restricted to household consumption and commercial sales have been banned—as was done for bamboo. Over the past two decades the villagers have also united to take up community development activities for forest regeneration and watershed management, these having been decided on at gram sabha meetings. The cleaning of forest ponds and seeding with fish fingerlings has led to immense gains in fish populations which are for local use. The thousand gully plugs constructed over the past ten years have stemmed soil erosion, especially at the edges of the forest and in eroded areas.

One of the most important commercial products of the village is the honey of the rock bee (*Apis dorsata*), whose production peaks in spring and autumn, coincidental with the flowering of forest trees. A unique form of honey harvesting has been developed and propagated throughout the village; this is called *ahinsak* (non-violent) honey. By this technique bees are not driven out by smoke for honey collection, as is normal. Smoking causes bees to abandon their hives, leading to loss of further honey production for that season. Instead, here, hives are tackled at night, when the bees tend to be passive and slow to react to disturbance. Further, only the part of the hive that holds the honey is cut and carefully collected, leaving the area which harbours the grubs and larvae. After extraction, the bees in such hives tend to quickly rebuild the honey-carrying part of the hive rather than abandon it. This allows repeated honey extraction in a single season—at least three times—rather than just once, resulting in considerably increased honey production in Mendha. The honey collectors process and bottle the honey locally, so there is no adulteration. The honey is then sold in the local town Dhanora and district headquarters Gadchiroli. The whole process ensures that there is considerable value addition within the village. A training programme is also in place to recruit more young people to perform these tasks.

The Ecology of Participatory Management

It was obvious to me that Mendha's villagers spent a lot of time deliberating on forest conservation issues and constantly adapted their rules to take into account changing pressures, both from within the village and from outside. But, given all these efforts, to what extent has Mendha been successful in conserving the biodiversity values of its forest? For instance, what is the current regeneration status of intensively used commercial tree species in the forest? Is a healthy population of wild herbivores and carnivores, for instance, compatible with grazing, fuelwood extraction, and NTFP collection? What has been the effect of common management practices on trees and shrubs?

There were indications that all was not well in the Mendha forests despite the controlled harvest and patrolling in place. A visiting biologist, in fact, could not be blamed for scepticism about the value of community forestry in preserving biodiversity. Casual walks through the forest revealed ample signs of habitat degradation. Good quality forest, as is seen in the presence of distinct layers of vegetation and dense regeneration, could be encountered only in patches, such as on the tops of the hills and steep slopes. The village–forest interface, in fact, was marked by an almost empty understorey and visible soil erosion, apparently caused by intensive cattle grazing. I saw several amla trees hacked mercilessly by collectors of fruit, despite the injunctions imposed by the Mendha gram sabha. Hacked saplings of the hardy garadi (*Cleistanthus collinus*) and ain (*Terminalia alata*), two tree species that resprout readily from stumps and roots, dominated the understorey.

I was also concerned that despite the worry about commercial NTFP species, there did not appear to be any rules in place to govern the levels of their extraction. Villagers reported that collection of NTFP takes place all over the forest area on a first-come-first-served basis. Grazing too is not bound by any restrictions on sites (Pathak and Gour-Broome 2001). During my first visit in 2000 I felt that the lack of control on geographic extent and quantity of extraction would likely lead to shortages of NTFP in future.

The Biodiversity Register for Mendha confirms the trends that a biologist would expect. Many of the important NTFP species, as many as 46 of 56 species, are perceived to be declining in productivity. Amla, mahua, and tendu patta have the locals most worried. The Biodiversity Register notes that the number of tendu-collecting days had dropped from 12 in 2001 to just 9 in 2003. The income per family from tendu patta has come down to Rs 2341 in 2003 from Rs 3212 in 2001. More than one discussion that I had with both women and men revealed the growing worry among people about their declining NTFP stocks and productivity. Grasses suitable for livestock fodder and the variety and quantity of fish species is also perceived to be declining steadily.

Related to NTFP collection is the extensive use of fire within the Mendha forests, which is obviously influencing forest structure and tree composition. Fires are ignited intentionally from February to April each year, mainly to facilitate the collection of tendu leaves used in cigarette manufacture. Firing advances the budding of new leaves on tendu trees to the dry season so that leaf-processing can be completed before the monsoon sets in (Saha and Howe 2003). The practice of using fire is said to have started in 1906, coincidental with the rise of the global cigarette industry (ibid.). Fire is also used for clearing the leaf litter and shrubbery under the mahua trees in the month of April so that falling mahua flowers can be more easily collected. The chronic use of fire has always been suspected by ecologists to be one of the practices most destructive of forests in Central India. The firing of tendu trees leads to low-intensity fires that sweep through the understorey, destroying the seedlings and saplings of many species, so that fresh regeneration is affected. While the Mendha gram sabha has supposedly banned the use of fire, the ban has obviously not been effectively imposed as fires are commonly seen in the dry season (Pathak and Gour-Broome 2001).

Since my first visit to Mendha in 2000 a number of ecological studies have been carried out that now give deeper insights into the sustainability of forest management in Mendha. Sonali Saha, an ecologist then with the University of Illinois at Chicago, undertook a two-year quantitative study to analyse the effects of forest fires on plant species composition and forest regeneration (Saha and Howe 2003, 2006).

Her finding was that fires used for NTFP collection in Mendha were causing significant mortality of seedlings and saplings, which could lead to severe lack of tree regeneration in future. Over a period of two years mortality was only 21 per cent in sample plots protected from fire as compared to those subjected to experimental fire: here sapling mortality was as much as 66 per cent. The growth rates of saplings (as measured in annual increase in length) were severely reduced by fires as well. Interestingly, the same study showed that seedlings of different tree species reacted differently to understorey fires, with root-sprouters,[12] such as tendu and ain, easily re-establishing after fire, and root-crown resprouters mostly failing to revive from the roots.[13] These results decidedly point to both reducing tree species diversity as well as changing tree composition in future. Chironji and mahua are two of the root-crown resprouters that are adversely affected indirectly by fire on account of reduced competitive ability in fired landscapes. One of the reasons for decline in the productivity of these two NTFP species as well as their regeneration could, therefore, well be the chronic use of fire.

In 2007 the honey collection business had also run into trouble because of lack of finances to buy the new equipment needed to safely carry out the job, such as uniforms, gloves, and masks. It had turned out not to be a financially sustainable operation because the buyers in town were not paying up in time. Being forced to sell honey at very low prices in the village itself, for the villagers the economic viability of the whole operation was coming into question. On the other side destructive honey collection practices by villagers elsewhere were being reported again: large trees were being cut to get at the hives, smoke was being used to drive out bees, and entire hives were being harvested.

[12] These are hardy species that have the physiological capacity to sprout again from roots after the plant is damaged or cut, such as garadi (*Cleistanthus collinus*) and tendu (*Diospyros melanoxylon*).

[13] Root-crown resprouters are tree species that do not easily revive from the root once the external plant is damaged by fire or browsing, such as chironji (*Buchanania lanzan*) and mahua (*Madhuca indica*).

Mendha's animal diversity was also reported to be declining, as seen in the loss of several wild mammal and bird species from the area, a process that had been set in motion over the past few decades. Populations of the flying squirrel, red junglefowl, and peacock had declined visibly during the lifetime of the villagers. This could possibly be ascribed to hunting, habitat degradation, or simply the disjunction of the Mendha forests from other surrounding forest areas. Discussions with local people who were knowledgeable about wildlife confirmed that they had begun to feel the effects of declining plant and animal populations.[14] While cheetal, wild dogs, and gaur had been rare for several decades, langur and sambar deer had shown a recent decline. Smaller mammals such as wild boar, porcupines, and black-naped hare, still exist, mainly because they have adapted to raiding agricultural fields. The People's Biodiversity Register has additionally recorded that grey langur, scaly anteater, leopard, mongoose, four-horned antelope, and nilgai have all declined during very recent times. The loss of access of wild mammals to the river, which is now surrounded by agricultural fields, is cited by the locals to be an important factor affecting wild species.

Some of the wildlife decline could be related to the widespread extraction of fruits and seeds from the forest: this does not leave much for frugivores and herbivores. Several herbivore species depend on fruit such as amla for vital nutrients, and mahua flowers are utilized by deer, squirrels, and wild boar. One wonders how far the clean sweep of the NTFP collection would have affected the reproductive rates of mammals in the long term.

The role of hunting is also felt to be important by the locals in causing species decline, along with the increasing use of pesticides, habitat loss, and the inaccessibility of the river Katthani to animals. Hunting is too close to the people's hearts and culturally important to them. Rucha Ghate, who has been researching forest conservation in the region, recounts several tales of how entire groups of people go after animals as small as the black-naped hare, just for the thrill of the hunt. Young boys sheepishly admitted to hunting birds as a common

[14] People's Biodiversity Register, Mendha (Lekha), 2005.

pastime. Pathak and Gour-Broome (2001) report frequent hunting of most animal species.

Talking to older people confirmed my feeling that adverse changes in the forest are under way. While there is definitely an ocean change in the relationship with the forest department, there is an overall decline in feeling for the forest among villagers as well. An old inhabitant said to me: 'Both outsiders and Mendha dwellers have become less sensitive to the need for keeping the forests intact. The extent as well as quality of forests as well as wildlife have reduced tremendously during my lifetime. The new generation is not used to hardships and is therefore gradually growing more and more distant from a forest life.'

Compounding sustainability issues is the continuing encroachment into delineated forest areas, admitted to by several villagers as well as the headman of Mendha, Devaji Tofa. Shivram Duga confirmed that the inevitable expansion of families is leading to fragmentation of landholdings, which have now reached a point where they can no longer be further reduced. As more land is now needed to keep families going, many families have extended their parcels into the forest. There are no concrete steps taken towards family planning or population stabilization either. Forest boundaries are fast receding. The population has shown a 1.6 per cent increase over the nine-year period from 1998 to 2007.[15] In 2004 the per capita forest area in Mendha was 4.82 ha. (Ghate 2004), rather a large amount compared to the national average, which is 0.06 ha.[16] Yet, given current economics, it seems increasingly difficult for the people to eke out a satisfactory living from subsistence agriculture and forest products alone. Devaji Tofa admitted in a conversation: 'Unemployment and poverty still continue to haunt the village. Pressure on our forest base is increasing because of the need to grow more food. We still have to find the optimal balance between amount of agricultural land and forest land within our village boundaries.'

[15] In 1998 there were 70 households recorded with a population of 375 (Pathak and Gour-Broome 2001). In 2007 there were 84 families with a population of 434 (Hiralal and Tofa undated).

[16] United Nations Statistics Division (http://unstats.un.org/unsd/environment)

Illustr. 11: With the expansion of subsistence agriculture in Mendha (Lekha) village, Maharashtra, the forests are gradually receding.

A Rocky Balance

It would be difficult to predict which way the process of consensual conservation is going to proceed in Mendha. To me, the balance between conservation and development seems precarious here, as much as in the rest of India. On the positive side, it is very likely that this patch of forest, like millions of hectares in India, would have been converted to a wasteland long ago by the ravages of paper mills, commercial plantations, dams, or other infrastructure projects had it not been for the stewardship here of the local Gond people. In the future too, there is indirect long-term protection against the indiscriminate 'development' currently ravaging the Indian countryside. Such protection as there is, is because the local inhabitants have strong stakes in keeping their forests intact.

While the available observations indicate that the Mendha forests no longer harbour much of the mammalian diversity of the region, a large variety of smaller organisms—plants, birds, snakes, and insects—still exists here. The Mendha forest therefore contributes to landscape-level biodiversity, serving as a refuge for several species that might have otherwise gone locally extinct, and a corridor for mammals to disperse. Biodiversity inventories reveal that used forests are far superior to monocultural plantations, logged forest, or even intensively used forests in the variety of organisms that they do protect (Pathak and Gour-Broome 2001).

Visits to villages in the region reveal that Mendha may not be representative of the general situation, despite the fact that forest movements are said to have spread to as many as twenty villages in Gadchiroli district. For instance, Markegaon, a neighbouring village, is similar in most respects to Mendha. In fact, the per capita forest area is much larger in Markegaon, entailing less pressure on forest resources. Yet Mendha has fared much better in forest conservation than Markegaon due to its community-initiated movement, unique consensual form of governance, and long-term guidance by Hiralal. Markegaon, in comparison, has experienced only 'official' JFM, that too rather inadequately implemented by the forest department. A recent quantitative comparison reveals that signs of forest disturbance such as fire, lopping, and erosion have increased manifold in Markegaon but stayed stable in Mendha (Deepshikha Mehra, pers. comm.). So conservation in Mendha, at least overtly, appears to be on rather firm ground.

Yet there are subtle signs that Mendha might be a village in the middle of a fast-paced transition, like thousands of others in India. Talks with younger people revealed that their aspirations clearly lay elsewhere. What was keeping back the majority of the youth in agriculture, grazing, and forest-based activities was just the lack of good education that could integrate them with external vocations and propel them into the cash economy. In 2007 I met a few young people who are studying in high school and college, located several kilometres away from the village. They now interact much more intimately with the outside world, possibly learning more about the possibilities for employment out of their village. I noticed that several literate young women and men have been employed by government and non-governmental agencies for village development work and were travelling well beyond the confines of their *taluk* during the course of their work, something that would have been unthinkable just a decade ago. Today, quite a few families own mobile phones, enabling far better communication than even a few years ago. My host and friend Shivram Duga has renovated his mud-and-thatch house, which now has larger doors and extra rooms to accommodate his growing family. Maniram Duga's house now has concrete flooring where he can afford it and a small black-and-white TV. Most families have shifted to expensive tiled roofs from the original thatch, owing partly to a shortage of thatch grass as well as the ease of tile-roof maintenance. Cemented drains have been constructed in many of the better-off households, helping sanitation.

Will the winds of change affect the way these people manage their forest as well? Traditions have a way of crumbling in the face of modernization. There are already signs that some of the sustainable management traditions may slowly be breaking down. There is even a feeling among villagers about the futility of sticking to sustainable extraction practices when outsiders continue to destroy the forest. Although pressures from the corporate sector and timber smugglers have been stopped, extraction pressure for fuelwood and NTFP from the surrounding villages continues to lead to unpleasant showdowns from time to time. The perceived importance of external extraction can be gauged from the fact that the first decision taken by the Forest Protection Committee which was implemented was to impose a fine on all neighbouring villagers harvesting from their forest (Tofa and Hiralal undated). Coupled with clear signs that the use of fire by the village people themselves, and overexploitation of NTFP, are already causing adverse changes in the forest by way of forest tree composition and structure, the fate of the forests might appear to be sealed. A major disturbance takes place during the tendu collection season, when large groups of nomadic gatherers pass through the Mendha forests, setting fire to trees.

However, influential community leaders such as Hiralal and Tofa think that the only hurdle to a more complete commitment from local people towards sustainable forest management is lack of formal ownership over resources (Hiralal undated). Although the JFM agreement was signed more than ten years ago, the villagers are yet to receive their share of the economic benefits from the forest, as promised by the agreement. However, people continue to protect the forest and continue to follow their own crafted rules regarding the extraction of goods. Hiralal thinks that the breaking point will soon be reached. He has been campaigning for conversion of the RF in Mendha to 'village forest', as provided for in the Indian Forest Act 1927. In the event of conversion to village forest, the village gets absolute legal right for the management of its forest and will have far greater authority to keep out outsiders. The difference is that JFM is officially governed by a government resolution and implemented through the department, while village forest is governed by the villagers themselves: 'Only complete responsibility over the forest will create a deep and abiding interest in forest conservation. Forests will then be managed much better', says Tofa.

With increasing population and demand for agricultural land, coupled with visible overexploitation of the forest, it is difficult to see how forest ownership by itself will lead to better sustainability. To top it all, the threats from a long-term insurgency (Naxalism) in Central India often forces local peasants to give up precious foodgrain and income.[17] Village governance, too, is not without its share of problems and is far from smooth. Villagers often lag in participation, coming to meetings only when the issues involve them directly, and frequently paying back loans belatedly. Casual interviews in the village revealed some undercurrents of dissatisfaction over village decisions, particularly on the question of payments to the village fund. Apparently the issue of communal *vs* personal property has not been worked out to everyone's satisfaction.

By way of developmental infrastructure, too, not much has changed during the last ten years. Tofa informed me that school education had not improved despite much effort. A student of 18, Sheetal informed me that schoolteachers often played hookey, leaving the children to

[17] Naxalism refers to a mass insurgency that has now spread over more than 150 districts in India, mainly within the states of Andhra Pradesh, Bihar, Jharkhand, Chhattisgarh, Orissa, and West Bengal. The movement, which has a strong communist ideology, started in the 1960s with the aim of overthrowing feudal landlords and has a mass appeal among rural landless and oppressed castes.

fend for themselves. Drinking water continued to be a problem, with the wells drying up in summer. Women then had to travel long distances to wash clothes and fetch drinking water. Agricultural crops continued to be vulnerable to raiding by wild boar.

I left Mendha not much more enlightened than before. The locals seemed neither to be 'noble savages' nor simply 'opportunistic conservationists', as is claimed by most biologists who have visited the village. While the local people are looking after the forests because they realize their fate is closely tied to them, they also seem to possess a certain ethic of conservation, a certain contentment that allows them to subsist on probably a hundredth of what a city-dweller in India would typically consume. One villager, Shantabai, says: 'We depend heavily on these forests. Without forests we will have nothing. In the cities, people have to pay to get all these goods. Here we get them free. We do not have the money to pay for these goods. Here, many people do not understand that we have to conserve the forests for our own benefit, not for anyone else.' But it is hard to predict what will happen once this forest dependence is reduced by gradually growing educational skills and exposure to markets. And the pressures of extraction are only going to increase in future, given the reducing extent and quality of forests. Still, one thing is certain: as long as the people's connection with the forest remains, their role in greening the landscape will continue to be important, although perhaps not to the extent most biologists would like. With the correct incentives, a conducive policy framework, and demographic stabilization, the Mendha initiative might even continue and improve in effectiveness over the years.

As I left the village I asked Devaji Tofa what he felt about the future of their unique conservation movement. He said: 'We do not deny that we have problems here. People need still more strength, knowledge, and maturity to deal with these problems. There is still a long way to go in building capacities, and greater understanding among our people. Yet I am quite certain that this experiment will continue into the future, if not wholly, then at least in part.'

6

Crafting the Commons: India's Joint Forest Management Experience

Driving through the south-western West Bengal countryside on the smooth highways, one cannot be faulted for believing that a green revolution is under way. There are thatched huts, bamboo fences, and rainfed agricultural fields. There are people commuting on foot, motorbikes, and bullock carts, as anywhere in rural India. Small herds of cattle stalk the highways in search of fodder. But what is different about the landscape is the astonishing greenery—miles and miles of it—a mosaic of young regenerating forests, sal monocultures, eucalyptus and Australian acacia plantations, and even the occasional patch of relatively pristine forest.

West Bengal was the birthplace of one of India's largest socio-ecological experiments, Joint Forest Management, or JFM for short, initiated by the state government about thirty years ago. Since then the JFM programme, and other variants of community-based forest management, have caught on like wild fire in several other states of India.

Going Back in Time

South-western West Bengal lies in the relatively wetter forest zone of eastern India, receiving 1000–1500 mm of rainfall a year, enough moisture to sustain what is known in technical parlance as mixed dry deciduous forest.[1] The sal tree (*Shorea robusta*), extremely valuable for its durable timber, forms the majority of trees, while other useful trees such as mahua, kendu, salai, piya sal, haritaki (*Terminalia chebula*), palash, bahera (*Terminalia belerica*), and dhok make up the rest. During colonial times the sal stands of this area, known as the Jungle Mahals, were heavily exploited for shipbuilding and extension of railway tracks in India (Sivaramakrishnan 1999). Most of the timber extraction took place through zamindars (landlords) who owned large private estates. Apart from timber, the zamindars also sold commercial NTFP to private buyers (Sivaramakrishnan 1999) and fuelwood to locals at nominal rates (Banerjee 2007).

After Independence, with the abolition of zamindaris and the conversion of their forests to nationalized status—protected and reserved status—there was literally a free-for-all in the appropriation of forest resources. Between 1950 and 1980 these forests, for all practical purposes, turned into open-access areas, leading to their rapid degradation. The fact that the process of nationalization itself was fraught with administrative irregularities, such as the lack of settlement of existing customary rights (considerable in themselves), did not make the transition easier. Pressures for fuelwood and fodder from a rapidly expanding population further contributed to the reduction of forest cover and quality in the state. The newly formed West Bengal forest department found it increasingly difficult to preserve the forests under its control, being faced with hostile local people who often resorted to 'stealing' to meet their subsistence needs. The crisis over biomass reached breaking point in the 1960s and 1970s.

In a surprisingly far-sighted move, the government of West Bengal began an attempt towards the regeneration of degraded forests in the early 1970s. This was initiated by a pioneering forest officer named

[1] This description mainly pertains to the belt of sal-dominated dry deciduous forest stretching across the south-western part of West Bengal at the eastern edges of the Chhotanagpur plateau, a fairly homogeneous forest type. This region includes the five contiguous districts of Midnapore, Birbhum, Bankura, Purulia, and Burdwan in West Bengal.

Ajit Banerjee, who realized the futility of continuing with the same policies.[2] For the first time the support and co-operation of local communities was enlisted in forest regeneration through the JFM scheme. Although the exact arrangements varied from place to place, the basis of the new approach was to allow local people access to a demarcated forest area near their village for the collection of plant products and biomass, in return for their assumption of responsibility for its protection and regeneration. The locals were also promised a share of revenues from timber and commercial NTFP from the forests.[3]

Following the decision over joint management, officials of the forest department worked with local people all over the state to form Forest Protection Committees (FPCs) through which the resource-sharing arrangement was formalized for each village. Though the scheme has been experimented with since 1971, it was formalized only in 1989 through a state-wide government order. In many cases, formal MOUs were signed between forest departments and each village committee. It was envisaged that 'micro-plans' for forest management and regeneration, specific to each village, depending on its ecological and economic conditions, would be developed through a consultative process. Meetings were planned to be held every few months to resolve emergent conflicts and problems. A forest official of the rank of beat officer was to be made the ex-officio secretary of the village FPC, responsible for keeping records.[4]

Even before JFM began in this region, the majority of the sal forests in the area had been managed as coppice stands, that is, forests regenerated from left-over stumps and roots of old sal trees, rather than from seed. This practice continued after JFM began and led to swift regeneration because of an abundance of sal stumps. In most areas a rotation cycle of ten years or more for the felling of sal trees for timber and poles was established. Local people today collect a diverse range of plant

[2] Dr Ajit Banerjee continues to advise and study JFM to this day, and has been involved in some of the insightful studies on the ecology and economics of the programme, some of which are referred to in this chapter.

[3] Fixed at 25 per cent of net sales of timber after the costs of processing are deducted.

[4] Beat officer: usually of the rank of forest guard or range officer.

products both for commercial and household use, including fuelwood, livestock fodder, timber, medicines, fibre, and food items from the regenerating sal stands. Most important among these products are the sal leaves: they are processed into plates in homes and provide the largest amounts of cash income locally. Commercially, the other important forest products are sal seeds, mahua flowers, mahua fruit, mushrooms, tendu leaves, tendu fruits, honey, kalmegh (*Andrographis paniculata*), and satamuli (*Asparagus racemosa*) (Government of West Bengal 1997). Apart from the sal-dominated forests, considerable areas of previously barren lands have been planted over with exotic species such as Australian acacia (*Acacia auriculiformes*), eucalyptus (*Eucalyptus spp.*), and cashewnut (*Anacardium occidentale*) for industrial use.

Over the years the impact of the JFM scheme has overtly been impressive. According to official estimates, by 1999 large areas of degraded forest land had been regenerated to some extent through community protection and artificial plantations across West Bengal. In 2001, 44 per cent of West Bengal's forest areas covering 5240 sq. km were officially administered under JFM through as many as 3593 FPCs (Banerjee 2007). There were noticeable increases in tree regeneration, plant species diversity, and forest biomass due to the protection afforded by FPCs (Ravindranath *et al.* 2000, Tata Energy Research Institute 1999). JFM has emerged as one of the most extensive experiments in active community-based forest management anywhere in the world, given its spatial extent and level of engagement with local people.

Hopes Gone Awry

Just a few years after JFM had been initiated,[5] its first independent evaluations and analyses starting trickling in. They pointed to several

[5] While informal protection aided by forest officers and self-initiated protection began in the early 1970s, it was only in June 1990 that the formal government notification was issued for the entire country. Different states actually adopted it formally, again as government resolutions, in the following years.

disturbing trends related to the management and outcome of JFM. Clearly, things were not turning out as they had been envisaged.

The primary goal of JFM, as originally envisioned, was to empower local communities to manage forests for their subsistence and livelihoods through joint management with the forest department. However, by the 1990s it was becoming increasingly evident that the real power to decide what kind of management would take place in the JFM forests was still really in the hands of the department. Villagers' participation was found to be limited to mundane matters such as choice of species—and not even in every case—or how often to patrol forests for protection. Recent studies indicate that to this day the forest department still holds power over forest micro-planning, the sale of timber and forest products from protected forests, as well as the accounts of FPCs (Banerjee 2007). Importantly, only forest officers have legal powers to deal with offenders and encroachers, often leaving the villagers themselves helpless in the event of incursions by timber mafia or local thieving.

It all starts with the process of micro-planning. Simple as the process was envisaged to be, micro-planning has been transformed into a mere formality, usually being completed by the forest officers themselves without the stipulated process of discussion with village representatives (Banerjee 2007). In attempting to meet annual targets of FPC formation, and because they do not see local participation as important,[6] forest officers generally give short shrift to micro-planning. It is not surprising that these documents often do not have the required detail or prescribed apportioning of rights and benefits. Studies have documented that, in many cases, even when microplans are drawn up in consultation with locals, they are abandoned when they do not match with the FD's working plans for the forest (Sundar 2000).

The unequal relationship between managements and people is made worse by the fact that most FPCs do not have legal recognition

[6] A.K. Banerjee, who is himself from the Indian Forest Service, estimates in an interview that not more than 15–20 per cent of the local forest guards are convinced of the importance of JFM (*Down to Earth* 2000).

of any sort, and therefore little security of existence. Few conservationists in India are aware that JFM is still not formally legislated for. As yet, there are no legal amendments in the Indian Forest Act 1927 to enable it. Rather, JFM is undertaken simply on the basis of a government order in every state.[7] According to this arrangement FPCs are 'registered' with the forest department rather than as legal entities with the respective state governments. Only in Gujarat and Haryana do they have any legal standing—as co-operatives and registered societies, respectively (ibid.). Further, the department reserves the right to dissolve FPCs if they are believed to perform unsatisfactorily. This ensures an inherently top-down relationship between the forest department and the FPCs (ibid.).

Benefit-sharing and power-sharing arrangements are often not clearly stated in the MOUs signed between the department and FPCs, leaving existing rules open to reinterpretation or arbitrary change when new government rules are promulgated. For instance, when benefit-sharing norms were changed without discussion or notice for the Hill Resource Management Societies in Haryana, FPCs were required to plough back as much as 40 per cent of the earned revenues into training and forest management relating to JFM (Sarin, undated). Compared to pre-JFM days, when people had paid no dues, the new situation actually left them fewer financial benefits. It is also worth noting that if the forest department alters a JFM agreement, the community has access to neither monetary compensation for past investments of labour and time nor to penal action (Sarin undated). Such uncertainties in governance, understandably, reduce the faith of villagers in the forest department and the local incentive for long-term forest protection, resulting in declining levels of participation by local people.

The perfunctory participation by local villagers in the working of the average FPC was documented by a field study undertaken by

[7] A recent proposed amendment to the Indian Forest Act 1927 did not even mention JFM despite the widespread nature of the programme. Rather, the amendment proposed to restrict the demarcation of village forests, an existing provision in the act, to areas *outside* existing reserved forests. This move was met with widespread protests by civil society organizations and subsequently abandoned (see Raju 1997).

Banerjee (2007) in ten FPCs spread across three different districts, based on questionnaire surveys. This was the first study to quantitatively evaluate the attitudes towards and participation in the JFM model by local villagers anywhere in India. Banerjee found that only 19 per cent of 167 interviewees had ever been to an FPC meeting during the previous year while only a minuscule 11 per cent felt that their opinions mattered for final decisions taken in FPCs. In several other villages that the researchers visited during the course of the study, FPC meetings were, in fact, rare and sporadic. They found that village participation is reduced in part by the opaqueness of the financial dealings—these being usually managed entirely by the relevant forest officer (Banerjee 2007, Kashwan 2003).

The dominance of the forest department in management right from inception has led to a rather timber-centred approach to JFM, an approach that tends to neglect local household needs such as fuelwood, fodder, and NTFP (Khare *et al.* 2000). Thus, most of the micro plans are centred around the sale of sal timber—to be harvested every 5–10 years. This sort of unbalanced micro-planning ultimately results in strengthening the power of relatively well-off landed people (who were able to forsake immediate consumption needs for fuelwood and fodder from their forest patch) *vis-à-vis* those with immediate biomass needs, usually the poor and landless (Sarin undated). However, Banerjee (2007) found that currently the largest part of local forest-based income comes from NTFP sales rather than from either the sales of timber, the sales of wood products from thinning operations, or from daily-wage labour.

For most observers a very relevant question is whether the local institutions formed as part of JFM will be robust enough to continue functioning even after external project funding comes to a halt.[8] It stands to reason that only those FPCs that have developed true autonomy and sufficient financial reserves will be able to sustain themselves in the long term. Some state governments attempted to use innovative methods for sustaining JFM after World Bank funding

[8] The World Bank supported the JFM programme, with the resources being mostly used for associated village development work.

came to an end in 1999 (Mahapatra 2000b). One of the ways that was envisaged was to lease out existing JFM lands to industrial groups for plantation in buy-back agreements. Such an arrangement was likely to marginalize locals even more in the process of decision-making over forest use and conversion (ibid.). This trend towards 'public-private partnerships' is visible in many other parts of India. For instance, the JFM programme mediated by the Foundation of Ecological Security in one FPC of Udaipur district is being jeopardized because of insistence by the forest department on planting *Jatropha* (an important biofuel species which is an exotic) on village common lands.[9] This plan was opposed tooth and nail by the locals but, as of 2007, they have been only partially successful in fending off this threat (Foundation for Ecological Security, pers. comm.).

Traditionally disempowered groups such as women and the landless are even more sidelined in decision-making processes at the FPC level (Banerjee 2007). For instance, none of the current JFM projects, including those funded by the World Bank, had planned any systematic compensation for the opportunity costs expected to be incurred by the poorest villagers during the initial phases of forest protection, when biomass protection needed to be controlled (Khare *et al.* 2000). As an instance, sale of fuelwood for income—an occupation resorted to mostly by poor villagers—is an activity that is instantaneously criminalized in most JFM forests after micro-plans come into force (ibid.).

Another unexpected difficulty came up during the implementation of JFM in many parts of India. In many of the project sites, boundary conflicts arose between adjoining villages over the demarcation of forest land for each FPC. Some of these conflicts were a result of earlier poor implementation of land settlement and demarcation of forest boundaries by the forest department, that often ignored customary rights (Kashwan 2003, Sundar 2000). Another factor overlooked during the planning stages of JFM was the use of natural habitat by a section of people who do not have formal access rights, such as groups of nomadic pastoralists and shifting cultivators who use various habitats seasonally. Conflicts with customary land use rights came

[9] Observed during a visit to the field site in December 2007.

up frequently when the forest department attempted to cordon off forests for specific FPCs (Sundar 2000, Khare *et al.* 2000). Ratna-Reddy *et al.* (2007) have documented the contentious issue of shifting cultivation in Andhra Pradesh which conflicted with JFM in varying ways. Shifting cultivation contributed as much as 20 per cent of the income of the poorest tribals in some districts of Andhra Pradesh, in addition to providing food security. With the initiation of JFM the forest department confiscated most of the land under shifting cultivation by tribals because they did not possess formal ownership documents.

In some cases JFM policies were found to obstruct self-initiated community forestry rather than encourage it. FDs have sometimes refused to register existing FPCs that were self-initiated, or to change their benefit-sharing norms. As a result village people already involved in forest protection have found themselves at the losing end when the actual registration took place, a long time after protection had started. In these cases, harvests were put off by several years, against the anticipation of the communities in question. Such an instance was Soliga village in Bharuch district of Gujarat, where the community was involved in forest protection since 1986, four years prior to the JFM order of 1990. By 1991 the bamboo forest was ready for harvest but the forest department did not allow harvesting on the basis that the working plan for the area that had been written in the interim period had different aims (Raju 1997). The condition that JFM is applicable only to 'degraded forests' has caused its own share of problems (Khare *et al.* 2000). This created hurdles for many FPCs that had been protecting high quality forest for several years, as happened in Gadchiroli, within the self-initiated conservation scheme (see Chapter 5). In the ultimate analysis there exist thousands of self-initiated forest protection groups in various Indian states whose existence is neither acknowledged by any of the state orders nor the overarching JFM order of 1990.

Does the Economics Work?

Another aspect of JFM requiring deeper study is the question of the scale of economic benefits flowing to local communities. It is pertinent to examine the break-up of economic and in-kind benefits available to local people to see how far this level of benefits has been important in keeping people bound to the JFM programme. The primary cash incomes from JFM come from commercial NTFP sales, wood harvest from forest-thinning operations, daily-wage labour inside the forests and plantations, and the stipulated 25 per cent proceeds from timber harvest after maturation. In-kind benefits to local people generally include fuelwood, fodder, and other minor forest products for household use.

Banerjee (2007) has carried out a detailed assessment of the total cash income generated by a household from the final timber harvest in three of his ten study villages. The average annual amount earned per household was as low as Rs 78, an extremely insignificant amount for a rural household. Labour employment for harvesting and thinning operations and NTFP collection, since the formation of the ten study villages, totalled 6370 days of work overall, which amounted to only 3.6 days of labour per household over the entire felling cycle. The survey also showed that none of the families had bought land or livestock with any additional cash earnings due to JFM. To make matters worse, the implementation of benefit-sharing agreements, in terms of the final timber harvesting itself, had been conducted in a very erratic manner, so that several of the FPCs had never experienced any harvest at all, despite several years of protection (Banerjee 2007). Clearly, there are next to no cash benefits from JFM.

However, when cash and in-kind benefits (including fuelwood, fodder, and NTFP) from the protected forest were totalled using the market values of these goods, Banerjee estimated that as much as Rs 22,142 to Rs 54,726 was earned annually by each household from forest activities, on the average. Further, poor and landless households, respectively, earned 27 per cent and 32 per cent of their total income from forest sources, in comparison to only 1 per cent for rich families and 15 per cent for middle-income families. Thus JFM *does* seem to have created an important source of livelihood for the poor and landless, apart from regenerating vital biomass sources that had declined over the years. The improved availability of fuelwood and fodder has also freed up time for women for more remunerative work, and thus improved their quality of life in many of the sites.

Many authors and foresters have suggested substantially expanding income from forests through the manipulation of vegetation, and more efficient extraction of forest products. The suggestions include growing turmeric, pineapple, medicinal plants, or cardamom within the FPC forests to enhance cash income (ibid.). However, it is highly unlikely that extraction from forests can be increased without significant ecological changes. Planting exotics or enriching the forest understorey with specific medicinal plants is certain to reduce the value of forests for biodiversity conservation as the natural species composition is then altered.

The government monopoly of forest produce is one of the critical factors keeping forest-based incomes low for years together. In Andhra Pradesh the simple act of turning over all sales proceeds from NTFP to FPCs has proven to dramatically popularize JFM because of high returns to villagers over a few years of protection (Mahapatra 2000a). Giving the FPCs a free hand to manage funds for the development of both forests as well as the village, and to market the forest produce, can tremendously improve incomes (Mahapatra 2000b). In many states, NTFP such as tendu patta and sal seeds are kept out of reach of villagers, which further reduces the returns to them, while other valuable NTFP such as bamboo are restricted, with villagers receiving only 25 per cent of the revenues from them (Khare *et al.* 2000). Commercial plantation products such as eucalyptus and cashewnuts continue to be restricted for FPCs, despite the fact that ownership rights over all NTFP in Schedule V areas are supposed to be handed over completely to panchayats and other local societies (ibid.).[10] Most scholars suggest open marketing for NTFP, rather than nationalization, to improve returns to local communities.

Apart from the legal web surrounding NTFP, people also believe that timber sales are mismanaged, resulting in products being sold at lower-than-market prices (Banerjee 2007). The lack of transparency in financial procedures at the village level does not help matters. For instance, while project funding from the World Bank introduced

[10] Schedule V areas have been demarcated in tribal-dominated districts where local people are given special rights over natural resources and autonomy in governance.

entry-point activities (such as the repair of approach roads, the construction of earthen dams and wells, and training in income-generation activities to encourage participation in the JFM programme), FPCs had little say in how the money was spent. For this reason, among others, the entry-point scheme has had a minimal impact on village development in most sites (ibid.).

Intensively Used Ecosystems

Early in the 1990s biologists across the country began to question the biological outcome of JFM. After all, the purpose of JFM was as much to restore and conserve natural forests as to revive forest-based livelihoods. It is this important question to which I now turn.

In the euphoria over achievements in forest regeneration, it is easy to forget that JFM forests are intensively used ecosystems from where people collect a variety of plant products. For instance, in a study of NTFP utilization in Midnapore district, as many as 73 per cent of plant species occurring locally were found to be used by local people and included leaves, roots, bark, seeds, fruits, shoots, and flowers of various plant species (Malhotra *et al.* 1991b). Apart from direct extraction, there is considerable disturbance to forest vegetation on account of accompanying practices, such as the use of fire for facilitating NTFP collection, livestock-grazing, and sweeping the forest floor for dry leaves and twigs (Malhotra and Poffenberger 1989, Ravindranath *et al.* 2000). The sal trees themselves are managed for subsequent pole harvests by thinning. All the emerging shoots, apart from a central one, are cut away during the initial years of growth. These managed sal stands are then clear-felled on a rotation cycle of ten years or more for the harvest of timber and poles. Cut-back operations are also carried out in between to convert the uneven sal coppice growth into an even growth to make harvesting easier (Palit 1999).[11] In addition, the sal trees are harvested round the year for their leaves during the first three years of tree growth.

In ecological terms the extraction of forest resources is considered sustainable if the harvest has no long-term deleterious effect on the

[11] A stand of trees of roughly the same size or age.

local population of the species (Hall and Bawa 1993) or upon the functioning of the natural ecosystem. The effects of intensive forest produce collection in West Bengal may include decline in density, productivity, and regeneration of the targeted plant species, depending on the part of the plant that is utilized. Intensive extraction may also result in changes in species composition, diversity, and productivity of the ecosystem or reduced density of dependent fruit-eating, pollinating, or herbivorous animal species. Apart from the intensive management of sal stands, large areas of degraded forest land have been converted to monocultural plantations of exotic species. The proportion of forests under plantations can be as high as 50 per cent, and even 92 per cent in some instances, though it may not be present in some sites. The main species are Australian acacia or akashneem, eucalyptus, and cashewnut, all of which are non-indigenous (or exotic) species. These exotic species are planted in anticipation of quick commercial returns, such as from industrial sales. In other areas the forests are managed for specialized activities such as tassar cultivation or lac production. Thus, what is known as 'forest' in general parlance is actually a patchwork of regenerating sal forest of various ages, semi-natural stands managed for various purposes, degraded land, and plantations of exotic tree species. Only a tiny proportion of the natural mixed deciduous forest originally present in the region still exists. Here I attempt to summarize all the knowledge on the ecological aspects of forest management based on field visits, talks with scientists and government officials involved in JFM, and the available published research.

Changing Landscapes

There is no doubt that the landscape of south-west West Bengal has undergone dramatic change after the initiation of JFM. Large tracts of previously degraded and barren lands have been transformed by the regeneration of sal forests from rootstock. Yet it is obvious that management practices over the last century-and-a-half, including recent JFM-related ones, may have converted the originally multi-species sal-dominated forests to the almost monocultural stands of sal that one sees today. Continuous management of the forest has led to a weeding out of species that regenerate only from seed, are shade-tolerant, and which cannot tolerate repeated cutting, fire, or grazing (Palit 1999).

Several observations made by scientists support the hypothesis that intensive human use after large-scale timber extraction from 1850–1950 has maintained the coppice sal forests in low-diversity condition. Tapan Mishra, a professor of botany, found that in areas subjected to relatively lower rates of NTFP extraction, such as in Kakrajhor in Midnapore district, the density of sal is lower and the forest is more mixed in comparison to areas under heavy extraction pressure. Another researcher (Das *et al.* 2000) also reports low densities of tree species that regenerate from seeds, such as haldu (*Adina cordifolia*) and mahua, in JFM forest stands of villages in Midnapore district.

A number of comparative botanical studies of plantations, coppice sal forests, and relatively undisturbed forests give further insight into the processes responsible for declining forest diversity in this region of West Bengal. For instance, Mishra and Banerjee (1997) found evidence that several species are not reaching the canopy in FPC-managed areas due to repeated cutting. An example: *Cleistanthus collinus*, which commonly grows as a shrub in many coppice sal stands under heavy extraction, was seen as a tree in Sutan Preservation Plot in Midnapore district, one of the sites under long-term strict protection by the forest department. Also, the density of sal trees was much lower in the preservation plot in comparison to that in coppice sal forests. Another large-scale study of human impact (Ramnarayan *et al.* undated) compared vegetation in four sites located along a gradient of disturbance in Bankura and West Midnapore districts of West Bengal. The most disturbed study site (an 8-year-old sal coppice forest) had been subjected to biomass extraction, grazing, and floor-sweeping of a number of plant products; the least disturbed was a 23-year-old sal stand where there had been little forest use. It was found that tree species diversity was highly depleted in the most disturbed sites, with only sal and tendu reaching the adult stage. In contrast, undisturbed sal stands harboured up to ten species of trees.

Yet another study in Bankura North Forest Division (Lal *et al.* 1993) studied mature trees, saplings, and seedlings at sites located in three forest ranges, each of which was administered under JFM for some years. These sites were reportedly subject to intensive forest produce extraction, grazing, and fire. The low species diversity of these sites was brought out by the results: only 9 species of mature trees were recorded over all three sites. However, high diversity was found in the seedling and sapling classes, yielding between 14 and 33 species in the understorey. These observations are highly indicative of the renewed regeneration of a variety of tree species after a prolonged period of disturbance in the study sites. My interviews with elderly people in Midnapore District confirm the perception of a general decline in tree species diversity. Particular decline was noted in the case of mahua, a species whose regeneration is known to be susceptible to grazing and fire and that appears to be under threat in other parts of India as well.[12]

Forest Product Extraction

Among the most economically important items extracted from the forest lands under JFM in south-western West Bengal are sal poles. These have regularly been in high demand for construction scaffolding. Surprisingly, despite the wide prevalence of clear-felling for poles, there is still great controversy on its ecological effects (see, for example, Chaturvedi 1992, and Guhathakurta 1992), mainly because there has been no systematic long-term study as such. The issue of sustainability of sal pole extraction has been debated at length in the pages of *Wasteland News*, an Indian journal dealing with forest management, popular among forest managers. Guhathakurta (1992) contends that the management of coppice sal forests on short rotations of 10–12 years must be sustainable since the practice has been going on for the last century and the sal stands are still producing poles. He feels that with the correct management practices, that is, the retention of standard trees and cutting multiple shoots from the correct place on sal stumps, it should be possible to maintain the current felling cycle for many years to come. Guhathakurta also believes that a longer rotation cycle may not lead to increase in productivity because, if left to age, older sal trees

[12] See chapter 5 of this book.

often develop fungal infestations in the heartwood, ultimately leading to low outputs. Sarkar and Chattopadhyay (1998) find that after coppicing, sal stumps produce lateral shoots from under the ground many of which develop into new independent trees. This causes gradual 'stump-shifting' in sal trees. They feel that this is one of the reasons sal forests have been able to survive intensive coppicing, over rotations as short as six years, in some cases, for over a century.

Several other foresters, however, are strongly opposed to the short rotation cycle and believe that after a few cycles, the productivity of the sal trees is likely to decline (Roychowdhury 1998, Chaturvedi 1992). It should be noted that in most sites, only one clear-cut has taken place so far. These authors believe that the clear-felling exposes the forest floor to micro-climatic stresses of various kinds and the trees to disease, all of which may slow down tree productivity and growth. Tapan Mishra, who has been carrying out ecological studies in forests under different management regimes, also believes that productivity of sal poles is bound to decline over the years given the large-scale export of nutrients from the system taking place with every round of pole extraction, which is not compensated by nutrient inputs in any form. Sarkar and Chattopadhyay (1998) also report loss of vigour in sal coppice forests in Midnapore district on account of repeated cutting in 5–6 year rotation cycles.

Another very obvious problem relating to sal pole production is the loss of genetic variability amongst sal trees due to the almost complete lack of regeneration from seed. Local scientists observe that, like elsewhere in India, sal seeds do germinate during the monsoon but almost none survive the long and harsh dry season. Consequently, tree reproduction depends almost totally on vegetative propagation via coppicing and stump-shifting. The fact that natural selection (through seed reproduction) has virtually come to a standstill in these sal stands means that the ability of the species to adapt to changing environmental conditions or stresses in future is highly limited. The adaptability of sal is of concern in view of forecasted climate changes. There are many possible reasons for the lack of recruitment of sal saplings from seed (i.e. reaching a stage where the sapling is likely to grow into an adult tree), such as lack of sufficient soil moisture due to the open canopy, compacted and infertile soil conditions, die-back due to fungal infections, grazing by livestock, and the trampling of young seedlings and saplings by humans and livestock.

The collection of sal seeds is yet another practice whose ecological impact is little known, although commercially it is one of the most important products in the region. Anecdotal observations suggest that both seed collection and the practices accompanying the collection process, such as the burning and sweeping of the forest floor, cause considerable loss of seeds that might regenerate (Rai 1996). Since sal seeds are highly nutritious, containing about 19 per cent fatty acids, they are likely to be a 'keystone' food resource for herbivores such as squirrels and deer during the harsh dry season (ibid.).[13] Complete removal of seeds during the mass-fruiting of sal could likely lead to drastic population decline amongst the bird, mammal, and insect species that depend on this resource. The commercial collection of sal seeds began in 1974 (ibid.) and so it may be too early to observe the impact of collection on animal diversity.

The collection of sal leaves may form the only source of cash income for many families. Leaves are collected from sal saplings up to about three years when the coppice is thick and thinning operations have not yet begun. During leaf collection the apical leaves are left on the saplings while lateral shoots are harvested for leaves.[14] In possibly the only study on the extraction of sal leaves, Deb (undated) believes that leaf collection from sal trees is not harmful to the trees, since only 5 to 8 per cent of the leaves on any tree are actually collected by a harvester, the rest being inaccessible. There is also a limit on the number of leaves a family can collect per day, this limit being imposed by the exigency of having to stitch plates overnight, in time for supply to the market before the leaves dry up. Based on simple calculations, Deb concludes that the collection of sal leaves is not likely to have a deleterious impact upon the productivity or growth of sal trees. In addition, leaves are

[13] 'Keystone' species refer to species of plants and animals whose removal from the ecosystem is likely to result in drastic decline in a number of many other species (see Terborgh 1986 for illustrations).

[14] Apical leaves: those emerging from the top of the sapling.

collected from sal saplings only upto three years of age, after which the saplings become too tall to reach. Also, the vertical growth of sal shoots is not affected, as only the lateral leaves are collected. However, Deb's contentions are not backed by systematic study. It is possible that there are long-term effects of leaf collection upon growth and mortality of young sal trees which are not evident in plain observations. In addition, there may be accompanying management practices—that he has not considered—which exacerbate the effects of sal leaf collection on young trees, such as repeated leaf manure collection, changes in micro-climate and habitat structure, and the pollarding of trees.

Land-use change from forests to plantations of exotic tree species is another factor in depleting regional-scale biodiversity in the JFM tracts. A large percentage of the forest land managed under JFM has been converted to plantations that are known to be impoverished of both animals and plants. In a comparison of coppice sal stands with plantations, only 7 plant species were found to thrive in association with exotic species as compared to 122 in coppice sal stands (Malhotra *et al.* 1991a). Again, in comparison to sal and teak plantations managed by the forest department, forests under FPCs exhibit much higher species diversity in the understorey and amongst herbs. While some exotic species allow the regeneration of native plants under them, and thus pave the way for the regeneration of native forest in degraded areas, their planting has to be followed by the encouragement of native plant species in tandem with the development of a fertile topsoil layer and microclimatic conditions conducive for germination. Intermediate levels of disturbance caused by people's extraction in managed sal stands reduce dominance amongst competing species and possibly lead to the enhancement of shrub and sapling diversity (Banerjee and Mishra 1996, Mishra and Banerjee 1997).

There are a number of other ecological changes that have occurred in JFM forests that have not been taken note of. For instance, ecologists believe that the soils in the region have gradually become infertile due to floor-sweeping for twigs and dry leaves, which would otherwise decompose and contribute to soil fertility. Ramnarayan *et al.* (undated) compared soil fertility status amongst four sites located along a gradient of disturbance use in Bankura and West Midnapore districts.

Almost all indicators of soil fertility, such as organic carbon, nitrogen, and phosphorus, were highly depleted in the heavily used sites as compared to the least used ones. In perhaps the only quantitative study of microbial ecology in the area, Mishra and his colleagues found that useful populations of fungi, actinomycetes, and bacterial counts were generally higher in the soils of sal and teak plantations in comparison to those of *Acacia auriculiformes* and eucalyptus plantations (Mishra *et al.* 1993). This study shows that there may be an adverse impact of exotic trees on soil properties and also that there is a general depletion of soil flora and fauna caused by leaf litter extraction and clear-felling over the years. However, termites (insects of the order Isoptera) are common in coppice sal forests and appear to have taken over the functions of decomposition in this region (T.K. Mishra, pers. comm.).

The study of the ecological factors that influence productivity in the understorey (shrub layer) of coppice sal stands is also extremely relevant to management since the shrub layer is most accessible to people and utilized for livestock fodder. T.K. Mishra and his colleagues have studied the influence of strict forest protection on the net productivity of biomass in the understorey of regenerated coppice sal forest in four different FPCs in Midnapore district. It appears that the annual productivity in FPC-managed areas may actually be slightly higher than that in strictly-protected areas that are free of extraction (Mishra 1998). One of the reasons for this counterintuitive result is that due to sustained extraction the dominance of certain fast-growing understorey shrubs is reduced. In the absence of such 'disturbance', a single species, *Combretum*, begins to spread aggressively in the understorey, outcompeting other saplings and shrubs. *Combretum* is also a species that is preferred for fuelwood by local people, and that may contribute to its control in FPC-managed areas.

The impact of canopy cover on understorey productivity was also studied by T.K. Mishra and colleagues in one of the most comprehensive ecological studies in the region, covering 225 FPCs in southwest Bengal (Centre for Natural Studies, undated). It appears that moderately open canopy cover in the range of 25–30 per cent may allow maximum productivity amongst herbs and shrubs in the understorey. This implies that more open canopy conditions, as compared to that inside a natural forest, would be necessary to maintain a productive understorey. Thus, allowing sal trees to grow back to their natural sizes might force a trade-off in the amount of plant biomass that can be extracted from the forest understorey.

Invasive species, or weeds as they are more commonly called, have their own role to play in altering the habitat for wild animal and birds in this region. Two weed species of South American origin have pervaded these forests, namely *Lantana camara* and *Eupatorium spp*. (T.K. Mishra, pers. comm.). In some areas, these weeds have become so common that village people have begun to collect them for use as fuel. These species appear to invade mostly forests that are disturbed and plantation areas that tend to be more open. They proceed to gradually 'move in' from the edges, such as from forest trails. In a comparative study of plantation types in the study area, Mishra and Banerjee (1997) report that *Lantana* invades teak plantations more frequently than sal plantations that are managed by the forest department.

The adverse effects of exotic weed species on local biodiversity and productivity are well known and documented the world over. Invasion by exotic weeds can drastically (and often, irretrievably) change the local species composition of plants and habitat conditions for fauna, and result in local species extinction in the long run. It has been observed in many parts of India that no other plant species can grow under the thick shrubbery of *Lantana camara* (pers. obs.). The continued spread of these exotics may result in large-scale habitat deterioration which will likely affect both local biodiversity and the productivity of these forests for various NTFPs. The reasons for the relative commonness of these weeds across different management regimes could be related to soil conditions, the degree of exposure of the forest floor to the sun, the degree of habitat disturbance, competition with other shrubs, and the allelopathic effects of other plant species.

In terms of direct impact upon the species whose parts are collected commercially, I found that apart from a few plant products there has been no study of any plant species out of the nearly 200 that are exploited in the study area. Long-term researchers think that *Rauwolfia serpentina*, chiraita (*Swertia chirayita*), and kalmegh are in danger of extinction from the region, apart from many other species. Discussions with people at the Murakata FPC and experienced forest department personnel revealed that there is a general agreement on the decline in the former abundance of medicinal plants in the forest over the years.

Empty Forests

There is no doubt that, over the years, animal diversity has shown an increase due to the regeneration of coppice sal forests in the study area. In particular, small mammal diversity is reported to have improved. Wild dogs, pangolins, jackals, hares, and hyenas have reappeared in many areas (T.K. Mishra and Debal Ray, pers. comm.). Talks with people at Murakata village revealed that butterfly diversity has also increased over the years of protection. One of the prominent changes since the improvement of tree cover in Midnapore district is the appearance of herds of wild elephants in the area, reported to be migrating from Dalma Hills in the adjoining state of Bihar. The elephants appear to be encouraged by the presence of tree cover that provides shelter to them during the daylight hours.[15]

On the other hand it is also clear that the forests of the sal belt are still highly depleted of wildlife that would normally exist in a typical dry deciduous forest. Several deer species that are common denizens of dry deciduous forests in other parts of India are conspicuous by their absence, such as cheetal, sambar, and mouse-deer. Large carnivores such as tiger and leopards are not reported anywhere in these parts, which is understandable given the lack of prey. Birds that are dependent on standing/fallen dead trees, such as woodpeckers, and those that require tall forest stands, such as hornbills, are missing from the regenerating forests and plantations.

The lack of any sizeable mammal population in these managed forests can be ascribed partly to the practice of clear-felling. Clear-felling is likely to have adverse effects on faunal diversity because it opens up the canopy for long periods. Further, cutback and multiple shoot-cutting operations reduce the complex vertical structure of a sal-dominated mixed forest to a highly simplified stand of uniformly-sized trees

[15] In the absence of either compensatory or alleviatory measures by the department against crop-raiding , the elephant problem ironically led village people in some FPCs to begin cutting their regenerated forests.

of mainly sal, which ultimately resembles a plantation. It is well known that the simplification of forest structure (both in terms of numbers of tree and shrub species and of vegetation layers) drastically reduces the niches available to insects, birds, mammals, and reptiles (Greenberg *et al.* 1997, Thiollay 1995, Terborgh 1998).

The short rotations that are in place for timber cutting do not allow tree species to attain reproductive status and to produce fruit and seed (Terborgh 1998). Given that fruits and seeds are important food resources that support wildlife, the lack of reproductively mature trees is likely to cause a depletion in animal populations over time. Further, large-seeded trees that provide much of the food for wildlife in intact forests are unable to disperse and regenerate in large forest gaps that are created during clear-felling operations (ibid.). Therefore, fruit-feeding birds and mammals are especially vulnerable to population decline in such intensively managed areas because they need a diversity of plants.[16] The local decline of species of seed dispersers and pollinators due to lack of food resources, in turn, is likely to lead to spiralling impoverishment of the ecosystem in the long term.

In a situation where rural economies are so heavily dependent on forest products, it is surprising that there has been very little study of the impact of various management practices on the floral and faunal diversity of JFM forests. The sparse scientific literature available is riddled with problems associated with inadequate experimental design, and interpretation of data (see Shahabuddin 2003 for details). Even the Economics and Environment Research Network in India, though set up for this purpose, has failed to establish robust scientific studies towards this goal that could prescribe more exact management practices.[17] In the absence of systematically collected data, few concrete strategies can be derived for long-term forest management with specific goals.

The other problem in trying to delineate management practices is the lack of consensus amongst various stakeholders, namely the

[16] Surveys show that fruit-eaters are more diverse in forests harbouring larger numbers of tree and shrub species per unit area.

[17] For instance, success in forest regeneration (Ravindranath *et al.* 2000).

local communities and forest department, on the specific management goals for each FPC. For instance, management goals can be defined in many different ways. Some goals can be to maintain the harvest of a particular NTFP, to maximize ecosystem-level biodiversity, or to optimize sal pole production. Only with a management focus can suitable micro-planning be done, utilizing the existing knowledge of the local ecology amongst local communities and researchers. As mentioned earlier, most of the micro-planning undertaken under JFM revolves around timber extraction, and there is little mention of the need to optimize biodiversity values. The optimization of plant biodiversity would also better satisfy the day-to-day needs of the local people for diverse forest products. As can be gleaned from the available biological data, there is a clear trade-off between growing and maintaining straight sal poles for timber sale and maintaining a diverse set of trees and diverse shrub layer which yields more products for local use.

Since 1996 local NGOs have attempted to involve the people of a few villages in Midnapore district in vegetation-monitoring exercises designed by scientists (Sarkar, Roy, and Yadav 2000). The monitoring exercises were aimed at assessing the biodiversity of the forest area under protection and the status of commercial species. In these two villages, the villagers are monitoring their forests regularly at six-month intervals with the help of local NGOs, so that the effects of forest management can be ascertained. However, there remain several questions with respect to the sustainability of these monitoring exercises on a longer time-frame and over a wider area. For instance, will these communities possess the ability and interest to continue the monitoring on their own after the initial few years?

The Road Ahead

Joint Forest Management may represent one of the largest exercises in the decentralization of natural resource management in India. Given the high pressure on forest resources it has not been easy to implement it in India and the result has been a patchwork of successes and failures. While there has been considerable success in regenerating trees over wide swathes of degraded landscapes, stalling soil erosion, and rejuvenating hydrological cycles, JFM has not led to lasting local empowerment of local institutions, either economically or institutionally. So the long-term commitment of local people to JFM remains questionable. Moreover, the biodiversity conservation value of JFM forest tracts is doubtful. JFM forests are intensively used and managed ecosystems, barring the occasional case, that protect only a small proportion of regional flora and fauna. The long-term viability of the sal-enriched forest stands themselves is under question given the felling cycle that is in place, and the almost complete lack of regeneration from seed.

The way ahead is clear. There has been enough research on the reasons why JFM has not been able to fully achieve its mandate *vis-à-vis* institutional and financial sustainability. FPCs must become statutory bodies with clear linkages to local formal self-government, particularly panchayats, and with clearly laid-out rights and responsibilities for both parties in the agreement. The functioning of FPCs in terms of micro-planning, forest boundary demarcation, and financial management has to be open to local participation and public scrutiny. The marketing and value addition of forest products, open sales, and efficient marketing at the local level must be priorities if local residents are to benefit the most from JFM, as they were meant to.

Long-term biological conservation in JFM areas may not be a central concern, but maximizing it is important for supporting rural livelihoods given the linkages between NTFP diversity and forest diversity. Local diversity can be increased by putting aside and protecting small patches of natural forests in the form of sacred groves and preservation plots in every district, so that a greater proportion of regional diversity can be sustained. Regional tree diversity will contribute to the long-term viability of both forests as well as rural livelihoods. Without such pockets of preservation the seed sources for many of the native tree species may be lost forever. Additionally, a few large trees of each species should be marked for preservation in each FPC until they begin to flower and fruit. In fact I found this practice still prevalent in one of the villages I visited, where an old sal tree has been preserved as a 'sacred tree'. Greater diversity within JFM forests can be achieved by the establishment of a selective logging regime instead of the clear-felling operations currently in place. This would ensure that while there is a certain degree of openness in the canopy, a richer and more multilayered forest can exist that will harbour more plant and animal species. However, stopping clear-felling will require considerable political will on the part of the government, considering the astronomical loss of revenues from the sal poles alone. In some cases, extraction pressures on various forest products by local people may need to be managed locally, but this is possible only through their greater involvement in management planning. Locals already recognize the importance of maintaining plant diversity in their forest patches but seem trapped by the overwhelming mandate of the forest department for generating cash revenue. Ultimately, the biology of these vital forests has to be brought back into focus; the revenue lens has long obscured it.

7

India Ecodevelopment Project: A Fragmented Legacy

The 1980s saw a slew of participatory conservation ideas implemented all over the world. There was a distinct shift in global thinking about biological conservation: it was no longer simply about protecting species from extinction but also protecting ecosystem services to humans that are economically quantifiable (van Schaik and Rijksen 2002). This was manifest in numerous efforts to synergize development and conservation, such as in the form of International Conservation and Development Projects (ICDPs). The Indian government was not far behind. The last decade of the twentieth century saw rather innovative efforts on the part of the Indian government to synergize the needs of economic development with those of conservation. Among the prominent programmes of the Indian government in this direction was the India Eco-development Project (IEDP).[1] Framed on the ICDP model, ecodevelopment aimed to improve conservation in protected areas through local participation of and increased benefit to the people living in and around them. The two major objectives of ecodevelopment as enunciated in its project document (World Bank 1996) were to, first, 'improve the capacity of protected area managers to conserve biodiversity and to increase opportunities for local participation in PA management

[1] Hereafter referred to as 'ecodevelopment'.

activities and decisions.' And second, 'to reduce negative impacts of local people on biodiversity and conversely, of PAs on local people.'

The ecodevelopment project ranks among the most ambitious consevation projects ever undertaken in India, apart from Project Tiger. The total project financing amounted to $67 million (Rs 300 crores) during the official project period from 1994 to 2004.[2] Geographically, too, the project was spread widely, being implemented in nine PAs in nine different states for varying durations: Buxa Tiger Reserve (West Bengal), Gir National Park (Gujarat), Ranthambhore Tiger Reserve (Rajasthan), Rajiv Gandhi National Park (Karnataka), Palamau Tiger Reserve (Jharkhand), Pench Tiger Reserve (Madhya Pradesh), Kalakad-Mundanthurai Tiger Reserve (Tamil Nadu), Periyar Tiger Reserve (Kerala), and Great Himalayan National Park (Himachal Pradesh).[3]

Through its emphasis on local benefit and participation, ecodevelopment represented a considerable departure from the traditional exclusionary norms of conservation prevalent in India at the time. For the first time local conflicts between the needs of people and biodiversity were brought to the forefront rather than wished away. The programme was greeted optimistically by conservationists: finally, the scope of protected area management had officially been widened to include local interests that had long been neglected. The emphasis was admittedly on the need for preserving large mammal species that required large contiguous habitats, a goal that necessitated shifting out extraction pressures, particularly from core areas and national parks. Yet ecodevelopment stayed focused on developing robust village institutions that would act as interest groups for conservation inside and around

[2] The Global Environment Facility provided $ 20 million (Rs 90 crores or 30 per cent of total) and the remaining amount was co-financed through the International Development Association (42 per cent), the Government of India (8 per cent), state governments (13 per cent), and project beneficiaries (8 per cent).

[3] In two of these PAs, the Great Himalayan National Park in North India and the Kalakad-Mundanthurai Tiger Reserve in South India, the World Bank-aided Forestry Research Education and Extension Project was initially undertaken from 1994 to 1999, overlapping with the ecodevelopment project, to experiment with the community-centred biodiversity conservation approach.

PAs. Detailed procedures were worked out for engendering consensual village development that would move pressures away from forests and inculcate responsibility for ecosystem protection and restoration among local people. Community development and income generation schemes would be planned together with local people and one-time household benefits would be equitably distributed.

Ten years later, the ecodevelopment programme had left little impact in most of its project sites. The scattered available evaluations revealed that most of the official project aims remained largely unfulfilled (see Karlsson 1999, Baviskar 2003, Shah *et al.* 2002, Woodman 2002, Sethi 2004a, b, c, d, e, f, Das 2007, Varma 2007). In most sites people–management relations seemed to be as embittered at the end of the ten-year period as at the beginning. Only a few of the sites had developed effective village institutions for undertaking conservation work in the long term, such as the Periyar Tiger Reserve and the Kalakad-Mundanthurai Tiger Reserve. Even in these two sites the expected impact fell far short of the original target group in terms of social reach (Uniyal and Zacharias 2001). Many of the income-generation schemes started for local villages were far from financially sustainable by the end of the project period while most had closed down a few years later (Gubbi *et al.* 2009). While the ideas behind the initiation of ecodevelopment had been thought through in detail, the implementation had left a lot to be desired because the local staff of the forest department had not been trained adequately. Many remained unresponsive to the need for inclusiveness. Above all, there had been minimal independent monitoring of either the socio-economic or biological impact of ecodevelopment in most of the project sites, as would have been expected in an intervention of this scale (ibid.). Many conservationists felt that ecodevelopment actually had a destructive impact upon park management due to the mismanagement of funds that were used more for infrastructure development than for creating village-level rapport and economic independence.[4] Clearly, here was one more instance of a key component of the Indian state, the forest department, subverting yet again what could have been an important intervention in favour of biodiversity in the country.

[4] *Daily News and Analysis* report on new intervention by the World Bank.

So where did the ecodevelopment project go wrong? In this chapter I attempt to piece together the evidence that helps explain why such a well-planned and well-funded scheme had just a fraction of the impact it was meant to achieve across the country.

Operating Principles

Operationally, the crux of ecodevelopment was the creation and sustenance of village-level institutions that would be the anchor at the local level for reducing local dependence on natural resources and increasing local participation. Several different institutions, such as ecodevelopment committees (EDCs), Forest Protection Committees (FPCs), village forest committees (VFCs), self-help groups, and small savings and credit groups were planned to be formed in each of the nine project sites. While EDCs and FPCs were formed of entire villages or panchayats, self-help groups and small savings and credit groups were to be formed of smaller and occupationally homogeneous groups within villages.

Village-based groups such as EDCs were sought to be established with a bank fund made up of money contributed by village households (25 per cent) and from the project funds (75 per cent). From this sum, low-interest loans were to be provided to people to initiate microenterprises of various kinds, and community-level works for improving agricultural and forest productivity. The activities were aimed primarily at reducing dependence on forests for both income and consumption. It was thought that the collected fund would be embellished continually by people and set aside as a long-term corpus that could be managed by them after the term of the project.

Ecodevelopment was envisaged to work through a process of micro-planning to decide the exact development activities (from a list of indicative activities) at the village level, a process that would be carried out consensually between villagers and local forest officers. Given the historically strained relation between foresters and local villagers, considerable emphasis was given to the process of rapport-building through informal means. PA authorities and village communities would agree upon any proposed investment based on the likelihood of it resulting in measurable improvement in biodiversity.

Protection would then be enforced through a system of 'reciprocal commitments', which meant that villagers would voluntarily help forest protection and reduce their dependence on forests in exchange for development and alternative income generation.

It was planned that village groups would undertake alternative livelihoods and environmental improvement, and also benefit from household-level interventions. Income generation included activities such as bee-keeping, tailoring, repair shops, tourism, vermiculture, and tree nurseries—as appropriate to the local setting—all alternatives to forest-dependent livelihoods. Environmental improvement activities were more in the nature of community-level benefits and envisioned as those that would improve agricultural productivity. They were meant to give indirect benefits for forest restoration, such as watershed management, fuelwood plantations, and crop protection measures. The provision of household-level benefits was aimed at reducing the use of fuelwood for domestic cooking and heating by providing smokeless stoves, liquefied petroleum gas (LPG) cylinders, and solar energy installations. The improvement of protected area management was another important goal of ecodevelopment through the reduction of crop damage using modern techniques, the restoration of degraded landscapes, the development of park infrastructure, and the training of PA staff.

Lack of Ownership

The emphasis on village institutions as the via media for undertaking ecodevelopment activities meant that considerable investment had to be made in developing both the institutions and establishing collaborative relationships with park managers. However, evaluations soon after the beginning of the project revealed a widespread lack of feeling of ownership of the project by local people, the immediate beneficiaries. This can be ascribed to several reasons. First, the formation of EDCs and VFCs largely ignored existing institutions such as the panchayats and *mahila mandals* (Chhatre and Saberwal 2006): mostly the EDCs were created from scratch. In the Kailadevi Wildlife Sanctuary the existing conservation institutions, such as the *kulhadi bandh panchayat*, were subverted by the forest department through a process of takeover and gradually destroyed (Das 2007).

Another reason for the lack of involvement was that marginalized groups were often left out of the ecodevelopment planning process. Economically marginalized groups are known to be most dependent on forest resources both for income generation as well as household consumption. Equitable participation in EDCs across different economic classes was limited by making membership conditional on a 25 per cent financial contribution from each household. Numerous families belonging to the poorest strata of society could not even afford to pay the initial contributions in Gir or Pench (Shah *et al.* 2002, Woodman 2002), leading to several families being excluded in the initial stages of the programme. In Gir this included some of the Maldhari families, a nomadic group most dependent on park resources for grazing livestock (Shah *et al.* 2002). In Buxa only registered families were considered for participation in the ecodevelopment programme while others with no pattas or those living in forest villages were essentially left out (Karlsson 1999).[5]

Some other schemes, too, that intended to reduce pressure on firewood, such as the provision of LPG stoves and cylinders, became a failure (Shah *et al.* 2002). By the nature of the scheme taken up, the poorest people who were most dependent on firewood for cooking were least able to avail of the scheme as they could barely afford to refill LPG cylinders regularly. A survey in Periyar showed that only 42 per cent of the beneficiaries were still using their LPG cylinders two years after the end of the project period. Most people (58 per cent) cited unaffordability as the reason while others cited difficulties in transport (Gubbi *et al.* 2009). Another evaluation in Gir reveals that there was minimal adoption of LPG cylinders among the grazing community of Maldharis. This was mainly for cultural reasons but also because of a lack of commitment towards forest conservation (Varma 2007).

However, there were cases where an imaginative choice of low investment activities enabled a larger number of people to participate in ecodevelopment activities such as in the Great Himalayan National Park during the post-project period. For example, a

[5] Forest villages were established by the British government for forest labour activities such as logging and planting; they do not have official rights over land even now.

successful vermiculture-cum-composting scheme was initiated that required little to no investment on the part of the local people. This had begun to yield reasonable profits for the groups involved by 2004 (Pandey 2004, Sanjeeva Pandey, pers. comm.). Similarly, in Periyar small financial contributions by the park management enabled local EDCs to set up profit-making business enterprises along the route of the annual Sabarimala pilgrimage, equipped with solid waste management and cooking facilities (Uniyal and Zacharias 2001). In Gir some landed families in revenue villages successfully developed vegetable gardens as a supplementary income-generating option (Varma 2007).

Experience shows that the internal homogeneity of EDCs in terms of caste, economic activity, and economic stratum is important in determining the success of an ecodevelopment activity (Uniyal and Zacharias 2001, Pandey 2004, Annamalai 2004). Occupationally homogeneous groups have similar concerns and constraints and are likely to be able to relate better to each other. The formation of smaller sub-village groups for specific activities and schemes also made it practicable for members to attend meetings frequently and thus enabled closer co-ordination amongst them (Pandey 2004). Good communication within groups through frequent meetings and focused activities enhanced a feeling of involvement and cohesion. This could be behind the relative success and longevity of some of the EDCs in Periyar and small savings groups in the Great Himalayan National Park. In Periyar a programme to empower small agriculturists and their organization into a co-operative enabled them to get better prices in the market and led to substantially increased income (Uniyal and Zacharias 2001).

An important reason for the limited success in the earliest stages of ecodevelopment was the failure to consult local people. Frequently, activities were taken up without prior consultations with them, as had been envisaged through the micro-planning process (Woodman 2002, Baviskar 2003, Bandyopadhyay 2004). Examples of such activities were bee-keeping, the distribution of smokeless chulhas and Jersey cows in Buxa (Karlsson 1999), and the distribution of LPG stoves in Gir (Shah *et al.* 2002, Sethi 2004c). In such cases the perception of the people was that although they were consulted on the types and means of activities to take up, final decisions were effectively taken by the officials of the forest department (Shah *et al.* 2002). Often, the result of this non-participatory approach was that the eco-development activities initiated were not suited to local ecological conditions. For instance, biogas plants and orange orchards, which require heavy inputs of water, were initiated in Pench, where these activities were ecologically inappropriate due to low rainfall (Bandyopadhyay 2004). In Pench, where tubewells and pumps were asked for by villagers, bunds were constructed because of a shortfall in funds. These did not serve the purpose of providing water during the dry season and therefore were not maintained by the villagers (Woodman 2002).

The other result of a top-down approach was that many income generation activities never took off the ground, particularly since local managements were unable to match them to the existing skills available in specific villages. In the Rajiv Gandhi National Park 'a remarkably uniform set of activities was planned for each village, selected from the "indicative list" of income-generating and resource substitution activities in the initial concept plan' (Mahanty 2002). In fact in the Gir Protected Area, possible income-generating activities were identified only towards the tail-end of the project period (Shah *et al.* 2002, Varma 2007).

However, in the Great Himalayan National Park significant progress was made in developing the funds of women's savings and credit groups (WSCGs) (Pandey 2004). For example, by 2003, 95 WSCGs consisting of 1050 members had a collective fund of Rs 530,000 through monthly collections, income generation activities as well as PA contributions (Pandey 2004). Because their own savings were loaned by the women for production activities, the recovery of small loans was almost complete (Annamalai 2004, Pandey 2004). In Periyar, too, managements reported the successful creation of a community development fund of almost Rs 2 crores by EDCs towards the end of the project period through tourism-based activities (Sethi 2004e). Here, surveys indicated that 58 per cent of income generation benefits were still used and maintained two years after the project was over (Gubbi *et al.* 2009). The relative success in Periyar and Kalakad-Mundanthurai can be ascribed to greater delegation of powers to village members in decision-making over fund utilization. In contrast, in Gir people reported difficulties even in getting financial reports from

EDC presidents (Shah *et al.* 2002). In the Gir National Park and Great Himalayan National Park, EDC members found themselves with a limited role once micro-plans were finalized and the time came to organize the supply of various commodities for distribution through contracts (Shah *et al.* 2002, Chhatre and Saberwal 2006). In Gir National Park important issues, such as the supply prices of items required for ecodevelopment activities, were not sorted out in the initial stages of micro-planning. These discrepancies led to much distrust between the PA managers and village groups. There was also a lack of proper information imparted by field staff on basic project norms such as the scale of financial allocation to each household from PA management, leading to much confusion and fears of corruption. In contrast the innovative joint account system for VFCs in Kalakad-Mundanthurai, involving the joint operation of accounts by the VFC chairman and member-secretary (from the local forest department), was found to greatly increase people's sense of involvement and participation in ecodevelopment (Annamalai 2004).

Closely related to the issue of financial transparency is good reporting and the conduct of regular audits of village funds. Capacity has to be built for this so that EDCs don't suffer on account of delays in decision-making by PA management. Nor should village funds get utilized without the knowledge of PA management. However, a perusal of correspondence between the World Bank and field managements indicates that even until late 2003 none of the project sites had reported much progress with this aspect.[6] In most of the PAs fund collection for EDCs at the village level was completed only in late 2003, almost at the tail end of the project. A lot of emphasis has been placed on refining the concept of the village development fund, particularly in relation to guidelines for using it as a revolving fund at various levels such as for PAs, EDCs, and eco-units. This had been envisaged as the main source of financial sustainability after the project came to an end (World Bank 1996). Further, sustenance of the momentum of activity in the ecodevelopment programme necessitated quick release of funds to user groups once a micro-plan/given activity was decided upon. In

[6] World Bank 2003 a, b, c, d, e, f.

the Gir National Park, in particular, the delayed flow of funds was found to be one of the major reasons for waning interest in ecodevelopment at the village level (Shah *et al.* 2002). However, in Kalakad-Mundanthurai there was a direct flow of funds to the VFC accounts, rather than being channelled through the PA management, a procedure that led to elimination of delays (Annamalai 2002). In Kalakad-Mundanthurai the extent of involvement of village groups and pace of activities was relatively fast, as also the loan recovery percentage (Annamalai 2004).

Surprisingly, tourism was not seriously explored as an income-generating activity for villages in most of the project sites, though this would likely have brought in most of the profits for EDCs. The development of tourism is particularly important since income-generating activities based on it have a lower damage potential for forest structure and diversity and are relatively easier to monitor and manage. Easy-to-implement tourism strategies, such as the purchase and running of tourist vehicles, the employment of local nature guides for trekking, and running small co-operative lodges and eateries, were never explored. However, there was an exception in Periyar where the EDCs today set up food stalls for religious pilgrims visiting the Sabarimala temple (Sethi 2004e, Uniyal and Zacharias 2001). Yet it was obvious by the end of the project period that tourism had hardly been given the kind of importance it deserved. Only 0.8 per cent of local households were benefited by nature-guiding in Periyar at the end of the project period (Gubbi *et al.* 2009). Similarly, co-operative schemes such as the formation of local LPG supply companies, which could have brought in revenues for EDCs and simultaneously contributed to forest conservation, were never thought of.

Given the lack of feeling of participation in decision-making relating to the project and low success in generating alternative incomes, it is not surprising that even after several years of the project there was little commitment among villagers to forest protection activities in most of the project sites. In the absence of income alternatives for local people, little or no adherence or follow-up on reciprocal commitments could have been expected. In Gir, some Maldhari settlements continued to have a substantial impact on the PA even during the final year

Illustr. 12: The overexploitation of leaves and branches for use as livestock fodder has contributed to widespread forest degradation in the Sariska Tiger Reserve. Ecodevelopment sought to resolve such conflicts between human use and biodiversity conservation in protected areas, but was largely unsuccessful.

of the project and several years later (Shah *et al.* 2002, Varma 2007). The Rabha tribals of Buxa were forced to patrol and give up their extraction of forest produce at a time when ecodevelopment activities had not yet taken off in the area (Karlsson 1999). The restrictions on forest access that the ecodevelopment project entailed were looked on with suspicion for similar reasons in the Great Himalayan National Park, Pench, and the Rajiv Gandhi National Park, a situation not helped by the lack of transparency (Bandyopadhyay 2004, Baviskar 2003, Mahanty 2002). In fact ecodevelopment initially met some resistance from local people who believed they might lose their rights over land or access to forest resources without appropriate compensation (Shah *et al.* 2002, Baviskar 2003). In the Great Himalayan National Park, political kinships frequently took over the project money and led to partisan development activities favouring a few influential groups over others (Chhatre and Saberwal 2006). In Periyar, none of the crop protection measures initially invested in by the forest department were maintained by local communities, possibly because of the expense or their lack of effectiveness (Gubbi *et al.* 2009). In the Rajiv Gandhi National Park it is believed that the socio-economic interventions carried out under the ecodevelopment project did not make any real impact on livelihoods, so that the basic attitude of people towards the park remained unchanged (K.U. Karanth 2002).

The traditional attitudes of PA staff towards villagers have been thought to be a major constraint in the successful implementation of ecodevelopment: working in a co-operative way with village groups is very different from the purely punitive role in forest protection. Close observation revealed that villagers and the forest department were shackled by hegemonic power relations (Woodman 2002). Even in Periyar the hierarchical structure of the forest department has not internalized the basic concepts of ecodevelopment (Uniyal and Zacharias 2001). Woodman (2002) quotes forest staff: 'Guards with patrolling and EDC responsibilities are often in a position where they spend their days chasing the very people that they sit with for EDC meetings in the evenings!'

The effectiveness of ecodevelopment was further constrained by the power relations within park managements because all too often they do not allow feedback on project processes from field staff to the highest decision-making tier. Given their daily interaction with local people and supervision of development schemes, field staff often have useful insights into how projects function. However, interviews with field functionaries found that their views were not being taken adequately into account in the planning of interventions (ibid.).

There were other reasons for the near failure of ecodevelopment in most of the project sites. Awareness about ecodevelopment was at a premium, resulting in rumours and misinformation at the village level. In the Rajiv Gandhi National Park, villages and local voluntary groups had varying perceptions of what the project was about: these related to poor communication and information links with NGOs and the forest department (Mahanty 2002). Woodman (2002) reports a similar situation in Pench even at the tail end of the project period and Varma (2007) for women in Gir. Periyar was among the places where beneficiaries had a narrow view of ecodevelopment, though partially correct: that its primary aim was to reduce the negative impact of people on parks (Gubbi *et al.* 2009). At the other extreme, in the Rajiv Gandhi National Park many of the local villagers expressed complete lack of awareness of the ecodevelopment project even after several years of project initiation (Sethi 2004a).

Forest functionaries themselves were often not clear about the objectives of the ecodevelopment project. Questionnaire surveys indicated that while EDC secretaries (forest functionaries) felt village development was the primary aim, decreasing forest dependence was a secondary aim of IEDP (Woodman 2002). During an interview with a senior officer in 2004 at the Project Tiger directorate the officer said: 'Ecodevelopment is unsuccessful because we have created a one-way street—we keep giving doles and the villagers have got used to taking them.'

Obviously, even high-level officers were not completely clear about the objectives of the ecodevelopment project and often sceptical of its potential benefits. This was symptomatic of the official view of ecodevelopment: it was seen more as a way to hand out doles to local villagers who had lost access to PA resources rather than as a way to build bridges with them for better PA management or robust institutional partnerships. Discussions with field staff in Gir also revealed that they were not fully convinced of the efficacy of a project such as ecodevelopment and this affected their motivation to establish relationships of trust with local groups (Shah *et al.* 2002).

Further, the transmission of project ideas, ethos, and methodology was severely limited due to lack of effective mechanisms for concept transmission (Woodman 2002). The training of forest staff was fragmentary and when staff were trained appropriately they were not always posted into the appropriate roles. Some were transferred out during the project cycle, leading to discontinuities in the process of rapport-building. People in the villages often saw this as yet another rural development scheme because the linkages of planned activities with forest conservation were not always clear or emphasized (ibid.). In the initial stages of the project at the Gir National Park, in an attempt to increase the attractiveness of the project, the entire scheme was showcased by the intermediary NGO as one that would primarily provide household-level benefits rather than as one aimed at community-oriented development and conservation (Shah *et al.* 2002, Sethi 2004a, Bandyopadhyay 2004). This approach went against the concept of community-oriented consensual action right from the discussion stages.

However, some of the project sites laid great emphasis on awareness-creation and educational activities in the target villages (Annamalai 2002). Kalakad-Mundanthurai had an active educational programme with high levels of village participation. During the awareness programmes biodiversity conservation was linked deliberately to visible symbols such as sources of drinking and irrigation water; the concept of conservation of a 'river-sanctuary' was widely propagated where the importance of the sanctuary-to-town water supply was emphasized (Dutt 2003). This led to a high level of awareness among the target villages regarding the aims and objectives of the ecodevelopment project and to an informal creation of consensus regarding the need for a project of this nature.

Floundering PA Management

The impact of the programme was further weakened in several of the sites due to rather weak PA administration. Many Indian PAs still exist without a rationalization of their boundaries or final settlement of the rights of people living within and on their peripheries (Pabla 2005). In such a situation, interventions under the project are likely to be ineffective because, if the status and rights of people *vis-à-vis* the PA remain unclear, the identification of communities for intervention is difficult and relationships between PA staff and local communities continue to be conflicted. This is true whether one considers recognized communities with formal rights or 'unrecognized' groups without formal land or access rights. In the Rajiv Gandhi National Park, for instance, the ecodevelopment project was initiated in an atmosphere of uncertainty over modes of conservation and the question of tribals' rights to live in and use the forests within (Mahanty 2002). In Pench the World Bank had proposed bringing all the disparately managed forest areas, that is, wildlife sanctuary, national park, and reserved forest, under a single administrative control. But those steps had yet to be undertaken even at the tail end of the programme period. As another example, final notification for Palamau was yet to be issued in November 2003 despite this having been recommended strongly by donor agencies right from the start.

While ecodevelopment in fringe villages around a protected area can potentially reduce pressures on forests, such programmes can turn out to be unsustainable if other government departments are working at cross-purposes with the aims of ecodevelopment in the larger landscape surrounding it. Through ecodevelopment, PA management was supposed to develop linkages with other government agencies such as revenue, animal husbandry, agriculture, and finance through the formation of regional committees (World Bank 1996), so that PA issues could be integrated into regional planning. Fodder development, water conservation, and afforestation are activities that can be taken up under a large number of other existing development schemes and can be dovetailed with ecodevelopment programmes. For example, in Ranthambhore significant progress was made by the PA management towards building linkages with other government programmes, including famine relief, during the ecodevelopment project. In Gir a regional planning committee incorporating state secretaries from the departments of revenue, animal husbandry, agriculture, and finance was constituted by the government of Gujarat. However, these committees lost much of their significance soon after the end of the project period. In the Great Himalayan National Park much larger development forces were at work, whose significance to ecodevelopment was not evident even to the park managers. A proposed hydel project over the river Parbati threatened to take away a major chunk of valuable habitat for endangered species within the national park, even as ecodevelopment and village relocation were being implemented to reduce extractive pressures (Chhatre and Saberwal 2006).

Park Management Institutions

In terms of park management it was planned that ecodevelopment would use and build upon existing organizational structure rather than create new positions. The state forest departments felt that the assignment of eco-development responsibilities would not adversely impact the adequacy of staffing of existing non-project conservation activities (World Bank 1996). This was because the PA staff was expected to become more productive due to 'greater accountability and increased public profile' (ibid.), implying that currently PAs may be overstaffed and their field staff under-worked.[7] In the end, in most of the sites, existing staff were diverted to ecodevelopment functions either as an additional responsibility (as in Gir, Shah *et al.* 2002), and only sometimes as an exclusive function, as in Kalakad-Mundanthurai (Annamalai 2002). The diversion of existing staff to ecodevelopment thus further reduced the staff strength for routine functions, already depleted in most cases.

Experience showed that having exclusive staff for ecodevelopment activities in some of the sites greatly increased the efficacy of the project at the local level (ibid.). This is because exclusive responsibility allowed far more frequent interactions between PA staff and villagers, and more effective follow-up on specific activities, many of which were quite complex to begin with. It also allowed PA staff to focus on duties that went closely with co-operative management, rather than having to fulfil two conflicting roles necessitated by forest protection on the one hand and village-level interactive activities on the other (ibid.). Further, several existing management staff who took up the task of ecodevelopment in a focused manner in some PAs have contributed substantially to the success of the project and have developed specific skills and expertise that they originally did not have (Annamalai 2004). The work of rapport-building with local communities and awareness-creation requires a certain level of sensitivity and training

[7] This goes against my observations of the field duties of guards and foresters, who are mostly highly overworked, uninsured, and underpaid, and do not get many of the basic facilities required to carry out their duties, nor any compensation in the event of injury.

that can only be built up with experience. Though the World Bank strongly recommended that the positions initiated under the ecodevelopment project should be sustained even after the project period, so that the approaches at the local level remain consistent through time, the posts were discontinued in most sites. In Gir, where staff were not exclusively devoted to ecodevelopment activities, the micro-planning process was greatly constrained by dilution of the protection role and lack of adequate time in the field (Shah *et al.* 2002).

Hard Lessons

Ecodevelopment represented a considerable departure from traditional norms of PA management in India. In the many individual innovations that were started in the different project sites and that continued after the initial project period, the IEDP left behind a valuable legacy, however limited in its reach. In the Periyar Tiger Reserve many locally trained forest-product smugglers-turned-naturalists today offer some of the best wildlife experiences to tourists. EDCs in Periyar benefit from the religious pilgrimage to Sabarimala each year. In the Great Himalayan National Park local women's savings and credit groups working on vermiculture-composting and apricot-oil extraction offer a template to expand ecodevelopment activities to the larger group of beneficiaries. Other user groups have been organized in other PAs to benefit from forest resources and improve their own livelihoods.

Yet ecodevelopment failed visibly in a large proportion of its original aims, mainly due to serious flaws in the way it was implemented on the ground. It could have benefited from much greater community representation, more involved participation by local people, longer periods of rapport-building, and more training among PA staff. One of the major drawbacks that limited participation was the inability of local villagers to raise the 25 per cent contribution for the ecodevelopment fund (Jha 2000). The inability to recognize the social heterogeneity of village societies before designing specific activities thus became a major constraint (see also Varma 2007). The Periyar Tiger Reserve and the Great Himalayan National Park showed the efficacy of developing user-group and social group-based strategies for conservation.

The Periyar case also showed the importance of giving special attention to the involvement of marginalized people, usually tribals, who tend to be most dependent on ecosystem resources, a group largely overlooked in some other sites. A radical attitudinal change among field officers is required: this can be effected by intensive training and allowing a few field staff to dedicate their time to ecodevelopment over long periods. Much greater transparency and flexibility in financial management and decision-making is required through allowing direct financial flows to village institutions and joint accounting systems. This goes along with devolution of financial and decision-making powers to people in a real sense.

It is interesting to note how little emphasis there is in most of the original project documents on tourism as a valid and remunerative source of alternative income generation for local communities, particularly in sites with high tourist footfalls. Ecotourism has a real chance of succeeding in the fringes of PAs, given that many local villagers have tremendous knowledge of wildlife and ecosystems and can easily develop the managerial skills necessary for such enterprises (Uniyal and Zacharias 2001, Davenport *et al.* 2002). Even in Periyar, the only site to take advantage of ecotourism, a tiny percentage of the originally targeted households took up this livelihood successfully (Gubbi *et al.* 2009). Yet it is still unclear to what extent the highly seasonal and unpredictable nature of tourism-related jobs can sustain the large number of people living at the fringes. It is increasingly clear that far greater investments are required to meet the challenges at the park-village boundary than most developing country governments are willing to invest.

Simultaneously, gearing up other PA management functions, such as the development of essential management infrastructure, the rationalization of PA boundaries, and the settlement of rights are essential as a backdrop for effective ecodevelopment activities (Pabla 2005). Without getting their own house in order, the forest department cannot engender the morale or conviction to undertake activities so sensitive and difficult as those related to ecodevelopment as they would in cases where the rights of local stakeholders are clearly defined (see also Pandey and Wells 1997).

I would also question the value of international funding for something as basic as ecodevelopment, a necessary part of PA management anywhere in the world in so far as it includes the reduction of people–park conflicts and the redistribution of park benefits. Ecodevelopment activities need to be an essential part of PA management rather than provided for by temporary donor funding a few years at a time, if they are to have any continuity. The process of rapport-building between managements and local people takes years together and continued interaction is required between them as new challenges keep appearing on the horizon and specific new programmes need to be designed (Uniyal and Zacharias 2001, Rathore 2003). Further, the large infusion of funds, in many cases representing over eight times the normal budget of a PA, tends without adequate oversight to lead to waste and misappropriation. In 2008 funding by the World Bank for a proposed extension of the ecodevelopment project was vehemently opposed by leading wildlife biologists and advocates in India, given its mismanagement and in some cases, even adverse impact on PA management (K.U. Karanth 2008).[8]

More than one critique of the ecodevelopment programme attributes its failure to the fact that it does not challenge the basic exclusionary paradigm of diverting people's incomes from parks (Kothari 1998, Badola 2000, Woodman 2002, Chhatre and Saberwal 2006). They feel that it is not possible to harmonize the needs of wildlife and people while working within the current preservationist framework. Some feel that taking people 'away from nature' will reduce their respect and affinity for it, and their knowledge of it, therefore indirectly hampering the cause of conservation (Kothari 1998). They question the assumption that reducing poverty through developmental activities in the vicinity of PAs will automatically reduce environmental degradation inside PAs (Badola 2000).

I disagree with this critique of ecodevelopment for three reasons. One, the few successful ecodevelopment activities have to do with ecotourism, forest-based handicrafts, and NTFP processing, activities

[8] 'World Bank Offers India Loan to Save Tigers', *Times of India*, 30 May 2008.

that depend on forests with minimal impact and without creating additional dependence on park resources. Under ecodevelopment, controlled access rights to certain forest resources were also given to local people where other forms of livelihood were not possible (Gubbi *et al.* 2009). Second, many of the activities in ecodevelopment use people's traditional knowledge of ecosystems, such as in ecotourism, beekeeping, medicinal plant cultivation, and designing crop protection schemes. Where appropriate, income-enhancing schemes, such as sustainable agriculture, shopkeeping, and tailoring take people away from forests but only where people do choose to take these up. Ecodevelopment therefore does not propose to completely separate people's livelihood from forests. Indeed that would be impossible in a country with India's population density. The aim, rather, is to *manage* these existing pressures better. It is to ensure that existing PA benefits (such as from tourism or plantations) are redistributed from a small elite group (such as city-based tourism companies or cosmetics industries dependent on rare plants) to the poorest local stakeholders who pay most dearly for wildlife conservation. Ecodevelopment is about giving dependent people choices rather than straitjacketing them into forest-based traditional occupations, many of which are no longer sufficiently remunerative. The long-term vision of ecodevelopment, as I see it, is to involve fringe villages in a 'protective garland' around protected areas so that outsiders (such as poachers, timber-smugglers, and city-based tourist operators) can be excluded effectively.[9] And third, there is no escaping the fact that Indian society is rapidly undergoing a transition from rural to urban. The proportion of urban to total population in India grew from 19.91 per cent in 1971 to 28.54 per cent in 2001. How India as a whole manages this transition is the important issue because it cannot be wished away under any circumstances. Any person conversant with life in small remote villages in India is aware that more and more young people are aspiring to a better

[9] However, it remains to be seen how realistic any utilitarian scheme for sharing park benefits among 'local beneficiaries' can be, given the large numbers of people typically surrounding Indian wildlife reserves (K.U. Karanth 2002).

education and moving into jobs in towns and cities (Hegde and Enters 2000, Ghate and Beazley 2008). Apart from highly uneven development in rural-urban areas, this is partly because forest- and land-based livelihoods can no longer support even basic needs in a globalized world (see Shahabuddin *et al.* 2007). In this respect ecodevelopment can play an important role in dampening the sometimes cruel effects of a tribal family's shift to the city: this through a generational improvement of incomes and educational standards and, consequently, a change of livelihood.

Ecodevelopment promised a lot, achieved a little, but surely showed the way ahead in better managing Indian protected areas. The challenge is to recognize the failures as much as the achievements of this rather complex enterprise so that the Indian conservation movement can save itself from groping in the dark when such interventions are restarted in future.

8

Reinventing Conservation: Creating Space for Nature

Circa 2008: Facing the Crisis

Today, the efficacy of India's nature protection paradigm is increasingly being questioned. There is considerable evidence that Indian PAs have not been effective in conserving the range of organisms that they were mandated to protect. Several cases of local extinction from PAs have lately come to light, such as that of the Great Indian Bustard from the Karera Wildlife Sanctuary and the gaur from the Bandhavgarh Tiger Reserve. Both are endangered species and their local extinctions were as much due to a lack of understanding of their ecological requirements as due to habitat degradation and fragmentation. Poaching of wildlife, particularly of tigers, rhinos, and large cats is on the rise, spurred by the demand for wildlife products in South East Asia and China. Poaching is only aided by local hostility against the state's conservation agenda and spurred by years of neglect of park–people relationships. There has not been much progress towards linking local economies around PAs with the aim of conservation—not since the largely failed experiment of ecodevelopment which ended in 2002. Further, the research expertise that is brought to bear upon critical management issues is inadequate because of the lack of involvement of non-governmental scientists and independent experts, coupled with limited research capability within the forest department. Above all, there has been very little effort to mainstream bottom-up conservation efforts through creating a conducive policy framework over the years. Important programmes such as JFM, with considerable potential for broad-based conservation, have to a large extent been subverted by non-transparent and hierarchical processes within state forest departments.

The turn of the century has seen an intensification of industrialization and infrastructure development in the country, and an attendant burgeoning demand for land, water, and minerals. The fragmentation of wild habitats, increasing pollution, and conversion of forest are natural corollaries of this development. Environmental protection laws, which could have served to stop the decline of wilderness, have been observed to become visibly weaker after 1990, both in letter and implementation. This can be seen in the unwarranted haste with which the union ministry of environment and forests has been clearing development projects since 2000, many of which could adversely affect endangered species (Menon and Kohli 2008). Environmental Impact Assessment (EIA) used to be a critical tool in decision-making that allowed cancellation or modification of projects deemed to be destructive of natural ecosystems. In 2006, however, the process of EIA was reformulated drastically to reduce its usefulness as an instrument for averting destructive projects (ibid.).

In November 2006, close on the heels of the tiger crisis, another important environmental issue has challenged the country. The Forest Rights Bill was enacted into law as a result of the sustained campaign of tribal activists all over the country.[1] The social importance of this act lies in its aim to reduce the extreme disparity between historically marginalized forest-dwellers, particularly tribals, and the rest of Indian society. This is planned to be done through conferring land rights to people unofficially settled in and cultivating official forest land for a given number of years. For the first time in India, the issue of forest conservation now occupies the political mainstream because of its significance for social justice. The marginalized status of tribals that prompted this act cannot be doubted. For instance, of the total number of people displaced by various development projects in India,

[1] This being the popular name for Scheduled Tribes and Other Traditional Forest Dwellers (Recognition of Forest Rights) Act, enacted in January 2007.

tribals constitute more than half (Ramnath 2008). Another indication of tribal dispossession in the country is that between 1961 and 1991 the proportion of tribal people owning land had actually declined from one-half to one-third (ibid.).

After 2005 the decline in tiger populations across the country had spurred a dramatic increase in governmental activity and expenditure on PA protection. The imminent fear of tiger extinction only fuelled further concern about the implications of the new Forest Rights Act for biodiversity, leading to opposition to it in its present formulation by a large number of conservationists (Madhusudan 2005b). For biologists and foresters the greatest fear today is that as much as 15 per cent of India's forest land, including some inside protected areas, is likely to be written off for land allotments that have been mandated by this act. They doubt the efficacy of the act in reviving tribal livelihoods and foresee a large-scale takeover of forest lands by local timber mafia under the guise of tribal rights. The suggested modifications in the act with the aim of maximizing the number of beneficiaries and quantum of benefits continue to be furiously debated today, two years after its passage.[2]

The field implications of the forest act for wildlife are still rather unclear because many PAs have not completed the legal procedure for their final notification, leaving local people's rights in a grey zone. Therefore, few people, least of all officials in the MoEF, are sure of the exact area of forest land that is likely to be affected by this law, in itself an alarming fact. The estimates of forest land area to be affected by land settlements range from 1.91 per cent (Shah 2005) to as much as 15 per cent of the total (Ramnath 2008). This considerable discrepancy points to the neglect of due procedures of legal notification of RFs and PAs that have, in many cases, been overlooked by state forest departments.

The promulgation of the Forest Rights Act overlapped in time with significant amendments to the Wildlife Protection Act, initially

[2] Social activists asked for an advancement of the cut-off date for regularizing settlements in the forest from 1980 to 2005; an increase in the area of land to be allotted to each family from 2.5 ha to 4 ha; and extension of the bill's provisions to non-tribal families.

prompted by the tiger crisis of 2005. These amendments make the implementation of wildlife laws more stringent than before. But more importantly, these amendments provide for the delineation of 'inviolate' zones of forest land, termed Critical Wildlife Habitat (CWH), that were proposed to be put off bounds for human use, whether land settlements or development projects. Through these amendments the government appeared to be aiming at averting the possibility of land settlements inside tiger reserves, which was very likely under the forest act. Thus, in January 2008 the MoEF declared all the twenty-eight tiger reserves as CWHs.[3] The area of forest land to be demarcated as CWH within longstanding PAs is today the topic of heated debate, specially as the implementation of this provision might result in large-scale relocation of people, given the large numbers of villagers living inside them. Social activists are opposing the demarcation of CWH as they believe that tribal dwellings do not hamper the overall cause of biodiversity conservation, arguing that coexistence between forest-dwellers and wildlife is possible. Against this backdrop an increasing number of violent clashes are being reported between forest authorities and tribal people in the process of implementation of the forest act. Many of the differences between activists and the government, unfortunately, appear to arise out of a lack of basic information on the human impact in forests, the needs of endangered species, the extent of tribal settlement in forests, and the amount of land involved.

The divide between the proponents of strict nature protection and those of people-based conservation has never been deeper. This chasm has been exemplified by the starkly opposed reactions of different groups to the Forest Rights Act. Against the backdrop of steadily declining biodiversity and the acrimonious stances taken by conservationists, the prospects for wildlife conservation today seem bleak. However, as I detail below, it is realistically possible to reconcile these opposing points of view and harness them towards a synergistic, productive approach that can include both people and wildlife.

[3] 'Eleven More Tiger Reserves Now Out of Bounds', *Indian Express News Service*, 1 January 2008.

Accommodating Disparate Visions

The core issue on which consensus is needed across the ideological divide is the way Indian landscapes, with all their pressures and dependencies, are managed for biodiversity conservation. The way to harmonize these opposing demands on the Indian wilderness is to develop a mosaic of differing strategies in conservation all of which are given equal importance. History indicates that both community-based conservation and strict nature protection can contribute in significant and complementary ways towards the larger goal of landscape-level biological conservation. Numerous instances outside India testify to success of the coexistence of multiple strategies in natural landscapes, as in the Chitwan National Park in Nepal (Dinerstein 2003) or the Ranomafana National Park in Madagascar (Wright and Andriamihaja 2002).

Through the examples in this book I have shown that used and strictly protected areas are serving slightly different yet complementary functions in the context of conservation. People-managed community conservation areas have effectively regenerated and maintained green cover and now serve as important sources of biomass for dependent people. They have been specially effective under conditions of secure tenure, low extractive pressure, and clearly-defined access rights. Along the way they have created a wildlife-friendly habitat matrix which reinforces the functions of wildlife protection in strictly protected areas—for instance, by providing corridors for large mammals. One can witness this change in the thousands of hectares under JFM and other forms of community conservation in India. Importantly, the regeneration of forests has also resulted in the protection of the natural water regimes of many areas and the preservation of soil fertility in downstream areas, though these functions are rarely acknowledged in the public discourse. In parts of India, such as described in Chapter 5, villagers have beaten off corporate interests that threatened to decimate precious natural resources. Yet, by their very nature, multiple-use ecosystems can preserve only a proportion of regional faunas, often excluding larger species such as the tiger, elephant, and leopard, and sensitive animal groups such as amphibians.

On the other hand, under good management, strictly-protected or inviolate areas have the potential to preserve a much wider range of micro-habitats, species, and ecosystem processes. They tend to improve the reproductive capabilities of large mammal species by providing substantial and contiguous breeding habitats that can sustain viable populations. The protection of rare and endangered megafauna necessitates the protection of larger natural landscapes, given their need for larger areas to maintain viable populations and for a variety of micro-habitats needed during their life-cycles. Habitat-restricted species, too, have a better chance of surviving in strictly protected areas due to the fact that their habitats, typically rare in the landscape, tend to have a better chance of inclusion when large areas are cordoned off for protection. Such biodiversity benefits are visible in national parks such as Corbett and Nagarhole, which are better managed and financed than most others, and which still harbour almost all their historically recorded mammal species. Yet, this government-sponsored model is surprisingly vulnerable to denotification in the face of competing commercial interests such as mining, given the almost complete lack of local public support that could fight off these interferences. As I have pointed out throughout this book, both of these paradigms already exist in India, to differing extents and with differing effectiveness. However, while strictly protected areas occupy centrestage, community forestry has continued to work despite all odds and without much legal backing. A mosaic of approaches can only work with the continual adaptation to new situations and changing environments, as also by developing new connections between the two approaches. In the rest of this chapter I lay out a tentative framework for making each of these approaches more successful, both independently and in tandem.

Strictly Protected Areas

Apart from a few high-profile tiger reserves, India's protected areas are in a shambles. Much of the reason for poor management of the PAs in India lies in their unclear foundations, both legal and administrative (Pabla 2005). A study on the management of PAs in Maharashtra from 1996 through 2003 revealed the extent of confusion that still exists regarding the boundaries of protected areas as well as the legal rights of local people (Pande 2005). This lack of clarity principally arises, as we noted earlier, from the fact that legal procedures for rights settlement have not been completed in a large proportion of PAs. In fact, very few PAs, apart from tiger reserves, have been finally notified after satisfactory settlement of rights, compensation to villagers, and/or relocation of villages. Consequently disputes over boundaries and rights continue to fester in many PAs. The lack of final notification of rights is due to the fact that the documents prepared by settlement officers charged with this task often do not match the records available with the chief wildlife warden of the given state. Another reason for delays in the completion of legal procedures for PA establishment is the lack of agreement between the revenue and forest departments on the compensation to be paid to villagers during the settlement of rights. And an extremely convoluted set of conservation laws regarding settlement of rights, caused by continual amendments to the Wildlife Protection Act, adds to the confusion (Pabla 2005).

The statistics compiled by Pande, updated to 2003, suggest considerable bureaucratic inertia, which can soon begin to cost India its remaining PAs. For instance, in Maharashtra, of the 35 national parks and wildlife sanctuaries, a meagre 8 have been finally notified in terms of their total area. Another 7 have had between 75 and 99 per cent of their areas finally notified under the Wildlife Protection Act. According to government statistics Tamil Nadu fares no better, with only 4 of 12 bird sanctuaries, 0 of 8 wildlife sanctuaries, and only 2 of 5 national parks finally notified.[4] This results in disputes, given the uncertain status of resident rights. For instance in a sanctuary in Andhra Pradesh villagers attempting to build roads and a school were stopped by the park warden. He had no legal grounds for stopping them as the final notification of sanctuary boundaries had not been issued.[5] We have already seen in the case of Sariska the level of confusion that exists even among forest functionaries in relation to the exact rights and privileges of people living inside the PA.

A key grouse relating to management among conservationists is the

[4] Data obtained from the Tamil Nadu forest department, June 2008.

[5] *Protected Areas Update*, vol. XIV, no. 2.

inefficient mechanism of financial transfers to PAs and its expenditure. Wildlife is a concurrent subject between the state and union governments. Consequently, half the budget of each wildlife sanctuary comes from the union government and the other half, as matching grant, from the state government. Bureaucracy stipulates that the sum of money received by a PA from the union government cannot be utilized until the state contribution is also received. While the planned financial allocation to wildlife areas is satisfactory, very often the state contribution is not received until much later in the financial year, which ends on 31March. As a result, a large proportion of the received budget is often left unutilized, leaving the management planning in disarray.

Another important reason for the poor biological status of Indian PAs is the lack of motivation and enthusiasm among the field staff. While it is common to meet a few committed forest guards in every PA, the norm is a dispirited and disinterested guard holding the fort at the field level. If one looks at the conditions under which forest field staff work, this is not surprising. They are a beleaguered lot, working with lower salaries than many other less skilled workers in India. For instance, in Sariska a forest guard is paid between Rs 3500 and Rs 7000 per month, depending on his seniority. Within this allowance, they have to support their families and also prepare their own food in the field. Often, I have come across forest guards eating the simplest of meals: *chappatis* (Indian bread) with lentils. Yet they are supposed to patrol a forest beat of an average of 20 sq. km, twice each day, apart from other duties in the field. For accommodation, it is common to see them use field checkposts, which are typically ramshackle structures built of bricks and thatch. Sometimes a checkpost is simply a tent which, in elephant or tiger country, makes a forest functionary rather vulnerable. A profession fraught with danger to life and limb needs to provide medical and life insurance: however, there is none for forest staff. The Orissa Forest Rangers' Association and the Orissa Non-gazetted Forest Services Association have been agitating for the provision of health and life insurance and better salaries.[6] They ask to be on

[6] Ibid.

par with the police service.[7] Forest personnel go through no training in the areas of wildlife law, ecology, or social surveys. The typical guard is just not equipped to carry out his diverse tasks that range from protection and tree-planting to social surveys and wildlife census. Understaffing is another issue that needs to be addressed. Given all this, it not surprising that field staff possess little motivation towards that extra effort to make parks work, whether it is to help form village committees or chase down armed poachers.

To many who are strongly opposed to strict nature protection anywhere in India, it is important to point out that the term 'strict protection' does not imply 'unmanaged' or 'wild'. Rather, strictly protected ecosystems also require management for the preservation of specific conservation values such as maintaining the specific habitat needed for an endangered species. Management is inescapable given the manifold external threats from adjoining agricultural landscapes, invasive species, and natural catastrophic events: fires, storms, earthquakes. However management in strictly protected areas has to be carried out according to the dictates of biodiversity rather than economic needs. If for biodiversity it is necessary to remove a certain amount of a grass species from a wetland each year in order to preserve its habitat characteristics—say, related to water level, grass density, and species diversity of plants—it must be done. This can of course be intelligently managed: the extracted grass could be useful to local livestock grazers and can be diverted for their use, as is being done in the Chitwan National Park (Dinerstein 2003). In the case of a strict nature reserve, however, such removal would be dictated by season of removal and quantum removed for a specific *biodiversity* goal, rather than maximized for the benefit of local livelihoods or commercial gain. There can be numerous locally useful avenues for controlled extraction from PAs: science-based management actually opens up means for community participation and involvement such as these (Middleton 2003).

Local people can turn into effective protectors when they become aware of the benefits accruing to them, when they are involved in decision-making over natural resources, and made sensitive to the

[7] Protected Areas Update, vol. XIV, no. 2

Illustr. 13: Tourists from Delhi watch birds in the Corbett Tiger Reserve, Uttarakhand. Birdwatching in wildlife areas is becoming increasingly popular with tourists and can generate significant revenues for state governments.

long-term importance of biodiversity (see Powell *et al.* 2002, Terborgh and van Schaik 2002, Wright and Andriamihaja 2002). The feature common to all successful instances of public participation in PAs is that local communities necessarily benefit in some way from biodiversity conservation. Economic benefits with minimal ecological damage is possible through non-consumptive uses, the most promising being ecotourism. We have noted earlier that official tourism revenues for local developmental work can play an important role in changing local people's attitude towards PAs in their vicinity. Cases of such development can be seen in the Ranomafana National Park in Madagascar where local people are increasingly involved in research and protection activities (Wright and Andriamihaja 2002) and the Monteverde National Park in Costa Rica (Powell *et al.* 2002). Widespread community support for the reserve in the latter case has also helped deflect the challenge from invasion by squatters. What is clear is that community involvement and benefit cannot be separated from the long-term protection of inviolate areas.

In India there have been a few innovative efforts to increase community involvement in PA management. While ecodevelopment failed in most of the project sites, a diversified strategy was adopted in the Periyar Tiger Reserve to enhance benefits to groups of people that possessed different sets of skills. Tribal villagers once involved in poaching and illegal NTFP collection were persuaded to train as tourist guides. Village committees simultaneously monitor and manage pollution and physical disturbance along the pilgrimage route. Loans have been extended to pepper plantation owners in the buffer zone by the reserve managers to improve the productivity of the plantations and, in turn, incomes from pepper sales. Co-operatives have been formed for pepper sales so that middlemen are eliminated and net income to pepper-plantation owners enhanced. Such initiatives have visibly improved park–people relations and continue to open up new avenues for co-operation. In the Corbett Tiger Reserve, regular training and awareness programmes have been building capacity among local farmers to develop and manage ecotourism concerns. While none of these measures address livelihood issues comprehensively, they have engendered feelings of stewardship for the reserve, especially in instances when these programmes have been coupled with an awareness campaign highlighting the other benefits of proximity to the PA.

The appropriate model of tourism in strict nature reserves that can maximize local benefit is a system of co-operatives in which people are trained to manage businesses rather than simply fill daily-wage positions. A number of employment opportunities relating to tourism, such as home-stays, tour management, cafe management, and meal preparation can be delegated to local people after basic training. My experience is that in every village there are several capable people who can take on organizational roles with a little training. This approach was adopted in Nepal's Annapurna Conservation Area Project: training courses in lodge management, renewable energy installations, cooking, and account-keeping were held for locals. These led to considerable employment generation. Such a vision of tourism necessarily involves restrictions on non-local interests from operating in the same area so that competition for local villagers is minimized.

While ecotourism cannot be the mainstay of any park management scheme, given the vast numbers of potential beneficiaries in a country like India, the available figures in more popular protected areas indicate that there *is* scope for considerable enhancement of existing park revenues. In Sariska as much as Rs 35 lakhs was collected as tourist entry fees through a single gate during 2003–4. The entry fee paid today by an Indian visitor is as low as Rs 25, an amount that has not changed for at least twenty years. A doubling of the fee would double revenues without being a disincentive to tourism. Currently, the reserve's Nature Interpretation Museum is lying unused. If usefully deployed it can generate welcome additional revenue. And if the privately-owned tourist resorts pay even a small percentage of their annual revenues to the state forest department, even more revenues can accrue. Imaginative approaches replacing bureaucratic procedure can galvanize any PA.

Preference must naturally be given to local people in forest labour work and protection duties, particularly those who do not have assets outside PAs, as well as the poorest. Such people are normally far more familiar with the local wildlife and terrain, and much more likely to be content with their jobs close to home. Economic analysis based on socio-economic data and discussions with villagers has often resulted

Illustr. 14: Tribal people have a vast knowledge of forest plants and their uses. This knowledge can be profitably used for improving conservation in both national parks and community reserves through innovative planning.

in ideas for other livelihood alternatives in the area. An important rule of thumb, as we saw in Chapter 7, is that employment opportunities have to be developed *before* curtailing rights inside the PA.

Well-designed buffer zone management has to be seen as essential. Casual visits to most PAs reveal the tremendous extractive pressures on most of the Indian PAs from villages and towns located sometimes as far away as 10–30 km. Madhusudan (2005), for instance, documents the dependence of villagers in 159 villages for livestock grazing (the livestock numbering as many as 116,000) within the 5-km radius of the Bandipur Tiger Reserve. The Corbett Tiger Reserve, covering 1316 sq. km, has a population of 62,982 people in 92 villages living within 3 km of its boundary.[8] Although these villagers are not primarily dependent on the reserve, they do face frequent problems of crop damage, personal injury, and livestock loss caused by wildlife. The principal aim of buffer zone management is to create positive interaction between reserve managers and local communities and defuse antagonistic ones. Timely compensation for injuries from carnivores and for crop-raiding by wild ungulates is an essential ingredient of buffer zone management. Development of compensatory mechanisms for such local losses have always been inadequately funded and implemented even in India's best-funded tiger reserves. As another instance, in the high alpine zone abutting the western border of the Great Himalayan National Park, more than 15,000 people depend on the collection of medicinal plants, edible mushrooms, and livestock grazing to supplement their income from agriculture (Chhatre and Saberwal 2006). Given these high levels of dependence of local people on PA resources, increasing biomass productivity and the creation of employment opportunities in the buffer zone around PAs are obviously vital for their viability. It is eminently possible to restore forests and grasslands using the JFM framework on degraded village lands and reserve forest areas adjacent to PAs, activities that could also provide extra employment to local villagers. Unfortunately, JFM has largely been geographically divorced from wildlife sanctuaries and national parks. The juxtaposition of JFM and strict nature protection can be used for maximum complementary effect; and the legal

[8] See the Project Tiger website: projecttiger.nic.in.

Illustr. 15: Being dependent on the continued existence of natural forests, bee-keeping can be an important remunerative activity for local villagers and can support conservation goals. (*Photo: Courtesy Palni Hills Conservation Council and Development Alternatives*)

category of 'community reserves' could also play an important role in buffer zone management.

In some cases controlled access to forest resources via a licensing system can be allowed for the most marginalized communities, as long as extraction is monitored and controlled. Other means to establish rapport with local villages can be fodder aid during the summer drought period and regular livestock vaccination programmes. State forest departments need to play a part in the improvement of developmental infrastructure such as roads, health, and educational facilities in peripheral villages through closer co-ordination with the district administration. Interventions in buffer zones need to be backed up by strict controls on encroachment into PAs, a system that can be strengthened with the participation of local villagers. Such comprehensive buffer zone management requires a long-term engagement on a village-by-village basis and has to be connected with other rural development programmes in the adjacent areas.

In India there is no legal requirement to create buffer zones or undertake buffer zone management. Sometimes, of course, the very existence of a buffer zone is precluded by the juxtaposition of human settlements with the wildlife area. Where they do exist, buffer zones are mostly managed as a part of the protected area itself, with an inflexible set of rules rather than as zone for creative management. This means that the essential tasks required in buffer zones, such as controlled extraction, tree planting, and creating fuelwood and fodder plantations are ignored or carried out in a half-hearted way. In contrast, neighbouring Nepal has a law mandating park managers to implement buffer zone management, specifically through sharing half of park revenues with villages in the buffer zone. In the past, tourists brought in as much as US$ 350,000 annually to village committees in the buffer zone (Dinerstein 2003). While the field-level effectiveness of this scheme is still far from satisfactory, the existence of a legal framework as well as a source of finance gives room to PA managers in Nepal to develop linkages between the local economy and the objectives of the park.

While effective buffer zone management and benefit-sharing with local people can mitigate much of the local animosity between reserve managers and local people, there are cases where the displacement of villages from inside strict protected areas cannot be wished away. Displacements are required where this facilitates the consolidation of hitherto fragmented habitats, reduces life-threatening conflicts with wildlife, and reduces extractive pressures that threaten the long-term viability of the ecosystem. Yet, without ensuring the livelihood security of oustees from PAs, village displacement is likely to do more harm than good to the larger cause of wildlife conservation, as was pointed out in the cases of Tadoba-Andhari and Sariska. Incomplete and coercive rehabilitation has already caused considerable local hostility towards wildlife in and around PAs. In some cases, it has permanently damaged the long-term prospects of conservation.

There is now considerable scope and public pressure for improving the quality of resettlement so that already marginalized communities do not suffer the additional costs of wildlife protection. The financial allocation for resettlement has recently been enhanced to Rs10 lakh per household from the earlier paltry amount of Rs 1 lakh by the central government.[9] If utilized properly, and if village representatives are adequately consulted on the process and outcomes, the results can be rewarding. The implementation of relocation plans cannot be left to the forest department: the collaboration of local NGOs and development agencies with professional expertise in rehabilitation is essential. The primary stakeholder, the proposed oustee, needs to be involved in the exercise right from the outset and treated as a participant rather than an adversary. Forest villagers are often willing to move out from remote locations if the alternative prospects include better employment, but ultimately oppose relocation because of a poor rehabilitation package and lack of trust in the forest department. With greater accountability, transparency, public discussion, and technical guidance, village displacements can become an important and legitimate tool in PA management. In the absence of a formal relief and rehabilitation policy for the country, public hearings and consultation assume even more importance.

Strengthening People's Movements

India has a rich history of people's participation in environmental movements, particularly those that attempted to regenerate local natural resources, such as the Chipko movement (Guha 2000, Gadgil 2001). Today these traditions are manifest in the various forms of community forestry and wildlife conservation which are spreading rapidly through the villages and towns of India. In many cases villagers are responding to development threats in their neighbourhood in order just to protect their natural resources. In others, specific animal species that are endangered are being protected: the golden langur in the Chakrashila Sanctuary in Assam and the spotted-billed pelican in the village of Kokkrebellur in Karnataka being cases in point. In yet other cases locals are reacting to the perceived decline in their natural resources base—as described for Mendha village earlier. In north-eastern India the heads of seventeen villages bordering the Pakhui Tiger Reserve in Arunachal Pradesh have formed a joint protection force

[9] Ministry of Environment and Forests Press Release, 23 March 2008.

against hunting along with the reserve manager.[10] And a wildlife sanctuary has been created for the endangered Blyth's tragopan by the village of Khonoma in Nagaland.[11]

Given the increasing number of such instances of local wildlife conservation, both self-initiated and state-sponsored, interest seems to have awakened in the possible role that community reserves can play in supplementing the protective efforts of strictly protected areas. An amendment to the Wildlife Protection Act (1972) in 2002 allows the establishment of people-managed wildlife areas, named 'community reserves', where there is evidence of local interest in conservation, adjacent to existing national parks and wildlife sanctuaries. Community reserves represent a promising legislation that can revolutionize the participation of local people in long-term biodiversity conservation. Several such reserves have been declared since then: for instance, India's first Marine Conservation Reserve in Lakshadweep initiated by the Bombay Natural History Society in 2005, centred around the commercial importance of the giant clam. While the limitations of community reserves will become clear only after some years, there is likely to be a great deal of variation in the way these measures will play out in the future. The efficacy is likely to depend on the process of establishment of a reserve, particularly in the extent of involvement of local people. For instance, in Lakshadweep the collaborators went through a deeply consultative process with more than 400 public meetings being held before the reserve was formally notified.[12]

What is still missing in India is a system of incentives and encouragement to such efforts. Rather, in many cases, the forest department does all it can to create obstacles. Simply taking over existing community reserves in the guise of the new categories created under the Wildlife Protection Act, without a sensitive framing of rules that are locale-specific, will destroy them.[13] Such community initiatives have to be recognized and nurtured for their conservation value rather than

[10] *Protected Areas Update*, vol. XII, no. 4.

[11] www.iied.org/Gov/mdgs/documents/mdg3/ch3_24pp.pdf.

[12] *Yahoo India News Portal*, 10 June 2008.

[13] See also Das 2007, which shows how existing community institutions can be subverted and weakened through misguided interventions.

discouraged. In other cases it is clear that state forest departments do not take the concept of community-led conservation seriously. The Jayamangali Blackbuck Conservation Reserve, a stronghold of the blackbuck in Karnataka, is currently threatened by the widening and paving of a cart-track that will fragment the protected area into two. Local groups allege that the widening has been undertaken in contravention of the Forest Conservation Act (1980) as well as supreme court judgments. Further, eucalyptus plantations have been started along the roads without any consultation with local villagers. It is clear that community reserves are unlikely to make a dent in the conservation value of forest tracts unless they are established through a participatory process, whether initiated by the locals, the forest department, or voluntary groups. Unless financial and technical support is extended to the local villages for maintaining the reserve and ensuring its biological contribution, unless specific management interventions are planned and undertaken towards this end, and unless some form of compensation is offered to locals to make up for the opportunity cost of land-use change to agriculture or loss of hunting, this new venture will not succeed. There has to be a plan backed up by legal rules towards making community reserves work.

Designing an Alternative Future

The new paradigm, whereby a definitive mosaic of strategies is emphasized, has to be based on equity principles. It is only by placing community-based conservation on an equal footing with strict protection paradigms—while recognizing the weaknesses of both—that one can hope to strengthen nature conservation in India. As I have emphasized earlier, it is necessary to work towards *strengthening* both multiple-use *and* inviolate areas rather than argue for multiple use *or* inviolate areas. Acknowledging the importance of both types of management, however, is only the first step. As discussed above, the way forward is to focus on the socio-economic and ecological linkage between multiple-use and inviolate zones that can be constructively used to bolster both: it is this linkage, tenuous at present, that will likely make or break our future conservation efforts.

Despite the visible limitations, India can boast of expanding innovations in conservation. Historically, conservation initiatives in the country have ranged from the very local, where a small hamlet of tribals tends a sacred grove, to a large-scale national programme such as Project Tiger which aims to protect a vast diversity of ecosystems across the country. Yet if such a wide range of initiatives are to continue and succeed in the long term, they need increasing engagement with genuine science. In the fragmented and managed landscapes of today, often facing contested uses, there is a central role for science—in identifying issues, devising working approaches, and providing ways to predict and monitor ecological change—without losing sight of sociological contexts.

India possesses a growing number of scientists with the training, skills, and commitment to help resolve environmental conflicts. Today's ecologist is far removed from the 'authoritarian biologist' of the past.[14] A typical ecologist today possesses a long-term vision that takes into account not only the complex web of ecological and socio-economic relationships that exist in nature but also the rich history in which these relationships are embedded. A better understanding of socio-economic context has recently allowed collaborations between ecologists and social scientists in both research and intervention. The special role of the independent scientist in neutrally assessing conservation outcomes and processes, as also in advising management, has been recognized.

Recent effective conservation has been founded on partnerships among different interest groups that find common cause. There are increasing numbers of partnerships between the forest department and non-governmental actors, so that cumulative knowledge and experience in conservation on both sides can be capitalized upon.[15] Partnerships between corporate bodies and NGOs also have the potential to expand and spatially replicate local conservation initiatives. High economic growth over the last decade is now allowing socially sensitive corporate bodies to contribute to nature conservation projects in co-operation with local bodies. With the country's comfortable foreign

[14] See Guha 2003.

[15] See, for instance, Bhatnagar (2008), who has written about joint efforts by government, biologists, and local people to preserve inviolate zones in a larger landscape of used grasslands in the trans-Himalayan region of Ladakh.

exchange position, it may not be necessary to borrow from international aid agencies to develop and maintain our environmental conservation machinery.

So, India does not lack in human resources that can engage in continually moulding and improving conservation. The country harbours one of the most informed set of civil society actors in the developing world. Some of these are attempting to deflect environmental mistakes and increase public participation in decisions affecting biodiversity. In contrast with many other developing countries, India's democratic framework does allow contrary positions to be heard. The public has some impact on policy, for Indian conservationists can count on a relatively sensitized judiciary and an increasingly vocal media to back their cause. Grassroots environmentalists work continually against the odds to ensure the accountability and transparency of governmental interventions in natural resources, a necessary first step in promoting public participation. The activist has played a particularly important role in finding a balance between development and conservation, and in advocating alternative forms of economic development that can reduce the burden on the biological world.

India's rich heritage of ecological knowledge and action, if properly harnessed, has the potential to rejuvenate its living world. India's wildlands have given birth to diverse cultures which were intricately linked to the biological cycles of plenty and scarcity, feast and famine—until very recently. The Asiatic lion, the one-horned rhinoceros, the majestic elephant, and the supremely graceful Bengal tiger are not only powerful cultural symbols for the Indian public but also signify the existence of immensely diverse and important ecosystems that have nurtured humans for eons. Yet without a radical shift in the current conservation paradigms that addresses issues of both equity and ecology, we cannot hope to safeguard nature. And to lose it all would mean not only the end of nature as we know it, but also an irretrievable and tragic loss of everything important that the country stands for. It is time to reframe conservation, renew our connection with the earth, and reinvent the ecology that has sustained humans and wild nature alike.

Bibliography

Agrawal, A. 2001. Common Property Institutions and Sustainable Governance of Resources. *World Development* 29 (10): 1649–72.

Alves, J.P. 1999. Men and Tigers in Sariska Tiger Reserve, India. *Cat News* 30: 10–12.

———, and R. Garcia-Perea. 1998. Tigers and People: Strategies for Tiger Conservation in Sariska Tiger Reserve, India. *Cat News* 29: 9–11.

Annamalai, R. 2002. *Ecodevelopment in Kalakadu Mundanthurai Tiger Reserve, India*. Status Report. World Bank.

———. 2004. Sustainability of Ecodevelopment Initiatives in Kalakad-Mundanthurai Tiger Reserve. Project Tiger, Kalakad-Mundanthurai Tiger Reserve, Tamil Nadu.

Asher, M. and A. Kothari. 2005. Unsettling: The Reality of Resettlement in Orissa. *Down to Earth*, 15 August: 40–1.

Badola, R. 2000. Local People Amidst the Changing Conservation Ethos: Relationships between People and Protected Areas in India. In T. Enters, P.B. Durst, and M. Victor (eds), *Decentralization and Devolution of Forest Management in Asia and the Pacific*. Bangkok: RECOFTC Report N.18 and RAP Publication.

Bagchi, S., C. Mishra, and Y.V. Bhatnagar. 2004. Conflicts between Traditional Pastoralism and Conservation of the Himalayan Ibex in the Trans Himalayas. *Animal Conservation* 7: 121–8.

Bandyopadhyay, A. 2004. In Mowgli's Land. *Down To Earth*, 31 August: 49–51.

Banerjee, A. 2007. Joint Forest Management in West Bengal. In O. Springate-Baginski and P. Blaikie, *Forests, People and Power. Political Ecology of Reform in South Asia*. London: Earthscan.

Banerjee, S.K. and T.K. Mishra. 1996. Extension of Forestry Research through Joint Forest Management: An Ecological Impact Study. *Advances in Forestry Research in India* 14: 11–25.

Baral, N., M.J. Stern, and J.T. Heinen. 2007. ICDP Life-Cycles in the Annapurna Conservation Area, Nepal: Is Development Overpowering Conservation? *Biodiversity and Conservation* 16 (10): 2903–17.

Barve, N., M.C. Kiran, G. Vanaraj, N.A. Aravind, D. Rao, R. Uma Shaanker, K.N. Ganeshaiah, and J.G. Poulsen. 2005. Measuring and Mapping Threats to a Wildlife Sanctuary in Southern India. *Conservation Biology* 19 (1): 122–30.

Baviskar, A. 2003. States, Communities and Conservation: The Practice of Ecodevelopment in the Great Himalayan National Park. In M. Rangarajan and V. Saberwal (eds), *Battles Over Nature: Science and the Politics of Conservation*. Delhi: Permanent Black.

Bhagwat, S., C. Kushalappa, P. Williams, and N. Brown. 2005. The Role of Informal Protected Areas in Maintaining Biodiversity in the Western Ghats of India. *Ecology and Society* 10 (1): 8.

Bhatnagar, Y. 2008. Relocation from Wildlife Reserves in the Greater and Trans-Himalaya: Is it Necessary? *Conservation & Society* 6 (3): 263–70.

Bhatia, V.M. (ed.). 2000. *Dialogue on Sariska, Alwar, India*. Alwar, Rajasthan: Tarun Bharat Sangh.

Bombay Natural History Society. 2001. The Important Bird Areas (IBA) Programme in India. *Buceros* 6 (2).

Bray, D.B., L. Merino-Perez, P. Negreros-Castillo, G. Segura-Warnholtz, J.M. Torres-Rojo, and H.F.M. Vester. 2003. Mexico's Community-Managed Forests as a Global Model for Sustainable Landscapes. *Conservation Biology* 17 (3): 672–7.

Brockington, D. 2002. *Fortress Conservation: The Preservation of the Mkomazi Game Reserve, Tanzania*. UK: James Currey Publishers, and Bloomington: Indiana University Press.

Bunsha, D. 2005. Left High and Dry. *Frontline,* 21 May (online edition).

Centre for Natural Studies. Undated. Our Achievements. Midnapore, West Bengal: Raja N.L. Khan Women's College.

Chase, L.C., D.R. Lee, W.D. Schulze, and D.J. Anderson. 1998. Ecotourism Demand and Differential Pricing of National Park Access in Costa Rica. *Land Economics* 74 (4): 466–82.

Chaturvedi, A.N. 1992. No, it is Non-Viable and Unsound—A Rejoinder. *Wasteland News* 8 (1): 37–9.

Chhatre, A. and V.K. Saberwal. 2006. *Democratizing Nature: Politics, Conservation and Development in India*. New Delhi: Oxford University Press.

Choudhary, K. 2000. Development Dilemma: Resettlement of Gir Maldharis. *Economic and Political Weekly*, 22 July: 2662–8.

Cinner, J.E., S.G. Sutton and T.G. Bond. 2007. Socio-Economic Thresholds that Affect Use of Customary Fisheries Management Tools. *Conservation Biology* 21 (6): 1603–11.

Das, A., J. Krishnaswamy, K.S. Bawa, M.C. Kiran, V. Srinivas, N. Samba Kumar, and K.U. Karanth. 2006. Prioritization of Conservation Areas in the Western Ghats, India. *Biological Conservation* 133 (1): 16–31.

Das, N., S.C. Mahapatra, and R.N. Chattopadhyay. 2000. Joint Forest Management in Five Villages of Nayagram Range, Midnapore, West Bengal. In N.H. Ravindranath, K.S.Murali, and K.C. Malhotra (eds), *Joint Forest Management: An Ecological and Institutional Assessment*. New Delhi and Calcutta: Oxford and IBH Publishing Co.

Das, P. 2007. The Politics of Participatory Conservation: The Case of the Kailadevi Wildlife Sanctuary, Rajasthan. In G. Shahabuddin and M. Rangarajan (eds), *Making Conservation Work: Securing Biodiversity in this New Century*. Delhi: Permanent Black.

Datta, A. 2007. Threatened Forests, Forgotten People. In G. Shahabuddin and M. Rangarajan (eds), *Making Conservation Work: Securing Biodiversity in this New Century*. Delhi: Permanent Black.

Davenport, L., W.Y. Brockelman, P.C. Wright, K. Ruf, and F.B.R. Del Valle. 2002. Ecotourism Tools for Parks. In J.Terborgh, C. van Schaik, L. Davenport, and M. Rao (eds), *Making Parks Work: Strategies for Preserving Tropical Nature*. Washington: Island Press.

Deb, D. Undated. An Estimation of the Possible Effect of Community Leaf Harvesting on the Productivity of Sal Forests in West Bengal. Technical Paper 5. Indian Institute of Bio-Social Research and Development (IBRAD).

Dharmakumarsinhji, K.S. 1952. Report on Rapid Survey of Wildlife and Game in Rajasthan. In Office of Regional Commissioner and Advisor, Rajasthan, Jaipur File 47/G/52. National Archives, New Delhi.

Dinerstein, E. 2003. *The Return of the Unicorns. The Natural History and Conservation of the Greater One-Horned Rhinoceros*. New York: Columbia University Press.

Divyabhanusinh. 1987. Sariska Tiger Reserve. In S. Israel and T. Sinclair (eds), *Indian Wildlife*. Singapore: APA Publications.

———. 2005. *The Story of Asia's Lions*. Mumbai: Marg Publications.

Down to Earth. 2000. Community Forest Management is the Future. 31 October: 56.

Du Plessis, M.A. 1995. The Effects of Fuelwood Removal on the Diversity of Some Cavity-Using Birds and Mammals in South Africa. *Biological Conservation* 74: 77–82.

Dutt, S. 2003. Co-management in Indian Parks: The View this Far. Draft paper presented at the World Parks Congress, Durban, South Africa.

Endress, B.A., D.L. Gorchov, M.B. Peterson, and E.P. Serrano. 2004. Harvest of the Palm *Chamaedora radicalis*: Its Effects on Leaf Production and Implications for Sustainable Management. *Conservation Biology* 18 (3): 822–30.

Forest Survey of India. 1993. *Status of Forest Cover in Project Tiger Reserves.* Dehradun.

Freese, C.H. 1997. The "Use It or Lose It" Debate: Issues of a Conservation Paradox. In C.H. Freese (ed.), *Harvesting Wild Species: Implications for Biodiversity Conservation.* Baltimore: Johns Hopkins University Press.

Gadgil, M. 2001. *Ecological Journeys: The Science and Politics of Conservation in India.* Delhi: Permanent Black.

———. and R. Guha. 1992. *This Fissured Land: An Ecological History of India.* Oxford: Oxford University Press.

———. 1995. *Ecology and Equity: The Use and Abuse of Nature in Contemporary India.* New Delhi: Penguin Books.

Ganeshaiah, K.N., R.U. Shaanker, K.S. Murali, U. Shankar, and K.S.Bawa. 1998. Extraction of Non-Timber Forest Products in the Forests of Biligirirangan Hills, India: 5. Influence of Dispersal Mode on Species Response to Anthropogenic Pressures. *Economic Botany* 52 (3): 316–19.

Gaoue, O.G. and T. Ticktin. 2008. Impacts of Bark and Foliage Harvest on *Khaya senegalensis*. *Journal of Applied Ecology* 45 (1): 34–40.

Garcia, C.A. and J.P. Pascal. 2005. Sacred Forests of Kodagu: Ecological Value and Social Role. In G. Cederlof and K. Sivaramakrishnan (eds), *Ecological Nationalisms: Nature, Livelihoods and Identities in South Asia.* New Delhi: Permanent Black.

Gardner, T.A., T. Caro, E.B. Fitzherbert, T. Banda, and P. Lalbhai. 2007. Conservation Value of Multiple-Use Areas in East Africa. *Conservation Biology* 21 (6): 1516–25.

Gell, F.R. and C.M. Roberts. 2003. Benefits beyond Boundaries: The Fishery Effects of Marine Reserves. *Trends in Ecology & Evolution* 18 (9): 448–55.

Ghate, R. 2004. Uncommons in the Commons. Community Initiated Forest Resource Management. New Delhi: Concept Publishing Company.

—— and K. Beazley. 2008. Aversion to Relocation: A Myth? *Conservation & Society* 5 (3): 331–4.

Ghimire, M. 1999. The Royal Chitwan National Park and its Impact on the Indigenous Peoples of Chitwan and Nawalparasi, Nepal. In M. Colchester and C. Erni (eds), *Indigenous Peoples and Protected Areas in South and Southeast Asia. From Principles to Practice.* Copenhagen: IWGIA.

Government of Rajasthan. 2004. *Management Plan for Sariska Tiger Reserve (2004–2014).* Sariska, Rajasthan.

———. 2005. Report of the State Empowered Committee on Forest and Wildlife Management. Jaipur, Rajasthan.

Government of West Bengal. 1997. Proceedings of National Workshop on Recent Trends in Joint Forest Management. Bankura, West Bengal: Government of West Bengal.

Greenberg, R., P. Bichier, A. Angon, and R. Reitsma, 1997. Bird Populations in Shade and Sun Coffee Plantations in Central Guatemala. *Conservation Biology* 11 (2): 448–59.

Gubbi, S. and D. MacMillan. 2008. Can Non-Timber Forest Products Solve Livelihood Problems? A Case Study from Periyar Tiger Reserve, India. *Oryx* 42 (2): 222–8.

Gubbi, S., M. Linkie, and N. Leader-Williams. 2009. Evaluating the Legacy of an Integrated Conservation and Development Project around a Tiger Reserve in India. *Environmental Conservation* 35 (4): 331–9.

Guha, R. 1985. Scientific Forestry and Social Change in Uttarakhand. *Economic and Political Weekly* 20: 1932–52.

———. 2000. *Environmentalism: A Global History*. New York: Longman.

———. 2003. The Authoritarian Biologist and the Arrogance of Anti-Humanism: Wildlife Conservation in the Third World. In V.K. Saberwal and M. Rangarajan (eds), *Battles over Nature: Science and the Politics of Conservation.* Delhi: Permanent Black.

Guhathakurta, P. 1992. Is Management of Coppice Sal Forests on Short Rotations Sustainable? *Wasteland News* 8 (1): 31–3.

Gupta, R. 2005. Maneaten. *Down to Earth,* 15 March: 26–8.

Hall, P. and K. Bawa. 1993. Methods to Assess the Impact of Non-Timber Forest Products on Plant Populations. *Economic Botany* 47 (3): 234–47.

Hegde, R. and T. Enters. 2000. Forest Products and Household Economy: A Case Study from Mudumalai Wildlife Sanctuary, Southern India. *Environmental Conservation* 27 (3): 250–9.

Hiralal, M.H. Undated. Gateway to Sustainable and Participatory Community Forest Management. Village Forest with Draft Rules under Sec. 28 of Indian Forest Act 1927. Chandrapur: Vrikshamitra.

Holloway, C. (ed.). 1978. *Decline and Restoration of the Central Indian Barasingha.* Morges, Switzerland: International Union for the Conservation of Nature.

Jha, S. 2000. Conservation and Preservation through Community Participation in Two Indian Projects: A Policy Perspective. *Ambio* 29 (8): 527–8.

Johari, R. 2003. Of Sanctions and Sanctuary-Making: The Cultural Politics of Nature in Sariska Tiger Reserve, Rajasthan, India, 1850–2000. MS thesis, York University, Canada.

———. 2007. Of Paper Tigers and Invisible People: The Cultural Politics of Nature in Sariska. In G. Shahabuddin and M. Rangarajan (eds), *Making Conservation Work: Securing Biodiversity in this New Century*. Delhi: Permanent Black.

Johnsingh, A.J.T. 2006. Twenty Years in Rajaji National Park. In A.J.T. Johnsingh, *Field Days: A Naturalist's Journey through South and Southeast Asia*. Hyderabad: Universities Press.

———, K. Sankar, and S. Mukherjee. 1997. Saving Prime Tiger Habitat in Sariska Tiger Reserve. *Cat News* 27: 3.

Joshi, N.V. and M. Gadgil. 1991. On the Role of Refugia in Promoting Prudent Use of Biological Resources. *Theoretical Population Biology* 40 (2): 211–29.

Kabra, A. 2007. Impact of Displacement on Poverty and Livelihood Security: The Case of Kuno Wildlife Sanctuary, Madhya Pradesh, India. Unpublished PhD thesis, Jawaharlal Nehru University, New Delhi.

———. 2008. Conservation-Induced Displacement: A Comparative Study of Two Indian Protected Areas. Paper Presented at Research Conference on Nature, Knowledge and Power at Uppsala, Sweden, 15–17 August 2008.

Kalpavriksh Environmental Action Group. 2007. Review Paper on Displacement. Pune: Kalpavriksh.

Karanth, K. 2007. Making Resettlement Work: The Case of India's Bhadra Wildlife Sanctuary. *Biological Conservation* 139: 315–24.

———, L.M. Curran, and J.D. Reuning-Scherer. 2005. Village Size and Forest Disturbance in Bhadra Wildlife Sanctuary, Western Ghats, India. *Biological Conservation* 128: 147–57.

Karanth, K.U. 2005. Joining the Dots but Losing the Cat. *Cat News* 43: 4–7.

———. 2006. *A View from the Machan*. Delhi: Permanent Black.

———. 2008. A Tiger in Your Bank. *Down to Earth*, 15 June (online edition).

———, J.D. Nichols, J. Seidensticker , E. Dinerstein, J.L.D. Smith, C. McDougal, A.J.T. Johnsingh, R.S. Chundawat, and V. Thapar. 2003.

Science Deficiency in Conservation Practice: The Monitoring of Tiger Populations in India. *Animal Conservation* 6: 141–6.

Karanth, K.U., J.D. Nichols, N. Samba Kumar, William A. Link, and James E. Hines . 2004. Tigers and Their Prey: Predicting Carnivore Densities from Prey Abundance. *Proceedings of the National Academy of Sciences* 101 (14): 4854–8.

Karanth, K.U. 2002. Nagarhole: Limits and Opportunities in Wildlife Conservation. In J. Terborgh, C. van Schaik, L. Davenport, and M. Rao (eds), *Making Parks Work: Strategies for Preserving Tropical Nature*. Washington: Island Press.

Karlsson, B.G. 1999. Ecodevelopment in Practice: Buxa Tiger Reserve and Forest People. *Economic & Political Weekly* 34 (30): 2087–94.

Kashwan, P. 2003. Conflicts in Joint Forest Management. Cases from South Rajasthan. *Community Forestry* 2 (4): 12–17.

Khare, A., M. Sarin, N.C. Saxena, S. Palit, S. Bathla, F. Vania, and M. Satyanarayana. 2000. *Joint Forest Management: Policy, Practice and Prospects*. Delhi and London: World Wide Fund for Nature—India, and International Institute for Environment & Development—UK.

Kothari, A. 1998. Ecodevelopment and Joint Management of Protected Areas. Legal and Policy Implications. Seminar on Ecodocumentation, Wildlife Institute of India, Dehradun, 26–27 November.

———. 2000. Conserving Nature with Communities: Lessons from Real Life Experiences in South Asia. Paper Presented at the Second World Conservation Congress of IUCN, Amman, Jordan, 3–11 October.

———, N. Pathak, and F. Vania. 2000. Where Communities Care: Community Based Wildlife and Ecosystem Management in South Asia. New Delhi: Kalpavriksh, and London: International Institute of Environment and Development.

Kramer, R., C. van Schaik, and J. Johnson. 1997. *Last Stand: Protected Areas and the Defense of Tropical Biodiversity*. Oxford: Oxford University Press.

Kumar, R. and G. Shahabuddin. 2005. Effects of Biomass Extraction on Vegetation Structure, Diversity and Composition of an Indian Tropical Dry Forest. *Environmental Conservation* 32 (3): 1–12.

Lal, J.B., V.K. Bahuguna, Hilaluddin, and S. Hussain. 1993. Ecological Studies of Sal Forest in Bankura North Forest Division, West Bengal. *Van Vigyan* 32 (1–2): 15–22.

Lele, S. and R.B. Norgaard. 1996. Sustainability and the Scientists' Burden. *Conservation Biology* 10 (2): 354–65.

Lewis, M. 2003. Cattle and Conservation at Bharatpur: A Case Study in Science and Advocacy. *Conservation & Society* 1 (1): 1–22.

———. 2005. Indian Science for Indian Tigers? Conservation Biology and the Question of Cultural Values. *Journal of the History of Biology* 38: 185–207.

Lohr, S.M., S.A. Gauthreaux, and J.C. Kilgo. 2002. Importance of Coarse Woody Debris to Avian Communities in Loblolly Pine Forests. *Conservation Biology* 16 (3): 767–77.

Madhusudan, M.D. 2005a. The Global Village: Linkages between International Coffee Markets and Livestock Grazing in a South Indian Wildlife Reserve. *Conservation Biology* 19 (2): 411–20.

———. 2005b. Of Rights and Wrongs: Wildlife Conservation and the Tribal Bill. *Economic & Political Weekly*, 19 November (online edition).

———, K. Shanker, A. Kumar, C. Mishra, A. Sinha, R. Arthur, A. Datta, M. Rangarajan, R. Chellam, G. Shahabuddin, R. Sankaran, M. Singh, U. Ramakrishnan, and P.D. Rajan. 2006. Science in the Wilderness: The Predicament of Scientific Research in India's Wildlife Reserves. *Current Science*: 91 (8): 1015–19.

Mahanty, S. 2002. NGOs, Agencies and Donors in Participatory Conservation: Tales from Nagarhole. *Economic and Political Weekly* 37: 3757–65.

Mahapatra, R. 2000a. A Quiet Revolution. *Down to Earth*, 31 March: 24–6.

———. 2000b. Seeking Reliance. *Down to Earth*, 15 September: 46–90.

Malhotra, K.C. and M. Poffenberger. 1989. Forest Regeneration through Community Protection: The West Bengal Experience. Proceedings of the Working Group Meeting on Forest Protection Committees, Calcutta, 21–22 June 1989.

Malhotra, K.C., D. Deb, and T.S. Vasulu. 1991a. Restitution of Natural Biodiversity in South West Bengal Forests. Delhi: Ford Foundation.

Malhotra, K.C., D. Deb, M. Dutta, T.S. Vasulu, G. Yadav, and M. Adhikari. 1991b. Role of Non-Timber Forest Produce in Village Economy: A Household Survey in Jamboni Range. Calcutta: IBRAD.

Maraj, R. and J. Seidensticker. 2006. Assessment of a Framework for Monitoring Tiger Population Trends in India. A Report to the IUCN. World Conservation Union and Project Tiger, India.

Mayaram S. 1997. *Resisting Regimes: Myth, Memory and the Shaping of a Muslim Identity*. Delhi: Oxford University Press.

McElwee, P.D. 2006. Displacement and Relocation Redux: Stories from Southeast Asia. *Conservation & Society* 4 (3): 396–403.

Mehra, D., S. Ghate, R. Ghate, A. Chaturvedi, P.K. Garlapati, A. Bose, S. Hate, and R. Humaane. 2004. Impact of Relocation on Forest-Dependent Communities: A Case of Protected Area of Vidarbha Region in Maharashtra State, India. Mimeo, Nagpur: SHODH.

Menon, M. and K. Kohli. 2003. A Conservation Strategy. *Frontline* 20 (12) (Online Edition).

———. 2008. Re-Engineering the Legal and Policy Regimes on Environment. *Economic & Political Weekly*, 7 June: 14–17.

Middleton, B. 2003. Ecology and Objective-Based Management: Case Study of the Keoladeo National Park, Bharatpur, Rajasthan. In V.K. Saberwal and M. Rangarajan (eds), *Battles Over Nature: Science and the Politics of Conservation*. New Delhi: Permanent Black.

Ministry of Environment and Forests. 2005. *Joining the Dots. Report of the Tiger Task Force*. Government of India.

Mishra, T.K. 1998. Users Become Managers: Indigenous Knowledge and Modern Forestry. *Economic & Political Weekly*, 7 February.

———, and S.K. Banerjee. 1997. An Ecological Reconnaissance of Lateritic Forest of South-West Bengal. *Advances in Forestry Research in India* 16: 5–43.

Mishra, T.K., P.K. Das, B. Behari, and S.K. Banerjee. 1993. Microbial Distribution in Relation to Soil Attributes in Lateritic Region under Different Vegetations. *Indian Journal of Tropical Biology* 1: 249–57.

Mittermeier, Russell A., N. Myers, C.G. Mittermeier, and H. Ford. 1997. *Hotspots: Earth's Biologically Richest and Most Endangered Terrestrial Ecoregions*. Monterey, Mexico: CEMEX.

Mukherjee, S. 2000. Habitat Use by Sympatric Small Carnivores in Sariska Tiger Reserve, Rajasthan, Western India. PhD thesis, Saurashtra University.

Murali, K.S., U. Shankar, R. Uma Shaanker, K.N. Ganeshaiah, and K.S. Bawa. 1996. Extraction of Non-Timber Forest Products in the Forests of Biligirirangan Hills, India: 2. Impact of NTFP Extraction on Regeneration, Population Structure and Species Composition. *Economic Botany* 50 (3): 252–69.

Murphree, M. 2004. Communal Approaches to Natural Resource Management in Africa: From Whence and to Where? *Journal of International Wildlife Law and Policy* 7: 203–16.

Nagendra, H. 2007. Drivers of Reforestation in Human-Dominated Forests. *Proceedings of the National Academy of Sciences* 104 (39): 15218–23.

———, B. Karna, and M. Karmacharya. 2005. Examining Institutional

Change: Social Conflict in Nepal's Leasehold Forestry Programme. *Conservation & Society* 3 (1): 72–91.

National Tiger Conservation Authority and Wildlife Institute of India. 2008. *Status of Tigers, Co-predators and Prey in India*. New Delhi.

Negi, A.S. 2003. Case Study from Corbett Tiger Reserve, Uttaranchal. In *Proceedings of National Seminar-cum-Consultation on Relocation of People from Protected Areas in India: Policy and Process*. New Delhi: Council for Social Development.

Pabla, H.S. 2005. Strategies for the Protected Areas in India. In U.R. Sharma and P. Yonzon (eds), *People and Protected Areas in South Asia*. Kathmandu: IUCN-South Asia and Resources Himalaya.

Palit, S. 1999. Bonds of Amity: Joint Forest Management in West Bengal Has Come to Stay. *Wasteland News* 14 (3): 21–7.

Pande, P. 2005. *National Parks and Sanctuaries in Maharashtra. Reference Guide. Volume II. Individual Profile and Management Status*. Mumbai: Bombay Natural History Society.

Pandey, S. and M.P. Wells. 1997. Ecodevelopment Planning at India's Great Himalayan National Park for Biodiversity Conservation and Participatory Rural Development. *Biodiversity & Conservation* 6 (9): 1277–92.

Pandey, S. 2004. Experiential Learning in Linking Rural Development with Local Livelihoods to Conserve Biodiversity at the Great Himalayan National Park, India. Official Report.

Pandit, B.H. and G.B. Thapa. 2003. A Tragedy of Non-Timber Forest Resources in the Mountain Commons of Nepal. *Environmental Conservation* 30 (3): 283–92.

Pathak, N. and V. Gour-Broome. 2001. *Tribal Self-Rule and Natural Resource Management: Community Based Conservation at Mendha-Lekha, Maharashtra, India*. Community Based Conservation in South Asia: No. 9. Kalpavriksh and International Institute of Environment and Development.

People's Biodiversity Register, Mendha (Lekha). 2005. Compiled by Vrikshamitra, Gram Sabha of Mendha (Lekha), and Centre for Ecological Sciences (Indian Institute of Sciences).

Peters, C.M., A.H. Gentry, and R.O. Mendelsohn. 1989. Valuation of an Amazonian Rainforest. *Nature* 339: 655–6.

Plowden, C. 2004. The Ecology and Harvest of *Andiroba* Seeds for Oil Production. *Conservation & Society* 2 (2): 251–72.

Poteete, A. and E. Ostrom. 2004. In Pursuit of Comparable Concepts and Data about Collective Action. *Agricultural Systems* 82: 215–32.

Powell, G.V.N., S. Palminteri, B. Carlson, and M.A. Boza. 2002. Successes and Failings of the Monteverde Reserve Complex and Costa Rica's System of National Protected Areas. In J. Terborgh, C. van Schaik, L. Davenport, and M. Rao (eds), *Making Parks Work: Strategies for Preserving Tropical Nature*. Washington: Island Press.

Prathapan, K.D., P.D. Rajan, T.C. Narendran, C.A. Viraktamath, K.A. Subramanian, N.A. Aravind, and J. Poorani. 2006. Biological Diversity Act: Shadow of Permit-Raj over Research. *Current Science* 91 (8): 1006–7.

Prathapan, K.D., P.D. Rajan, T.C. Narendran, C.A. Viraktamath, N.A. Aravind, and J. Poorani. 2008. Death Sentence on Taxonomy in India. *Current Science* 94 (2): 170–1.

Rai, A.M. 1996. Ecological Aspects of Seed Collection of *Shorea robusta* with Reference to Uttar Pradesh. In M.P. Shiva and R.B. Mathur (eds), *Management of Minor Forest Produce for Sustainability*. New Delhi: Oxford and IBH Publishing Co.

Rai, N. and C.F. Uhl. 2004. Forest Product Use, Conservation and Livelihoods: The Case of *Uppage* Fruit Harvest in the Western Ghats, India. *Conservation & Society* 2 (2): 289–314.

Raju, G. 1997. Joint Forest Management: The Dilemma of Empowerment. Working Paper. Anand: Institute of Rural Management.

Raman, T.R.S., G.S. Rawat, and A.J.T. Johnsingh. 1998. Recovery of Tropical Rainforest Avifauna in Relation to Vegetation Succession following Shifting Cultivation in Mizoram, North-East India. *Journal of Applied Ecology* 35: 214–31.

Ramnarayan, K., N.P. Melkania, P. Bhattacharya, and S.B. Roy. (Undated). Forest Floor Sweeping: A Case Study from West Bengal Forest Protection Committee. Technical Paper No. 7. Indian Institute of Bio-Social Research and Development (IBRAD).

Ramnath, M. 2008. Surviving the Forest Rights Act. Between Scylla and Charybdis. *Economic & Political Weekly*, 1 March: 37–42.

Rangarajan, M. 1996. *Fencing the Forest. Conservation and Ecological Change in India's Central Provinces 1860–1914*. New Delhi: Oxford University Press.

———. 2003. Parks, Politics and History: Conservation Dilemmas in Africa. *Conservation and Society* 1 (1): 77–98.

———, and G. Shahabuddin. 2006. Displacement and Relocation from Protected Areas: Towards a Biological and Historical Synthesis. *Conservation and Society* 4 (3): 359–78.

Rathore, B.M.S. 2003. Forging a Consensus in Rajaji National Park: An Interview. In V.K. Saberwal and M. Rangarajan (eds), *Battles Over Nature: Science and the Politics of Conservation.* New Delhi: Permanent Black.

Ratna-Reddy, V., M.G. Reddy, M. Bandi, V.M. Ravi Kumar, M. Srinivasa Reddy, and O. Springate-Baginski. 2007. Participatory Forest Management in Andhra Pradesh: Implementation, Outcomes and Livelihood Impacts. In O. Springate-Baginski and P. Blaikie (eds), *Forests, People and Power: Political Ecology of Reform in South Asia.* London and Stirling: Earthscan.

Ravindranath, N.H., K.S. Murali, I.K. Murthy, P. Sudha, S. Palit, and K.C. Malhotra. 2000. Summary and Conclusions. In N.H. Ravindranath, K.S.Murali, and K.C. Malhotra (eds), *Joint Forest Management: An Ecological and Institutional Assessment.* New Delhi and Calcutta: Oxford and IBH Publishing Co.

Reddy, G.V. 1994. Painted Spurfowl in Sariska. *Newsletter for Birdwatchers* 34 (2): 38.

Rodgers, A., D. Hartley, and S. Bashir. 2003. Community Approaches to Conservation: Some Comparisons from Africa and India. In V. Saberwal and M. Rangarajan (eds), *Battles over Nature: Science and the Politics of Wildlife Conservation in India.* New Delhi: Permanent Black.

Rodgers, W.A. 1990. A Preliminary Ecological Survey of Algual Spring, Sariska Tiger Reserve, Rajasthan. *Journal of the Bombay Natural History Society* 87 (2): 201–9.

Roychowdhury, P.K. 1998. Joint Forest Management in South West Bengal. In Proceedings of Workshop on Sustainability of JFM with Local Resources, Narendrapur. Loksiksha Parishad, Narendrapur; Forest Department, West Bengal and Ford Foundation, New Delhi.

Ruiz-Perez, M., M. Almeida, S. Dewi, E.M. Lozano Costa, M.C. Pantoja, A. Puntodewo, A. de Arruda Postigo, and A.G. de Andrade. 2005. Conservation and Development in Amazonian Extractive Reserves. *Ambio* 34 (3): 218–23.

Saberwal, V.K. and A. Kothari. 1996. The Human Dimension in Conservation Biology Curricula in Developing Countries. *Conservation Biology* 10 (5): 1328–31.

Saberwal, V.K., M. Rangarajan, and A. Kothari. 2000. *People, Parks and Wildlife: Towards Coexistence.* Delhi: Orient Longman.

Saberwal, V.K. and M. Rangarajan (eds). 2003. *Battles Over Nature: Science and the Politics of Conservation.* New Delhi: Permanent Black.

Saha, S. and H. Howe. 2003. Species Composition and Fire in a Dry Deciduous Forest. *Ecology* 84: 3118–23.

———. 2006. Stature of Juvenile Trees in Response to Anthropogenic Fires in a Tropical Deciduous Forest of Central India. *Conservation & Society* 4 (4): 619–27.

Sankar, K. 1994. The Ecology of Three Large Sympatric Herbivores (Chital, Sambar and Nilgai) with Special Reference to Reserve Management in Sariska Tiger Reserve, Rajasthan. PhD thesis, Department of Zoology, University of Rajasthan.

———, and A.J.T. Johnsingh. 2002. Food Habits of Tiger (*Panthera tigris*) and Leopard (*Panthera pardus*) in Sariska Tiger Reserve, Rajasthan, India, as Shown by Scat Analysis. *Mammalia* 66 (2): 285–9.

Sankar, K., D. Mohan, and S. Pandey. 1993. Birds of Sariska Tiger Reserve, Rajasthan, India. *Forktail* February 8: 133–41.

Sankaran, M. 2005. Fire, Grazing and the Dynamics of Tall-Grass Savannas in the Kalakad-Mundanthurai Tiger Reserve, South India. *Conservation & Society* 3 (1): 4–25.

Sankhala, K.S. 1964. Wildlife Sanctuaries of Rajasthan. *Journal of the Bombay Natural History Society* 61 (1): 27–34.

———. 1969. The Tiger in Rajasthan—A Study of its Habitat, Distribution and Status. *Indian Forester* 95: 763–70.

Sarin, M. Undated. Joint Forest Management in India: Achievements and Unaddressed Challenges. FAO Corporate Document Repository. http://www.fao.org/docrep/v3960e/v3960e06.htm

Sarkar, R. 2008. Decentralised Forest Governance in Central Himalayas: A Re-evaluation of Outcomes. *Economic & Political Weekly* 43 (18): 54–63.

Sarkar, S., S.B. Roy, and G. Yadav. 2000. Biological Diversity Conservation through Participatory Vegetation Monitoring Process. *Wasteland News* 15 (3): 28–30.

Sarkar, S.K. and R.N. Chattopadhyay. 1998. Rejuvenation of Sal Coppice Forest by Stump Shifting. *Wasteland News* 14 (3): 52–4.

Schwartzman, S., A. Moreira, and D. Nepstad. 2000. Rethinking Tropical Forest Conservation: Perils in Parks. *Conservation Biology* 14 (5): 1351–7.

Schwartzman, S. and B. Zimmerman. 2005. Conservation Alliances with Indigenous Peoples of the Amazon. *Conservation Biology* 19 (3): 721–7.

Seidensticker, J. 2008. Ecological and Intellectual Baselines: Saving Lions, Tigers and Rhinos in Asia. In L.L. Rockwood, R.E. Stewart, and T. Dietz (eds), *Foundations of Environmental Sustainability: The Co-Evolution of Science and Policy*. New York: Oxford University Press.

Sekhar, N.U. 1998. Crop and Livestock Depredation Caused by Wild Animals in Protected Areas: The Case of Sariska Tiger Reserve, Rajasthan, India. *Environmental Conservation* 25 (2): 160–71.

Sekhsaria, P. 2007. Conservation in India and the Need to Think Beyond 'Tiger vs. Tribal'. *Biotropica* 39 (5): 575–7.

Sethi, N. 2004a. Officially Bankrupt: One Stove, One Pot. *Down to Earth*, 31 July: 22–4.

———. 2004b. Imagining IEDP. *Down to Earth*, 31 July: 25–6.

———. 2004c. Lost in Transit. *Down to Earth*, 31 July: 27–30.

———. 2004d. Conserve or Pickle? *Down to Earth*, 31 July: 31–2.

———. 2004e. After Dosage. *Down to Earth*, 31 July: 33–4.

———. 2004f. Hold Tight. *Down to Earth*, 31 July: 34–5.

Shackleton, D.M. 2001. A Review of Community-Based Hunting Programs in Pakistan. Mountain Areas Conservancy Group.

Shah, A., A. Mukherjee, and H. Shah. 2002. Ecodevelopment Project in Gir Protected Area: A Study Based on Process Documentation Research. Ahmedabad: Gujarat Institute of Development Research.

Shahabuddin, G. 2003. Ecological Sustainability of Forest Management Practices: The Case of the Regenerating Sal Forests of South-Western West Bengal, India. *Social Change* 33 (2–3): 142–72.

———. 2005. Towards a New Paradigm. Review of: *Joining the Dots: Report of the Tiger Task Force. Project Tiger, Union Ministry of Environment and Forests, Government of India. Biblio* 10 (11–12): 21–3.

———, and R. Kumar. 2006. Influence of Anthropogenic Disturbance on Birds of Tropical Dry Forest: The Role of Vegetation Structure. *Animal Conservation* 9: 404–13.

———, and A. Verma. 2006. Annotated Checklist of the Birds of Sariska Tiger Reserve, Rajasthan. *Indian Birds*, 2 (3): 71–6.

Shahabuddin, G. and S. Prasad. 2004. Assessing Ecological Sustainability of Non-Timber Forest Produce Extraction: The Indian Scenario. *Conservation and Society* 2 (2): 235–50.

Shahabuddin, G., R. Kumar, and M. Shrivastava. 2005. Pushed over the Edge: Relocation from Sariska. *Economic and Political Weekly*, 6 August: 3563–4.

———. 2007. 'Creation of Inviolate Space': Lives, Livelihoods and Conflict in Sariska Tiger Reserve. *Economic and Political Weekly* 42 (20): 1855–62.

Shahabuddin, G. and M. Rangarajan (eds). 2007. *Making Conservation Work: Securing Biodiversity in this New Century*. Delhi: Permanent Black.

Shankar Raman, T.R. 2006. Effects of Habitat Structure and Adjacent Habitats on Birds in Tropical Rainforest Fragments and Shaded Plantations in the Western Ghats, India. *Biodiversity & Conservation* 15 (4): 1577–1607.

Shankar, U., K.S. Murali, R.U. Shaanker, K.N. Ganeshaiah, and K.S. Bawa. 1998a. Extraction of Non-Timber Forest Products in the Forests of Biligirirangan Hills, India: 4. Impact on Floristic Diversity and Population Structure in a Thorn Scrub Forest. *Economic Botany* 52 (3): 302–15.

Shankar, U., Ravi Hegde, and K.S. Bawa. 1998b. Extraction of Non-Timber Forest Products in the Forests of Biligirirangan Hills, India: 6. Fuelwood Pressure and Management Options. *Economic Botany* 52 (3): 320–36.

Sharma, A. and A. Kabra. 2007. Displacement as a Conservation Tool: Lessons from the Kuno Wildlife Sanctuary, Madhya Pradesh. In G. Shahabuddin and M. Rangarajan (eds), *Making Conservation Work: Securing Biodiversity in this New Century.* Delhi: Permanent Black.

Sharma, A.K. 1981. Birds of Sariska Tiger Reserve. *Newsletter for Birdwatchers* 21 (5): 7–10.

Sharma, D. 2001. Estimating the Density of Porcupines in Semi-Arid Sariska Valley, Western India. *Journal of the Bombay Natural History Society* 98 (2): 161–8.

Sharma, V.D. 1986. Sariska: Jewel of the Aravallis. *Sanctuary* 6 (2): 143, 164–9.

Sheil, D. and S. Wunder. 2002. The Value of Tropical Forest to Local Communities: Complications, Caveats and Cautions. *Conservation Ecology* 6 (2): 9.

Shrotiya, M. Undated. *Regenerating of Forest.* Alwar: Tarun Bharat Sangh.

Siebert, S.F. 2004. Demographic Effects of Collecting Rattan Cane and their Implications for Sustainable Harvesting. *Conservation Biology* 18 (2): 424–43.

Silvertown, J. 2004. Sustainability in a Nutshell. *Trends in Ecology and Evolution* 19 (6): 276–8.

Sivaramakrishnan, K. 1999. *Modern Forests: Statemaking and Environmental Change in Colonial Eastern India.* New Delhi: Oxford University Press.

Snodgrass, J.G., S.K. Sharma, Y.S. Jhala, M.G. Lacy, M. Advani, N.K. Bhargava, and C. Upadhyay. 2007. Beyond Self-interest and Altruism:

Herbalist and Leopard Brothers in an Indian Wildlife Sanctuary. *Human Dimensions of Wildlife* 12: 375–87.

Srikosamatara, S. and W.Y. Brockelman. 2002. Conservation of Protected Areas in Thailand: A Diversity of Problems, A Diversity of Solutions. In J. Terborgh, C. van Schaik, L. Davenport, and M. Rao (eds), *Making Parks Work: Strategies for Preserving Tropical Nature.* Washington: Island Press.

Struhsaker, T.T. 1997. *Ecology of an African Rain Forest. Logging in Kibale and the Conflict between Conservation and Exploitation.* Florida: University Press of Florida.

Sundar, N. 2000. Unpacking the 'Joint' in Joint Forest Management. *Development & Change* 31 (1): 255–79.

———, R. Jeffery, and N. Thin. 2001. *Branching Out: Joint Forest Management in India.* New Delhi: Oxford University Press.

Tata Energy Research Institute. 1999. Study on Joint Forest Management. New Delhi: TERI Project Report No. 98SF64.

Terborgh, J. 1986. Keystone Plant Resources in the Tropical Forest. In M.E. Soule (ed.), *Conservation Biology: The Science of Scarcity and Diversity.* Sunderland, Massachusetts: Sinauer Associates.

———. 1998. Wildlife in Managed Tropical Forests: A Neotropical Perspective. In. A.E. Lugo and C. Lowe (eds), *Tropical Forests: Management and Ecology.* New York: Springer Verlag.

———. 1999. *Requiem for Nature.* Washington: Island Press.

——— and C. van Schaik. 2002. Why the World Needs Parks. In J. Terborgh, C. van Schaik, L. Davenport, and M. Rao (eds), *Making Parks Work: Strategies for Preserving Tropical Nature.* Washington: Island Press.

Thapar, V. 2005. Note of Dissent. In *Joining the Dots: The Report of the Tiger Task Force.* New Delhi: Ministry of Environment and Forests, Government of India.

Thiollay, J. J. 1995. The Role of Traditional Agroforests in the Conservation of Rainforest Bird Diversity in Sumatra. *Conservation Biology* 9 (2): 335–53.

Thirgood, S.J., S.A.R. Mduma, J.D.Keyyu, and M.K. Laurenson. 2007. The Value of Long-Term Research: Conservation Science and Practice in Tanzania. *Conservation Biology* 21 (3): 576–9.

Tofa, D.N. and M.H. Hiralal. Undated. Mendha (Lekha). Vrikshamitra, Chandrapur, India.

Uniyal, V.K. and J. Zacharias. 2001. Periyar Tiger Reserve—Building Bridges with Local Communities for Biodiversity Conservation. *Parks* (11) 2: 14–23.

Van Schaik, C.V. and H.D. Rijksen. 2002. Integrated Conservation and Development Projects: Problems and Potential. In J. Terborgh, C. van Schaik, L. Davenport, and M. Rao (eds), *Making Parks Work: Strategies for Preserving Tropical Nature*. Washington: Island Press.

Varma, K. 2007. Conservation and Development in Gir: An Assessment of the India Ecodevelopment Project in Maldhari Nesses. Unpublished MS thesis, Cambridge University, UK.

Vijayan, V.S. 1991. Keoladeo National Park Ecology Study. Bombay: Bombay Natural History Society.

Weinberg, A., S. Bellows, D. Ekster. 2002. Sustaining Ecotourism: Insights and Implications from Two Successful Case Studies. *Society and Natural Resources* 15 (4): 371–80.

Weinstein, S. and S. Moegenburg. 2004. Acai Palm Management in the Amazon Estuary: Course for Conservation or Passage to Plantation? *Conservation & Society* 2 (2): 315–46.

Woodman, J. 2002. Ghosts in the Transmission: The Translation of Global Conservation Concepts to Local Scenarios: A Case Study of Ecodevelopment in Central India. Ninth Biennial Conference of the IASCP: The Commons in an Age of Globalisation, Victoria Falls, Zimbabwe, 17–22 June.

World Bank. 1996. India Ecodevelopment Project. Staff Appraisal Report.

———. 2003a. India Ecodevelopment Project: Supervision Mission Aide Memoire. Palamau Tiger Reserve.

———. 2003b. India Ecodevelopment Project: Supervision Mission Aide Memoire. Pench Tiger Reserve.

———. 2003c. India Ecodevelopment Project: Supervision Mission Aide Memoire. Periyar Tiger Reserve.

———. 2003d. India Ecodevelopment Project: Supervision Mission Aide Memoire. Ranthambhore Tiger Reserve.

———. 2003e. India Ecodevelopment Project: Supervision Mission Aide Memoire. Buxa Tiger Reserve.

———. 2003f. India Ecodevelopment Project: Supervision Mission Aide Memoire. Gir National Park.

Wright, B. 2005. Too Little, Too Late. *Indian Express*, 13 February.

Wright, P. and B. Andriamihaja. 2002. Making a Rain Forest Park Work in Madagascar: Ranomafana National Park and its Long-Term Research

Commitment. In J. Terborgh, C. van Schaik, L. Davenport, and M. Rao (eds), *Making Parks Work: Strategies for Preserving Tropical Nature*. Washington: Island Press.

Wunder, S. 2000. Ecotourism and Economic Incentives—An Empirical Approach. *Ecological Economics* 32 (3): 465–79.

Yadav, A.S. and S.K. Gupta. 2006. Effect of Micro-Environment and Human Disturbance on the Diversity of Woody Species in the Sariska Tiger Project in India. *Forest Ecology and Management* 225: 178–9.

Index

('t' after a number denotes occurrence within a table)